Claire Nahmad has written a numb⟨
spirituality, angel communication and esoteric secrets ⟨⟨⟨⟨⟨⟨⟨⟨
history, including *The Secret Teachings of Mary Magdalene* (2006),
The Coming of the Holy Grail (2012) and *Kick-Ass Angels* (2012).
The inner worlds of spiritual percipience have been open to her since
early childhood and her intuitive explorations inform her writing.
Her books, published in 30 countries and translated into 20 languages,
have a strong following worldwide and are frequently used in
mind-body-spirit courses and workshops.
She lives in rural Lincolnshire in a tumbledown cottage
with her cockerel Coleridge.

DEDICATION

For every member of the Sisterhood, past and present;
and for George Carver, because everything I do is always for you.

And I said to the man who stood at the gate of the year:

"Give me a light, that I may travel safely into the unknown."
And he replied:
"Go out into the darkness
And put your hand
Into the hand of God.
That to you shall be better than light and
Safer than a known way."

The Desert   M. Louise Haskins

This edition first published in the UK and USA 2014 by
Watkins Publishing Limited
PO Box 883, Oxford, OX1 9PL, UK

A member of Osprey Group

For enquiries in the USA and Canada:
Osprey Publishing, PO Box 3985
New York, NY 10185-3985
Tel: (001) 212 753 4402
Email: info@ospreypublishing.com

1 3 5 7 9 10 8 6 4 2

Typeset by Creative Plus Publishing Ltd/Mark Anstey
Printed and bound in China

A CIP record for this book is available from the British Library
ISBN: 978-1-78028-664-8

Watkins Publishing is supporting the Woodland Trust, the UK's leading
woodland conservation charity, by funding tree-planting initiatives and
woodland maintenance.

watkinspublishing.co.uk

PILGRIMAGE
TO
IONA

Discovering the Ancient Secrets
of the Sacred Isle

CLAIRE NAHMAD
FOREWORD BY LIONEL FANTHORPE

WATKINS PUBLISHING
LONDON

CONTENTS

FOREWORD

BY LIONEL & PATRICIA FANTHORPE

This profoundly deep and thoughtful book sets out on a true pilgrimage of the most meaningful kind. It is a pilgrimage from which every reader can benefit in both mind and spirit. It is a quest for truth, for knowledge and for meaning. Socrates warned us that "The unexamined life is not worth living." One great virtue of *Pilgrimage to Iona* is that it provides those essential philosophical and theological instruments with which we can examine life.

Claire has the gift of examining so-called myths and legends in depth and discovering their vital links with historical events, along with the true meanings beyond them. She also unravels many of the complex, entangled mysteries known to groups such as the Masons, Cathars and Templars.

One of the most powerful ideas in the book is the concept of Earth, and, in particular, sacred and special places such as Iona, being vibrant with divine life and power. If we think back on our lives, we may recall experiencing feelings of special spiritual depth when we visited such places. Iona optimises these feelings, but they are also reported from the Nile valley and Rennes-le-Chateau in France, which has been described by one sensitive and thoughtful researcher as a "gateway to the invisible".

Claire's expert knowledge of the Holy Grail enables her to fit this into her other extensive research and this helps to clarify the mysteries of Iona.

Among the other mysteries that are explored with such accuracy and integrity are the enigmas of gender and androgyny, and *Pilgrimage to Iona* penetrates and clarifies these brilliantly.

A particular mystery that has intrigued us as explorers of the unexplained for more than half a century is the mystery of the famous Emerald Tablets of Thoth, the Egyptian deity, also known as Hermes Triomegistus. Claire's treatment of this is absolutely fascinating.

Pilgrimage to Iona has been thoroughly and expertly researched, and Claire's excellent analysis of the many mysteries centred on the island has been synthesised into an excellent book.

A GIFT TO YOU FROM IONA

STEPHANIE SORRELL

I am going on a journey to a sacred place and because you cannot be with me, I want to bring you something back.

I have heard of this mystical isle, for many pilgrims have travelled there to be strengthened and refreshed. Some call it the 'Isle of the Saints'; for Saint Columba once travelled to its shores. Others call it the 'Land of the Druids' for they too moved upon its sacred shores. Still others call it the 'Isle of the Dove' as the Holy Spirit is believed to dwell here.

It was a long journey and when I set out I was weary and tense. Inside me was a hunger and thirst that nothing could satisfy. And pain had hollowed deep into my soul.

As the train took me across fields, through cities and towns, I looked at the houses and wondered if one of them was yours. Perhaps you were gazing out just then as I passed and I waved you a greeting from my heart.

Iona was at last before me and I felt its gentle welcome beneath my feet as I walked. There were many other pilgrims stepping onto its shores and the softly falling rains were like a benediction upon us, a holy baptism.

Here, where hearts were open, we gazed into one another's souls, and entered the magic of true communication. As our spirits touched we knew that we were inseparable and that we were one another.

The isle was beautiful. Each stone, rock and grain of sand glowed as though illuminated from within. The presence of the spirit was a holy fire in the landscape.

No-one there could remain untouched by its reality.

As I walked, I felt the strength of the rocks growing in me, gentle amethyst, dark basalt and dove grey. The white soft sands flowed through my veins and the turquoise seas pounded through my heart until I could no longer call myself a separate being.

Many of us journeyed to the Isle's sacred places and joined hands, becoming receptive to her heartbeat and offering our gratitude. On my lips was a song, a prayer for you so that you would hear it often in the deep recess of your heart.

We journeyed to the ancient sun temples where the white sands had once stretched out far beyond the sea that flowed there. Here, the rock columns became totems of power and the gentle coves resonated with the song of the spirit. Here, we dipped our hands into the crystal streams that flowed down the rocks and felt the hands of the devas and nature spirits beneath.

We climbed the hills where the angels of light and planetary masters had once stood and felt their presence. The wind upon our faces was the touch of their wings and the sun breaking through was the gentle radiance of their smiles.

As I lay on a rocky prominence gazing out to the small islands washed by the water, I thought of you and tried to create this picture in my heart for you. A picture of gulls poised on air pockets, their wings the colour of the sands, of great rocks pounded by the turquoise rhythm of the sea.

You see, I wanted to bring you something precious back from this Isle. Something to hold like one of the green or red feldspar stones here, or a shell touched by the moon. I wanted to show you the tame animals here and how a cow had allowed me to place my arms around her neck as she sat there. And as I gazed into the fearless jewel of her eye, I touched her spirit.

But what I have to give you is intangible as it is invisible. It is here, breathing through these words. If you close your eyes you will smell its fragrance pouring into your soul.

Dear friend, although we have never met, I already feel I know you. I experience the dance of your being, and know that it is my dance. And I know as you know that the hollow inside me that pain had made was really a chalice to hold this light without a name.

INTRODUCTION

The idea of pilgrimage is flooding back into the consciousness of our times. Largely abandoned in the West for centuries, its concept is beginning to resonate once again with our human need to celebrate our inner journeying and to mark as shrines along the way those points of inspiration and enlightenment that lead to the great beacon of destination.

That destination is interior and its dimensions are of the soul, whether it is completeness, achievement after striving, a sense that via the journey an inner cup has been hollowed to receive the spiritual mysteries of the site of pilgrimage, or all of these and more. Yet the outer journey and destination facilitate that deep inner process and are a mirror and antiphony of one another.

The intrinsic pilgrimage to Iona offered by this book reflects the essence of such a journey. Although it begins and ends on Iona, its circular passage requires a pilgrim's staff and pouch of provisions, and a heart that is open to mystery. These have been provided by Fiona Macleod, the Celtic mystic and writer who died in the first years of the 20th century. For those who do not know of Fiona, there is a story to tell and a secret to be revealed along with the many enigmas and mysteries of Iona, whose name her own reflects.

Fiona Macleod wrote a book about Iona which in its beauty, grace, and power of story and myth drawn from the folklore of the isle, has never been equalled. My book will follow her own in her role as leader and way-shower. The secrets and conundrums of the vision within her work can be revealed, over a century later, as fragments, echoes, hints of a shining truth that combine with Iona's history, and its future, to form a golden revelation about this tiny isle. Fiona's hidden revelation concerns our own times and our collective destiny, and its message needs to be understood in the context of now.

The greatest revelation given to King Arthur was that 'the king and the land are one'. It is a message for us all in that the supremacy or the highest within us will objectify as the living Earth, and the conditions of and on Earth, when we properly understand and honour that supremacy and let its life-blood circulate without obstruction.

By the same token, when our lowest essence is given free rein, the Earth becomes sick and racked with disasters, which is a growing threat today. These truths are realised deep within us, so that we know with an instinctive sense that the land is intimately connected to our spirituality and that its sacredness has its culmination points, which we recognise as sites of pilgrimage and, as pilgrims, strive to honour with our highest essence. The site itself, and our connection with it, help to unite us with that highest essence – our inner queenship, our inner kingship. The king and the land are one.

The aim of making a pilgrimage was always the offering of an act of devotion, for its own sake but also that the pilgrim might receive a healing, a blessing, an initiation or a revealed enlightenment. The sacred isle of Iona, 'rapt in dream', as Fiona expresses it, is dreaming the deepest dream of the human heart and soul for us so that we might receive its secrets and, in doing so, truly awaken.

CHAPTER 1

TIIE VERY BEGINNING

Who will tell the secret of Iona?" asked Fiona Macleod, the Celtic mystic, writer, and poet who died in 1905. "Who will reveal what it has hidden with such sweet poignancy for so many centuries?"

Many have said throughout Iona's history that this little Hebridean island, one of the western isles of Scotland, enshrines a secret; a spiritual mystery so profound that to tell its story is 'to go back to God, and to end in God'. Some have prophesied, perhaps with deeper vision, that the secret is not on Iona, but Iona itself. And, in undertaking this pilgrimage of revelation and inner striving to see and understand, the time seems right to seek to unveil the spiritual mystery of Iona at last, and to suggest that both renditions of Iona's secret are true.

Yet Iona's secret cannot be unveiled in a sequence of flat, stark facts. Her secret is factual and can ultimately be explained in factual terms, but, if we would approach such an unveiling via the route of true comprehension so that eyes can see and ears can hear, that approach must be an invocation of her spirit. Otherwise, facts will be rendered barren and meaningless, seeds that cannot burst into a true expression of their life potential.

To articulate this notion in Fiona's words: 'And that is why I would speak here of Iona as befalls my pen, rather than as perhaps my pen should go: and choose legend and remembrance, and my own and other memories and associations, and knowledge of my own and others, and hidden meanings, and beauty and strangeness surviving in dreams and imaginations, rather than facts and figures, that others could adduce more deftly and with more will.'

Nevertheless, there are some facts and figures about Iona that do not constitute the shackles of a mundane vision. 'It is but a small isle, fashioned of a little sand, a few grasses salt with the spray of an ever-restless wave, a few rocks that wade in heather and upon whose brows the sea-wind weaves the ancient lichen,' Fiona tells us. But what of its furthest origins? Even among the sturdy reality of statistics and science, the lamp of legends comes alight.

If we take a journey through time and space to see our planet Earth being formed in the vast expanse of our solar system five billion years ago, we can observe from our imaginal watch-tower that she remained as just a rock with iron at her core, washed over by immense oceans and played upon by the emanations of stars and star-mists and the forces of the elements for more than a billion of those years before Earth-life properly began.

Spinning to the sound of unimaginable symphonies, she voyaged in enthrallment whilst her heart – which was fire – wrought her inner and outer being. Within her oceans were isles of stone which lay silent, still, waiting, for there were no shifting tectonic plates in those unimaginably far-off days.

We can see that, eventually, those isles of stone that were her only land mass, responding to the fire at her heart, moved together to form the first supercontinent. Eventually, perhaps after seven separations and seven meetings, the last supercontinent, Pangaea, drifted apart at the rate of a single footfall in a single score of years to form the seven continents of today.

During that astronomical passage of years, the land mass of which Iona was a tiny point, like the pinprick of a star, was originally attached to what became known as North America. What is now Scotland broke away to conjoin with the remainder of the United Kingdom of today, and, in time, Iona detached to become a little island. But, before these land formations, as we have seen, there were earlier continents of which remain legends hazy with their span of time. What would eventually become North America, the United Kingdom, and of course Iona, were all an integral part of these continents: one conjoined area within them.

Delightfully, it is the secrets held within diamonds which tell us the scientific story; but it is the diamond light within the human spirit that contains and reveals the radiant significance of their primordial mythos.

The ancient rock strata comprising Iona are some of the oldest on the planet, estimated to be as much as 1,500 million years old. Prehistoric Native American creation stories tell us that this birth of land above sea level was the time when the stones walked out of the Earth – when the land itself was formed from the fire and the pressure and the materials within her core, and the stones were born.

The North American Indians know about the essence of stone. Their legends shine a light on its inner mysteries that will cast a beautiful effulgence over the rocks of Iona, which as pilgrims we are bound to explore.

Cultures all around the world believe that God, or Divine Spirit, or the Sun, came forth from a rock. Arthur pulled the sword – the Spirit – from a stone to claim his kingship – the supremity within him that was a symbol of the supremity or Spirit within each one of us. Even scientists, with their profound uncovering of the laws of matter and the strange doctrines and dogmas they have embraced regarding materiality and limitation, tell us that life on Earth began with the sacred marriage of water with stone. The living water fell on stone, remained present on stone, and the first bacterium was born from stone and water. Life came forth from the rocks, although its cradle was the water.

When you tread on Iona, whether in spirit or in flesh, commune with its stones and rocks as those early people of wisdom did – the Red race which knows about the Earth. The land where eventually their tribes ranged and settled (because they were not always nomads) once incorporated the sacred site of Iona. And the Celts, as well as their forebears before them, share this heritage of redness and a similar mystical connection to the land.

The Red people and the ancient Celts believed that stones are graced with each of the five senses, as well as profound empathy and the ability to see into the future and replay the events of the past. They are supreme record-keepers. It was taught that they have self-awareness and are home to spirits.

The storytellers of Iona, who sensed a truth and wove a tale, in gathering their stories were said to have listened to the rocks, and to the sound of the sea ever-present everywhere on the isle, and to the sound of the wind in the grasses. But what grounded the captured story, and allowed it to take shape and come forth, were the rocks and the stones.

There are no stone circles upon Iona, which abound everywhere else in the vicinity, although there is a little ring of stones on the holy isle believed to be the remnants of Saint Columba's cell. The reason, it is said, is because Iona gives rather than receives; and surrounding stone circles receive and hold powerful and mysterious forces which flow from her rather than being given to her from elsewhere.

An ancient Druid of the isle is recorded to have said disconsolately that all the stone circles were removed from Iona by its monks. But there are those who believe that the island itself is spiritually akin to a stone circle, and still others who imagine that there is a circle of stones that form a sacred temple deep within its subterranean structure, because, of all rocks on Earth, Iona's are most sacred.

As pilgrims, with open minds and hearts and a readiness to see visions, let us explore why this might be so.

CHAPTER 2

IONA, THE METROPOLIS OF DREAMS

In describing her impressions of the soul of Iona, Fiona tells a story from Ireland. She relates how Mochaoi, an abbot, was cutting wattles in a wood one day, in preparation for building a wattle and daub church for his community. 'He heard a bright bird singing on the blackthorn near him. It was more beautiful than the birds of the world.'

Mochaoi listened, entranced, and asked the bird: 'Who was thus delighting him.' The bird replied that it was an angel, come to encourage Mochaoi in his good work and, because of the love in the abbot's heart, to amuse him for a time with its sweet song.

'Thereupon, the bird sang a single sweet surpassing air, then fixed his beak in the feathers of his wing and slept. But Mochaoi heard the beauty and sweetness and infinite range of that song for three hundred years... yet to him it was less than an hour. For three hundred years he remained listening, in the spell of beauty: nor in that enchanted hour did any age come upon him, or any withering upon the wattles he had gathered; nor in the wood itself did a single leaf stir.'

The bird awoke and said farewell, and Mochaoi lifted his wattles and wandered home in a dream. Staring, he saw that instead of the little wattled cells of his community, a great stone church stood before his wondering eyes. A passing stranger told him that it was the church of St Mochaoi.

The abbot went into the church and spoke to the brethren assembled there, none of whom he knew, telling them the story of the bird and its song and his enthrallment in the wood. They told him of a legend, three hundred years old, that related how their first abbot had gone into the wood one fine morning and had been carried away by angels.

Acknowledging his story, they made him abbot again, and revered him as a saint, and built a shrine in the enchanted wood at the spot where for three hundred years he had been taken into the heart of God; and there 'surpassingly white angels' often alighted, and sang songs of great beauty in the trees, and in ecstasy carried the prayers of the faithful to the highest heavens.

This magical story not only resonates with the spirit of Iona because Iona was once known as 'The Isle of Birds', and because of the link between angels and birds and the songs of birds, and because angel sightings are legion there. Fiona tells it above and beyond these things because 'I am reminded of the story of Mochaoi when I think of Iona. I think she too, beautiful isle, while gathering the kelp of human longing and tears and hopes, strewn upon her beaches by wild waves of the world, stood, enchanted, to listen to a Song of Beauty. "That is a new voice I hear in the wave," we can dream of her saying, and of the answer: "we are the Voices of the Eternal: listen awhile!"'

Iona is dreaming a dream for us of a new era, a new age, so momentous and stupendous that from it, so her myths say, there will arise a new Earth and a new heaven. She dreams her dream to hold it for us in eternity until it can descend and be fully realised as a living entity within our waiting world.

People who have walked upon Iona speak of the isle as pure, virginal, encompassing a clear, undefiled space, just as in the region of Virgo the heavens are clearest of celestial phenomena, or just as Mochaoi listened to the angelic bird and, because of the love in his heart, became filled with the sanctity of God-consciousness.

When he awoke, as after a vast expanse of time Iona is now ready to wake, his temple had been built and was ready to be filled with his spirit. And perhaps, if he had not remained rapt in the magic of the angel's song, communing with heaven as he stood on Earth, his brethren would not have received as if through his channel the inspiration they needed to construct the temple as it needed to be constructed. When Iona offers up her secrets, as is her destiny in our own time, we shall see that she too was ever our link between heaven and Earth, and that her community is the whole world.

After relating the story of Mochaoi, Fiona goes on to make her most famous and most frequently quoted prediction:

'When I think of Iona I think often, too, of a prophecy once connected with Iona; though perhaps current no more in a day when prophetical hopes are fallen dumb and blind.

'...I believe that we are close upon a great and deep spiritual change. I believe a new redemption is even now conceived of the Divine Spirit in the human heart, that is itself as a woman, broken in dreams and yet sustained in faith, patient, long-suffering, looking towards home. I believe that though the Reign of Peace may be yet a long way off, it is drawing near: and that Who shall save us anew shall come divinely as a Woman...But whether this Divine Woman, this Mary of so many passionate hopes and dreams, is to come through mortal birth, or as an immortal Breathing upon our souls, none can yet know.

'Sometimes I dream of the old prophecy that Christ shall come again upon Iona, and of that later and obscure prophecy which foretells, now as the Bride of Christ, now as the Daughter of God, now as the Divine spirit embodied through mortal birth as a Woman...the coming of a new Presence and Power: and dream that this may be upon Iona, so that the little Gaelic island may become as the little Syrian Bethlehem. But more wise it is to dream, not of hallowed ground, but of the hallowed gardens of the soul wherein She shall appear white and radiant. Or, that upon the hills where we are wandered, the Shepherdess shall call us home.'

What is it about Iona that has inspired numerous reports, now seen only as old tales, of frequent visits to the isle by Jesus as a boy, with his mother Mary and his sister Naomi, all accompanied by Joseph of Arimathea; and by Mary Magdalene and Jesus in their adult youth; and by Mary Magdalene and John the Beloved after the crucifixion, and by one other, of whom more will be revealed?

And why is it that the secret they knew and cherished is a secret, not only for Christians, but for the adherents of all religions of the world, and the faiths of those who are close to nature, and those who have no belief? And what is it about the very rocks of Iona that makes them so sacred?

There exist legends, within the mystery schools of the past and within native traditions (which were in any case linked with these esoteric schools), relating to the earliest continents: continents that existed before they merged into Pangaea, and Pangaea divided into what would gradually become the seven continents of our present era. Among the first was what tradition refers to as Polaris, a lush, temperate land located at the North Pole.

Legend says that this continent of the far north was known as the land of the 'high places', and that within it lived a people known as the God Race, men and women of high evolutionary degree. They emitted light and were known as the 'shining ones', graced with extraordinary gifts of such wonder and magnitude that to Earthly humanity, just coming into being, they seemed like angels or deities. The mystery teachings say that they were in fact human beings, but human beings who had unfolded and perfected all the divine attributes which are given in embryonic form to every member of humanity.

This God Race came to our Earth from other planets so evolved in their vibrational essence that they were invisible spheres, pulsating in their transcendent life far above the slow, heavy, dense dimension which houses physical manifestation.

These invisible planets were numbered among what the ancient Egyptians called 'the imperishable stars', worlds of such exquisite evolution that they had become spirits, as the people who lived upon them were spirits, star-like in their essence and, with regard to the clan of the God Race who came to Earth, guided by Osiris, 'shepherd of brilliant stars'. Osiris, it is said, was known among the God Race as a guardian, a leader, a star fulsomely radiant among stars. He was appointed to come to Earth from Sirius, a shining world where he served as one of its Grand Masters.

The God Race were immortals. Their 'high places', the legends say, comprised the location where our planet rises in alignment with the celestial centre called the pole of heaven, the axis of the sky. The mystery of the North Pole and its lights were seen as an Earthly representation of this wonder. It was here, in Polaris, that the first notion of the unicorn with its celestial horned 'pole', sign and symbol of the God Race, was breathed out into the world, because the unicorn resembles enlightened consciousness honed to a single point of unification. The unicorn was known to tread the 'high places'.

The God Race, according to these legends, were our overseers. They nurtured Earth's new developing humanity. They were aided in their task by another race of human beings from an evolved planet belonging to our own solar system, a contingent of which travelled to Earth to take up their posts.

They were not as exalted as the God Race but were nevertheless highly advanced in their evolution. They were known by the people of Earth as demigods.

Eventually, these demigods fell from grace and embraced ethical darkness, and in so doing they destroyed Polaris, causing it to freeze over. Part of the continent sank beneath the polar seas, but part of it was saved from the waves and remained habitable. It was named Hyperborea ('extreme' or 'far north' or 'behind the north wind'), referred to in the Old Testament (*Book of Isaiah* 14:13, Revised Standard Edition) as 'the mountain of assembly in the far north', the place where heavenly beings held council, although by then the continents had changed again and Hyperborea with its mystic mountain was now the island of Britain.

Nevertheless, this legendary mountain that inspired awe among the ancients was definitely considered by the mystery schools and esoteric traditions as located in Britain. The same mystical northern mountain, referred to as 'Safon' in the myths of the Canaanites, is mentioned again in the *Book of Isaiah* when the prophet reproaches the King of Babylon: 'You said in your heart, "I will ascend to heaven; above the stars of God I will set my throne on high; I will sit on the mount of assembly in the far north."'

There are many holy mountains that grace our planet, and in effect our ancestors regarded every mountain as holy, although some were more revered than others. These especially blessed mountains were considered as the abode of the gods. Even so, 'the mountain of assembly in the far north' seems in almost all cultures to have reigned supreme amongst them. But exactly which mountain, among the sacred 'high places', was this hallowed peak?

On Iona's highest point, the famous medium Grace Cooke saw, in a vision of the far distant past, fiery rocks and islands descending into the sea. They seemed to be bodies from outer space, drawn to Earth by the force of gravity, which indicated to her that Iona, and perhaps all the British Isles, were delivered to the Earth from elsewhere in the cosmos. But, much later on and for a second time, Iona herself was hurled into the sea from her base on land 'in the far north', for human folly had set into motion the geological process by which she was displaced.

A truth which Fiona knew in her deepest heart was this: Iona was that holy mountain of assembly in the far north, and what remains of her today is its highest peak. For Iona, although she might appear to be a little island, is actually a mountain top; there came a day in our Earth's ancient past when, via natural forces that were hideously manipulated to enact such a ritual, Iona, or the mountain of which she was its summit, was decapitated; and her lovely head, most sanctified among the high places, now has its resting place in the sea, washed around by the passionate restless waves that constantly tell her story on the wind.

CHAPTER 3

'THE ONE BIT OF EDEN THAT WAS NEVER DESTROYED'

W ho tells of this revelation: that Iona is a mountain top, the most
revered and sacred mountain top our world has ever known?
Fiona tells of it, in veiled, half-realised vision; and we will see that a story
supports it, a story even now unfolding and reaching its culmination in
our own time. Many scattered references and ancient rumours point to it;
but, perhaps most poignantly, the poet of Iona sang of it.

The poet of Iona was Mary Macleod, 'the sweet singer of the
Hebrides'. She carried the beauty of her Gaelic language within her
like a secret flame, whose radiance was in her voice and also in her face
and form, for Mary could sing exquisitely, and made songs of her own
verses. It seemed that Mary Macleod's beauty was of a kind that men
dared not vulgarize in thought. Instead, they fell silent in its presence,
seeing within their soul-memory what womanhood was when, in a
distant time, men invented the salute by shielding their eyes as they knelt
before a woman who represented Goddess, indicating that the light of
her essence and purity was too brilliant for their mortal eyes to behold.

Mary Macleod said of Iona that 'it was the one bit of Eden that had
not been destroyed,' and that it held central place there as an exalted
temple of natural beauty and wilderness, where only angels' feet trod.
No Earthliness was allowed to encroach on its sanctity, and, within the
temple, bright angels waited to serve Earth's tender new humanity and
carry it towards its god status...

The wisdom of the heart, our inner Sophia, does indeed intimate
through exalted myth, esoteric legend and the dim memories of ancient
secret brotherhoods, that Iona was once the highest peak on a northern,
but temperate, continent called Polaris, and that the entire continent was
a paradise on Earth. The celestial Eden was located just above its earthly
dimensions, in the higher or heavenly realms; but that heavenly Eden
was linked directly to Earth via the sacred peak that is now the island
of Iona.

Around and upon and within Iona was set the jewel within the crown
of Polaris – the heavenly-Earthly city that was sited on Earth and in

11

heaven, and was a wondrous conjoinment of the two. Its name was Eden or Edin. But this city was not a city such as we know cities today.

It was a realm of wonder, where mystic confluences – consummations and configurations of divine force – played between bright angels, the radiant race of exalted humanity which had descended to oversee the development of the new humanity on Earth, and God. Its keynotes were joy, beauty, harmony, service, God-power, love's ecstasy and the expression of perfect brotherhood. There was no degradation, no darkness, within the city or upon Polaris. But the miraculous city shone brightest of all.

Even today it is remembered in the name Edinburgh, city of Edin and its surroundings. The original Edin or Eden was once just as real, although exalted, a city of heaven upon Earth. But what sustained it? What made such a surpassing miracle – that heaven could descend and pulsate in glory on Earth – possible?

Esoteric vision tells us that in her earliest days, the Earth received a baptism of divine forces. Above the North Pole, which connected Earth's heart with the heart of the universe and the heart of God, a circuit of polar stars inscribed, through sacred geometry, a special influence – a benediction of grace – deep into her core. It made vibrant and musical the invisible umbilical cord that attached Earth to the essence of God.

And out of the polar opening (pilots have reported such a disc-shaped opening above the North Pole which distorts the controls and technical apparatus within their planes) there came forth an eight-rayed being of great brilliance and beauty. It was an uprush and objectification of that descended force from the stars which carried a direct connection to Divine consciousness right down into Earth's heart. It was a gift and a manifestation of God.

Akhenaten, the radical pharaoh, spoke of this eight-rayed being that links us to God as the sacred Aten. Mary Magdalene taught of its mysteries in her gospel when she described the ascent of the soul into enlightenment as a rising gradient symbolised by an eight-stepped ziggurat.

The Knights Templar revered it with the emblem of the octopus, and especially with their eight-pointed red cross. Moses hinted of it as a numerical figure when his pharaonic rod became a coiling serpent.

Buddha gave signs of it through the holy symbol of the swastika with its double-ended arms (the one that turns in the right direction!) and through his eightfold path to perfection. Solomon's wisdom, which held the key to the mystery of love, breathed intimations of it when he gave an octagonal design to the floor of his Holy Temple.

The enigmatic country of 'Languedoc', meaning 'Nation of Eight', now part of southern France, whispers of it throughout the many mysteries she enshrouds within her history. King Arthur, whose signature was that of the Pendragon, bore its sacrosanct form as his standard, for the sign of the serpent or dragon is the continuous life-flow represented by the entwining serpents, feminine and masculine, which form the figure 8. The great symbol of the Caduceus, staff of healing and wholeness, remembered its mystery. But most of all its memory is preserved in the history of the Holy Grail, for the Holy Grail is exactly what it is.

Its fabled cup is the cup of our hearts, for we received that divine essence and connection in our own hearts when the Earth received them into hers; they are part of the magic of the sacred flame within us that is our source and our vital reality of being. We were not in physicality upon the Earth at that time, but we were souls in waiting, ready to fulfill our divine mission of descent into dense matter.

Within the cup is the force which lifts us to heaven, and yet ensures that our link with Earth is so blessed that we can travel like angels up and down it, entering heaven whilst we are still on Earth and walking the Earth whilst we are in heaven. This force is real. It is not symbolic or hallucinogenic or an enactment of a ritual at an altar. It is actual. It makes a nonsense of the question as to whether or not God and the heavenly realms exist, and is why, when the Holy Grail was active on Earth, such a question never even arose.

The Holy Grail was the reason why Eden was able to exist on Earth. And the first point where it rose from the North Pole and rooted itself into the outer body of the Earth was Iona. It grounded its essence in eight places, eight stations upon our planet. They created the form of a cross with forked ends to its arms, like the traditional Templar cross.

These eight stations enabled fully conscious, spiritual lift-off, with a guaranteed return ticket, for the humanity of planet Earth, even for her birds and creatures, even for her manifestations of nature. But Iona was its initial and supreme location, Iona that was once a sacred mountain and is today a mountain top, and which in her earliest days stood as a great holy peak at the point of the North Pole, upon the continent of Polaris, within the city of Eden.

CHAPTER 4

SORROWFUL SONGS

The saddest story ever told is the story of those far-off times, and their sorrowful songs can still be heard on the winds and in the tides of Iona. And yet Iona sings too of the unveiling of a joy of such magnitude that it will heal and redeem all those ancient wounds, still bleeding today. The time draws near, she whispers; the time is almost upon us; the time is your time, and mine.

Fiona tells a story of Iona that invokes the spirit of that older story, like a cave painting seen by the light and darkness of dancing flames and shadows. The tale is an interweaving of truth and symbols and actuality, like the myths of Ur and Troy, whose real presence upon the Earth have been uncovered and verified.

It starts with the fairies. The people of Iona distinguished between the diminutive fairies that children often encounter, and the noble people of the Sìdhe ('Shee'), who were once, it is said, a race that existed in a high-vibrational physicality upon our Earth. Because the Grail was active in those days, these gracious and dignified fairy folk of high degree were able to move with ease between the physical dimension and their true home within the etheric worlds, as could humanity, although our home on this planet was the material domain. As we shall see, what we lost when the Grail was cut off from us is truly incalculable.

Fiona learned from an islander of Iona that these noble fairies, who had once lived within the single hill and within the underworld of the isle, had now moved further north, although elusively and temporarily they graced Iona still with their presence, for they could not stay away from such sacred ground. Nevertheless, a long time ago they had gone north. That was their kingdom and queendom now.

Fiona wrote: 'Some say it is among the pathless mountains of Iceland that they are fled away. But my friend spoke to an Iceland man, and he said he had never seen them. There were Secret People there, but not the Gaelic Sìdhe.

'Their Kingdom is in the North, under the Fir-Chlisneach, the Dancing Men, as the Hebrideans call the polar aurora. They are always young there. Their bodies are white as the wild swan, their hair yellow as honey, their eyes blue as ice. Their feet leave no mark on the snow. The women are white as milk, with eyes like sloes, and lips like red rowans. They fight with shadows, and are glad; but the shadows are not shadows to them...There are no men of the human clans there, and no shores, and the tides are forbidden.'

These noble fairy tribes which moved so far north have grown cold, remote, almost cruel, the stories say. They constantly express and propitiate the unbalanced energies, the uncompromising light and shadow, that human folly has left behind, because it is their task to shepherd and manage the hidden force fields of the Earth, even those that we ourselves have damaged, or, in our foolishness, have actually created. In order to do this, as the stories of Iona tell, they have been compelled to form their kingdom directly around and within the North Pole, where once, many millennia ago, such a heinous human crime was committed.

Since the Grail was severed from Earth and from human consciousness, this battle between darkness and light has expressed itself as unharmonised forces of radiance and shadow, ranged against one another like vast hosts. Their point of balance is within the human heart, which contains all mystery. Yet, in failing the spirit and momentum of creation so disastrously by refusing to provide this point of balance, humanity's own heart centre, both collectively and individually, has been thrown off balance. It is, thankfully, a damage that can be healed, although complete healing will come only when we restore the Grail to its rightful point of function within our hearts and within our planet.

At each of the major stations of the Grail, this unsettling contrast between light and dark forces presents itself. It is encountered at Chartres and Rennes-le-Chateau, its southern (forked) arm. In the latter area, a colleague of Grace Cooke, the famous medium, lost his mind and stabbed a member of her party, and there are many tales of people who have visited the region and felt themselves pursued by demons.

The Grail's northern forked arm, in Iona and Rosslyn (near Edinburgh), is unique in that Iona, within her little ring of sacred space, still holds the balance to some degree, although in the valley beneath Rosslyn, dark forces seem to rise up to the cliff's edge, and its river in psychic vision runs with blood. Also, as we shall see, a murder occurred within the famous Chapel there, although it is a place sanctified on levels other than just the orthodoxy of formal religion

In Glastonbury and Stonehenge (with energies that encircle Avebury), which comprise the western forked arm of the Grail, the forces of darkness and light interlock and do battle; many people have spoken of their awareness of this light and shade at these two points; at the forks of its eastern arm, Jerusalem and Ur (the latter now Iraq), the same conflict is sorrowfully evident.

And in the ancient cathedral city of Lincoln, which is its quintessential (fifth) midpoint at the intersection of the cross – or, if the Grail is counted as a figure of 8, as it truly is because of its double-ended arms even though it also has a structure of 4, Lincoln may be seen as its central 9 or 'tower' position – the shadow and radiance contrast is very evident.

On retreats experienced within the grounds of Lincoln cathedral, a mighty demon has been seen and his forces experienced and struggled against; and the Dean of Lincoln cathedral, only just over a decade ago, requested that the cathedral be closed to the public so that it could be cleansed of evil spirits.

The particular Ionean story of the fairies of the aurora which Fiona tells concerns a pre-Columban Christian monk (for there were monks on Iona before Columba came), who sailed to their kingdom long ago.

'He sailed for thrice seven days till he lost the rocks of the north: and for thrice thirty days, till Iceland in the south was like a small bluebell in a great grey plain; and for thrice three years among bergs. For the first three years, the finned things of the sea brought him food; for the second three years, he knew the kindness of the creatures of the air; in the last three years angels fed him. He lived among the Sìdhe for three hundred years.

'When he came back to Iona, he was asked where he had been all that long night since evensong to matins. The monks had sought him everywhere, and at dawn had found him lying in the hollow of the long wave that washes Iona on the north. He laughed at that, and said he had been on the tops of the billows for nine years and three months and twenty-one days, and for three hundred years had lived among a deathless people.

'He had drunk sweet ale every day, and every day had known love among flowers and green bushes, and at dusk had sung old beautiful

17

forgotten songs, and with star-flame had lit strange fires, and at the full of the moon had gone forth laughing to slay shadows. It was heaven, there, under the lights of the North.

'When he was asked how that people might be known, he said that away from there they had a cold, cold hand, a cold, still voice, and cold ice-blue eyes. They had four cities at the four ends of the green diamond that is the world. That in the north was made of Earth; that in the east, of air; that in the south, of fire; that in the west, of water. In the middle of the green diamond that is the world is the Glen of Precious Stones. It is in the shape of a heart, and glows like a ruby, though all stones and gems are there. It is there the Sìdhe go to refresh their deathless life.

'The holy monks said that this kingdom was certainly Ifurin, the Gaelic Hell. So they put their comrade alive in a grave in the sand, and stamped the sand down upon his head, and sang hymns so that mayhap even yet his soul might be saved, or, at least, that when he went back to that place he might remember other songs than those sung by the milk-white women with eyes like sloes and lips red as rowans.

'"Tell that honey-mouthed cruel people they are in Hell," said the abbot, "and give them my ban and my curse unless they will cease laughing and loving sinfully and slaying with bright lances, and will come out of their secret places and be baptized."

'They have not yet come.'

Fiona's smiling touch of irony at the end of her re-telling of this fable surely shows that she understands the mysteries of the Earth better than the abbot did in his day, although the story of Columba, Iona's later abbot, and Columba's radiance of vision, is a vital component of the life-blood of Iona.

That life-blood contains also the tale of Black Angus. Fiona sets up a compelling atmosphere in her recounting of it.

'One night, a dark rainy night it was, with an uplift wind battering as with the palms of savage hands the heavy clouds that hid the moon, I went to the cottage near Spanish Port, where my friend Ivor Maclean lived with his old deaf mother. He had reluctantly promised to tell me the legend of Black Angus, a request he had ignored in a sullen silence when he and Padruic Macrae and I were on the Sound that day. No tales of the kind should be told upon the water.'

When Fiona came to his cottage, he welcomed her into the fire-glow of the warm interior, and they sat down together beside the hearth. Her friend should have been out in his boat, but, because of his undertaking to relate the story, Ivor, a fisherman by trade, would not venture anywhere near the running wave, due to the ill omen of telling the tale. "We were to go out tonight," he explained, "but no, not I, no, no, for sure, not for all the herring in the Sound."

After citing the ancient pedigree of the story as it had come down to him on Iona, Ivor began, giving his tale its traditional title of 'The Dark Nameless One'.

On a day of the days, the day of Brigid, which was the first day of February, Colum (St Columba) was walking alone by the sea shore. He was in deep meditation and praying as he wandered near the rocks. It was said that when Colum prayed aloud, miracles happened.

And so it was, for a great black seal with wicked eyes lying upon the rocks spoke up and answered him when, as was his wont, Colum greeted it kindly. But the seal's response was a rough curse to the saint's blessing. It then asked him if he knew where its woman was, and its little daughter, and Colum realised that it was of the seal people, those who are of the progeny of the seal, and yet can wear the guise of men.

It told Colum that its name was Black Angus, and that the woman it yearned for was Kirsteen M'Vurich. When Colum told it that he had no knowledge of where she was, Black Angus cursed him again and returned to the water, 'and the hoarse wild laugh of him sprang into the air and fell dead upon the shore like a wind-spent mew'.

Colum walked back to his brethren, disturbed by his encounter, repeating the rune 'God is good' to counteract its evil. As he approached the abbey he met Murtagh, 'an old monk of the ancient race of the isles', and asked him if he knew of Kirsteen M'Vurich. Old Murtagh replied that she was a good servant of Christ, a nun in the south isles, until Black Angus carried her off into the sea almost a thousand years ago.

"Where is she now?" asked Colum. "Is she dead?"

"No," said Murtagh. "She is the woman that weaves the sea-spells at the wild place out yonder that is known as Earraid: she that is called the sea-witch."

On asking why Black Angus sought her in vain if her whereabouts were known, Murtagh told Colum that it was his doom ever to seek and yearn for her, but never to find her. There then follows a strange exchange between the two, begun by Murtagh:

"It is Adam's first wife she is, that sea-witch over there, where the foam is ever in the sharp fangs of the rocks."

"And who will he be?"

"His body is the body of Angus, the son of Torcall of the race of Odrum, for all that a seal he is to the seeming; but the soul of him is Judas."

"Black Judas, Murtagh?"

"Aye, Black Judas, Colum."

Fiona ends her tale as ominously as she began it:

'But with that, Ivor Maclean rose abruptly from before the fire, saying that he would speak no more that night. And truly enough, there was a wild, lone, desolate cry in the wind, and a slapping of the waves one upon the other with an eerie laughing sound, and the screaming of a seamew that was like a human thing.

'So I touched the shawl of his mother, who looked up with startled eyes and said, "God be with us"; and then I opened the door, and the salt smell of the wrack was in my nostrils, and the great drowning blackness of the night.'

Why should a story of Lilith and Judas be part of the heritage of Iona's tales? Why should the story be known by the traditional title of 'The Dark Nameless One' if its characters were all named? And why should the sinister spirit of 'the Dark Nameless One' still bring a threat to the well-being of the islanders, and a breath upon the wind and in the sea and relayed through wild things, of lingering evil?

Taken as simply an eccentric story infused with the trappings of Christian orthodoxy, it makes little sense. But, when the history of Iona is truly known, both the story of Black Angus, and the story of the fairy people who grew cold and cruel and were compelled to move to the northernmost point of the world, make perfect sense.

It is time to tell the story of Iona, perhaps even as a tale akin to that of Orpheus, who after his decapitation sang the sorrowful song of his story as a melodious-mouthed head upon the running wave.

CHAPTER 5

THE GRAIL UPON IONA

What gives authenticity to the story about to be revealed? The living pulse of the story itself, its urgency of revelation in a time when its culmination is almost upon us, is a factor. Another is the confirmation that arises on every side in the timeline of our present-day history. Yet another comprises the artefacts which keep appearing and will, it seems, continue to do so, artefacts whose testimony we only dimly perceive at present, but which will be revealed in a sharpness and clarity of focus before long which will cause us to wonder why we never guessed it all in its fullness many centuries ago. But most of all, it is a story we know already, within our own hearts, within that centre which is the point of 'pure reason', as Blake terms it – reason that does not betray our innermost essence, the mystic source of our humanity. When that betrayal takes place, our hearts remain restless and uneasy, no matter what orthodoxy of science or of religion chooses to lay down as doctrine and declares incontrovertibly valid. And so this uncovering will be tested via the most authentic means of all – in the wisdom of the heart by Iona's pilgrims who are my companions on this journey.

First of all, imagine the worst scenario within the scope of human failings that could ever overtake our world. We might cite nuclear war; but many signs point to the fact that we have allowed nuclear war to rage in our far distant past, and have, albeit stuntedly and shakily, come back from it. We might think also of global barbarism, cruelty and horror running amok. This we have also witnessed in days long gone, although its phantoms persist and often take on flesh in our world of today.

Perhaps the loss of all hope would spell our surest doom? This, thank goodness, has never happened, although there are those who stand in the shadows, and plot and conspire to make it happen. Knowing this story (and, once known, it will be as if we have always known it) will help us to fend off that threat forever.

The very worst case scenario – apart from the loss of all hope – might be that some great teacher, filled with light, would come as a beacon for our world, some human being chosen as a vehicle of supreme light that could steer our destiny ineluctably towards blessed shores of ascendance – and yet fall and fail, and turn to the darkness, and kneel at its feet in worship, and collude with it in an effort to bring humanity to ruin and disintegration. Could something so heart-chilling really happen: something almost exactly similar to the hypothetical situation in which Jesus, having had an assault of temptation made on him by the forces of darkness in the desert wilderness, might have decided to take up their banner and forsake his true destiny? What if, in short, our greatest source of divine inspiration in human form, sent to us as a gift from the heart of God, had defied God and turned against us?

It seems that such a scenario did occur, in a time so distant that we can only summon it as a dream. Nevertheless, in dreaming, we might remember; for this story belongs to everyone. Some intimations of it have already been given. It is a story of Iona.

One cosmic day, on a day of days, our solar system came into being. Earth had her place within it in special relation to the great central sun (not our sun, but the sun at the centre of the universe), and because of this special placing, her destiny was to foster into being the densest material plane that the universe had ever known. We might call this plane the outermost frontier of God, and, once it was completed and perfected, the dynamic of creation would extend into new dimensions never before experienced.

The whole of the created cosmos partook of the material plane, but not to the profound extent that Earth would eventually express. When we look out into the majesty and drama of the cosmos today, despite its many wonders, we do not see what is truly there. We see only what we can perceive – the material plane, the outermost limit of creation – tantamount to being able to see only the hazy outline of the tip of a single toenail of a gargantuan being, never suspecting that the being exists, and drawing all our scientific conclusions from that misapprehension. But in fact the rest of the cosmos, whilst manifesting the dense materiality of the physical domain to us who inhabit that domain, is a spiritual expression of reality and is infused with Divine Spirit.

Within its many spheres, human evolution began; but this was an evolution within worlds and conditions that vibrated at a higher level than our dense Earthly physicality of today. Some planetary human communities made great strides in their evolutional odyssey, and became a God Race, beautiful, radiant, and attuned in perfect degree to love and harmony: of the very essence of the Divine. Others, born later from the heart of God, pressed close behind, making good headway. Some younger communities were a halfway-house, journeying at a slower pace in the footsteps of their shining brethren, but ever progressing into the light.

First of all, the God Race (mentioned in Chapter 3) came to Earth through the God-link that materialized as the mighty mountain which we will call Iona, for Iona it was, Iona that stood upon the continent of Polaris. Iona's name was Mount Heredom in those far-off days, meaning 'House of Inheritance', because she housed the Holy Grail, our most precious gift of inheritance from God. Mount Heredom stood directly above the North Pole.

The rocks from which Iona and part of the continent of Polaris were formed were not rocks of Earth. They came from the heavens, from outside our solar system whose materials had formed the rest of the planet in the normal way. They were infused with the inconceivable fire of the Divine. They came from the dimension of the God Race, those beautiful souls who were 'first home', so to speak: our cosmically primordial ancestors who were the first to return to the heart of God as realised, individuated, perfected beings; described as 'fully human' by Mary Magdalene in her mysterious and poetic gospel, discovered in 1896 in a dusty old antiquities shop in Cairo.

The God Race, from their home in higher dimensions far from Earth, forged these rocks with a special receptivity; and through their facilitation, God put 'the sword in the stone' by infusing Her-His essence into a concentrated dewdrop of Divine force that the rocks received in the manner of a Grail cup. They were directed to Earth and arrived safely by means of gravitational force, because Earth's heart longed to receive them. They became the larger part of Polaris and, especially, the holy mountain of Iona.

Earth's heart energies are contained within a huge white crystal, as big as a country, contained within her centre. The continent of Polaris, set at the North Pole, was formed and positioned above this immense white crystal, and Iona, the holy peak at the centre of Polaris, put down roots of purest light deep into its most profound point – Earth's heart of hearts.

The North Pole released its essence, an uprush of its descended God-force, by means of Polaris and the mountain that was Iona, and that force, which was the Grail current, arose and fixed itself into eight stations upon the Earth, as described above. Its first and supreme point was Iona or Mount Heredom, the holy mountain, which stood at the site of the North Pole. Iona was the custodian of the Grail energies, and its dispenser.

Because of its eight vital stations, the Earth was awash with the Grail forces, which formed a living ladder between heaven and Earth. The God Race could therefore live on Earth and occupy heaven simultaneously. Without the rising, refining power of the Grail, the density of vibration upon which Earth's body manifested would have rendered it impossible for them to inhabit.

Iona was the geographical connecting point between heaven and Earth; and the God people, together with the highest angels, dwelt on and within her sanctified ground. As Mary Macleod has told us, with the accuracy of an equation designed by Einstein, only the feet of angels and of God (the God Race) trod there. No earthliness was allowed to encroach on this holiest of sanctuaries.

Countless aeons later, Iona did become the point of connection between heaven and Earth for an advanced but less exalted humanity, after the God race had been forced to leave the Earth. And, of course, Iona or Mount Heredom was always the facilitator of the Grail, which included everyone in its loving power of upliftment.

Yet these were her beginnings – as the holy of holies, where only gods and angels walked. These shining ones oversaw the beginnings of life on Earth and its gradual progression into deepest matter. They chose simian bodies for Earth's new humanity and developed a human chakra system* for them, so that they could be seeded with human essence.

And then they put out a call to the furthermost planet of our solar system, the planet Nibiru, to come to Earth and seed them.

* See p. 107

24

CHAPTER 6

GOD'S HOLY MOUNTAIN

'The mountain of assembly in the far north'; this is the description given of the sacred mountain that was Iona in many ancient texts. Another name for her, and her ethereal dimensions, is 'Shambalah'.

We tend to think of Shambalah as mystically situated upon the utmost heights of the Himalaya mountain range. However, all the ancient texts relating to Shambalah place it in the extreme north, in the location of the British Isles; Tibet and the Himalaya do not have a north orientation.

There is certainly a beautiful connection-point to Shambalah or Eden above the peaks of the Himalaya, protected from the strife and contamination of the material Earth by a girdle of purest snow. But even though Shambalah is entirely etherealised today, the manifestation of heaven on Earth which was anciently Shambalah was, and continues to be, Iona.

Although still buried deep within the very soil of the country to the point where there is not much evidence that it exists, the light of Shambalah seeded all of Britain. And when that light rises again, as it will very soon, it will be a call from Iona's heart that summons it.

Iona was a mountain of assembly because the gods did indeed assemble there. They were human beings who had unfolded their God-nature, expressing all the gifts with which God has graced humanity in order that it may truly grow into the Divine image. Every one of those gifts – and even more, because God never ceases giving – dwells within us today like a secret folded bud, ready to burst into full flower as soon as we are ready to receive that Divine influx of light against which our inner blindness – and a network of sinister manipulations – shroud us so skilfully. But for life to change indelibly here on Earth, we must receive it together. We must collectively become a receptive cup.

The God Race called a certain chosen contingent of Nibiruan people here to planet Earth as stewards and custodians because they had made good spiritual progress within the level of materiality that obtained on Nibiru. Nibiru is very similar to Earth in many ways, although its physicality is less dense, more refined, in its vibrations. In this less spiritually taxing environment, a certain number of Nibiruans had reached a stage of evolution which was almost as developed as that of the God Race themselves.

There were two levels of evolutionary attainment on Nibiru. One, a minority, partook of this very high grade of achievement; the second, the majority, comprised a lesser degree: what we might think of as a 'halfway-house' humanity.

The humans of lesser degree on Nibiru were not less advanced due to their own culpability. They were, indeed, making good progress on their evolutionary path. The situation on Nibiru existed as it did because the God Race, initially overseeing the seeding of Nibiruan humanity just as they oversaw the seeding of Earthly humanity, had, by Divine decree, impregnated a number of Nibiruan women. These women were chosen for their courage and spiritual grace, and their committed receptivity to God's plan. The children to whom they gave birth grew up to form Nibiru's advanced humanity.

God's plan was that Her-His beloved humanity should be mercifully prevented from making laborious, stumbling and painful progress on its path by means of a Divine boost. God saw that it was possible for humanity to advance by a quicker, less harrowing, more beautiful route than the plodding, boulder-strewn course it would otherwise have to take.

The Divine strategy, given to us in grace, was implemented as described above, through impregnation by the God Race of certain members of the developing humanity on its designated planet. It was an exquisite outworking of Divine law, because it gave an opportunity for older humanity to give a helping hand to younger humanity, thus quickening the pace of their evolution; and it was a perfect expression of God's mercy and free-handed giving.

The spiritually and evolutionally enhanced members of the Nibiruan, or any other, planetary community that resulted from this process were not given their gifts so that they could selfishly exult in them and feel superior. They were born as kings, queens, ministers, healers, teachers, guardians and guides to their own planetary race, entrusted with a sacred mission to protect, educate and enlighten. Their lives were made golden by their gifts, but the gift of that gold was to be incessantly given. They were royal servants of their people.

It was a number of these enhanced Nibiruans, as well as a group of ordinary Nibiruans, who were summoned to Earth. They were called to be hosts of the Earth project because of their closeness in spirit to planet Earth, for Nibiru is Earth's planetary lover, masculine in essence as our Mother Earth is feminine. They are affinities.

Nibiru is also the founding member of our solar system, being its furthermost planet and therefore circumscribing it with guardianship. It has an enormous orbital cycle of 3,600 years, which creates an impressive sphere of protection! Nibiru is the shielding knight of our solar system. It was therefore beautifully appropriate that Nibiruans should host the great enterprise to develop Earth, with her special destiny, to perfection.

The enhanced Nibiruans were to dwell simultaneously in Eden and Polaris with the God Race in order to help to serve Earth's new humanity. The ordinary Nibiruans dwelt on Earth in their own sphere of vibrational resonance at first, which was not the densest material plane we know today, because that was still coming into being. It was in fact the same vibrational sphere they had inhabited whilst living on Nibiru, because of course these vibrational spheres or dimensions are levels of life, not planets.

Although the ordinary Nibiruans existed at an ethereal level of life on Earth that was lower in essence than the very high frequencies of Polaris which culminated in Iona and Eden, they could still share and bathe in these exalted frequencies from time to time because of the presence of the Grail. That was their joy and their inestimable gift from God.

The plan was that the ordinary Nibiruans would gradually penetrate matter until they could be fully grounded in the bodies that the GodRace (together with the enhanced Nibiruans, who were helping the God Race in their work) was preparing for them. As forecited, these bodies had been chosen from the simian family as the most suitable and adaptable animal bodies to facilitate the new humanity in their development and attainment of their highest potential on Earth in physical matter.

Animals are a vital element of the mystery, glory and majesty of the physical domain when it was first conceived of in the Divine mind: an element that the essence of humanity (which, although created, is also Divine) would be given as a part of their gift of evolution via matter. All this mystery, glory and majesty would be ours, by decree of God;

and it would be added to us by means of our evolutional journey within the vehicle of the animal. This is the true meaning of our sanctified investment with the dominion of animals – and it has nothing whatsoever to do with hunting, trapping, eating, degrading, or performing experiments on them!

Animals are the spirit, the potency, the beauty, poetry and wonder of the inner essence of the elemental forces: born of God, but not God-realised. It is our task to bring them – and ourselves through them – to God-realisation. And in doing so, the beauty and facilitation of creation is added to us in full measure.

The question therefore arises: which animal was it that was chosen for the Nibiruan line of human evolution?

The answer is that it was the serpent; and, as a further expression of the serpent: the dragon.

When the Nibiruans, both enhanced and ordinary, came to Earth, they immediately began to meld their etheric serpentine form into the form of the perfect Earthly human being. They did so because this perfect form was a principle which had to be held within their Divine imagination (for our imagination is Divine – our most powerful gift from God) before it could begin to gain expression on Earth through the simian body.

So, although both degrees of Nibiruans operated entirely within the etheric and spiritual dimensions of life on first coming to Earth, their bodies (for we always have a body on whatever level we function) began to assume the form of most beautiful human beings, even more refined than our own in the present day – representing how we shall look when we have finally perfected ourselves. However, in the case of the enhanced Nibiruans, these changing forms still held on to something of the serpent in their appearance. And in fact, intimations of the sinuous, flowing wave-form of the serpent will always be a beautiful inheritance of Earthly humanity.

It was only the ordinary Nibiruans who were to evolve into fully physical bodies walking the Earth. The enhanced Nibiruans were to oversee and overlight the process under the guidance of the God Race. However, both ordinary and enhanced Nibiruans were soon joined by others.

Races from other star systems came here to assist the Nibiruans with their great project. They were all human, and each race had evolved via its chosen planetary animal. Six peoples came here in those early days of the world. Two of these peoples originated from Nibiru, for Nibiruans had evolved through two races – a black and a white race. Both were, of course, serpentine in form, and were very closely allied, although also very different.

Some members of these star races joined the enhanced Nibiruans, being of equal spiritual stature. They lived on Polaris and, simultaneously, within the Edenic dimension whose link to Earth was Iona. Some, being of lesser spiritual stature, joined the ordinary Nibiruans about to venture deep into the densest physical domain and enter the bodies of the prepared simians; for, like the Nibiruans, all six star races were composed of two groups: 'enhanced' and 'ordinary'.

For a time – some thousands of years – a golden age reigned on Earth. There was no bloodshed; no animal was slain. The races merged in joy, though each remained clearly individuated. If contention ever arose it was directed and melded into an increased flow of compassionate tolerance and became a source of kindly and liberating humour. The people drew their spiritual vision from their heart, and knew God, whose presence walked among them continually, and continually brooded them like a mystical bird. The towering mountain, its sunlit peak a great symbol and a visionary spiritual teaching of joy, was a source of renewal, an ever-replenishing connection to the heavenly realms that all could partake of whenever their hearts grew weary. This was Iona's gift, although Iona herself during the golden age was touched by angels' and gods' feet only, so that her pristine forces could maintain their highest magnitude.

Nevertheless, though protected, Iona (Mount Heredom) was the key of admittance to the higher worlds. The people of Earth, the communities clothed in physical flesh, accessed the Grail forces that spread out from the mystical mountain, their pivotal point. Each individual could ascend by means of their own volition. Through Iona's dispensation, the gates of Shambalah, spoken of by the ancients as a 'fairyland', were open wide to all those who trod the Earth; and this gateway, of 'ivory and pearl and all things most wondrous and lovely', was upon Iona, and was Iona.

Then a shadow fell.

CHAPTER 7

THE KING AND QUEEN OF IONA

We can speak of a king and a queen of Iona or Mount Heredom: lord and lady over the assembly of the gods, those enhanced members of the six races which had come to Earth from the stars to oversee a great project; and over the ordinary communities among those races, whose members were to seed a selection of developing simian bodies with human essence in order that the great project might be carried out.

Above all and over all, dwelling with God and profoundly linked with the king and queen, presided the God Race, who directed from on high according to the ordinances of God, but who were subtle and gentle in their guidance. Their rod and rule served the principle of precision, never oppression or unwarranted interference.

The king and queen were not quite as we might think of them from our perspective of today. They were as one, for they consisted of a single androgyne. In those far-off times, human beings were androgynous. Both the male and female aspects of a single androgyne could manifest separately and function separately; but they were ever conjoined by an indissoluble bond.

The king and queen were God-appointed. They were the Divine couple, for they were a human reflection of the Daughter-Son of God, a supernal presence we know as Christ Consciousness or the Christic forces. But we should not think of these forces clinically as a concept. An ineffable Being, the Christ Being, heads them, just as we perceive that God is a Being from whom all things flow, including the Christ Being in the heavens.

The king and queen in question constituted an androgyne that was perfectly attuned to the Christ. This androgyne was not the great Christ Being itself, of course, but a human vessel for Christ, just as, inconceivably far off in the future, Jesus and Mary Magdalene would take up the same appointment, although their androgynous nature was ethereal. The decree was always that the Christ Being overlit the selected Divine human couple on any given planet, who in turn flooded with light the 'enhanced' community, which passed that light on to the 'ordinary' communities.

The God Race, who were individually Christed (fully receptive to the Christ Being), oversaw the selection of the Divine couple or Divine androgyne from among a planet's enhanced community, according to the most spiritually receptive among them. It was not until the coming of Jesus and Mary Magdalene that a Divine couple was chosen from among the God Race itself; one who, moreover, by a miracle of God descended into the furthermost realms of matter to actually walk amongst us in flesh on Earth.

Prior to this miracle, the Divine couple or androgyne, once selected and anointed, did not descend to the lower planes of life inhabited by the 'ordinary' communities. Instead, certain leaders and adepts from these communities were brought into their presence by ascending the ladder to the upper realms provided by the forces of the Grail. These forces were present on other planets, but not to the singular degree in which they took form on Earth, which required the unfolding of an unprecedented expression of their miracle because of its dense physicality. The Grail was a special gift to the children of Earth from God.

Although Nibiru naturally had its own Divine couple, the selection of the Divine couple for Earth was actually made on Nibiru from the enhanced Nibiruan community so that it would be in place from the beginning of Earth life. This was because things had to be done a little differently on Earth. Its challenges were to be greater than any which had yet come into existence.

Due to the density of matter on the Earth plane, it was ordained that the enhanced community from Nibiru should impregnate the ordinary community on Earth so that the planet could go on to develop her own enhanced community. The ordinary humanity on Nibiru had been enhanced by the God Race themselves, who had impregnated selected Nibiruan women, and in time had chosen the Divine couple from the community that emerged from these pregnancies.

This was normal procedure. But because of Earth's density, it was impossible for the high-frequency God Race to descend so far into matter as to be able to impregnate Earthly women. A level of mediation had to be created, which was supplied by the enhanced Nibiruans, of high vibration, yet not so high as their fathers among the God Race. They were the designated impregnators.

The androgyne that comprised the King and Queen of Iona (linking Eden with Polaris, the latter a few steps below the former in terms of dimension) bore the name of Anu. Individually, the king was called Annum, and the Queen, Antu. They were known as 'the Glorious Daughter-Son', 'the Vehicle of Heavenly Light' which had travelled to Earth from Nibiru – the chosen Divine couple for Earth.

They headed a democratic assembly comprising the enhanced members of the six star races that had come to Earth, and a majority vote decided all affairs of governance. This assembly was known later as the Anunnaki Council. 'Anunnaki' means 'those who came down'; the translation does not refer to space people who came from the skies, but to the enhanced brethren who descended to Earth and ascended again to their own higher (yet nevertheless Earthly) dimension of Eden by means of the Grail forces. Members of the God Race and 'angels most bright and beauteous' dwelt in Eden, and they overlit the Anunnaki Council.

During the golden age, there was no strife throughout the Earth, and Anu poured the blessings of Divine wisdom, power and love upon her-his domain in fullest measure. This domain comprised the Earth below (our Earth of today) and the higher sphere of Eden.

One important point to bear in mind is that beyond the loveliness of Eden there was a higher, deeper dimension still, which was more exalted even than Eden. This noble sphere of life was, we might say, the very highest dimension of the Earth. It was so beautifully resonant with Divine light that it was heaven; and yet it was also Earth. It represented the point where Earth transcended into heaven and was consummate with heaven.

We are connected with this Earth-in-heaven via the deepest point within our hearts, wherein a white eternal flame burns that we can magically summon into a star. This star, free from all taint of self-interest and ego, is the most powerful force within us because it is our direct connection to God; our inheritance of holy fire. It is the Holy Grail within.

This beyond-Eden dimension of the Earth was in itself ruled and sustained by a mighty queen who can only be described as a drop of the pure essence of Mother God, the All. It was because of the presence of this Great Queen that the Earth had been enabled to come into being and to maintain its planetary beinghood both within heaven and within the furthermost material sphere of manifestation.

The Great Queen was Divine, and yet she was simultaneously of Earth. In the deepest mystery of her being she was the Divine Earth. She was not the planetary spirit (the one we call 'Mother Earth') but something greater and more profound, although nevertheless intimately connected with the planetary spirit. She could assume human form, yet she was a drop of God. She was immeasurably beyond us all, and yet she was closest to us. She was known as Tiâmat's Daughter, Tiâmat who was Mother God, 'She who bore them all'.

Every being on Earth knew of her and sang her name; all in Eden held her in deepest reverence...until the darkness came. It is needful to remember her to properly understand this story, because what humanity imposed upon Tiâmat also happened to this supreme Daughter of Mother-God. Desecration could not fall upon one without falling upon the other.

The darkness first fell through self-doubt and fear. The conditions of Earth required that the male and female aspects of the human androgynes who had settled there should become more loosely connected in order to facilitate their adventure into physicality. Even the enhanced community in Eden, and therefore Anu too, were obliged to comply with this requirement. Although Anu – the androgynous king and queen – did not descend into the lower ethers (which were gradually becoming fully physical), those ever-materialising lower ethers were nevertheless connected to Anu's heart-sphere (Anu's area of operation, or home), so whatever affected them affected the king and queen.

Besides, as previously described, because of the power of the Grail, the enhanced community were able to descend directly into the lower spheres, and did so continually in their capacity as guides, educators, law givers and judicial overseers. And so it was that all felt the impact of this slackening of the androgynous bond. The men, however, were in a unique predicament.

It was universally recognised across the spheres that Mother God was the great Originator – that all had come forth from the Great Mother. Father God was with her and of her and came forth from her. There was no imbalance or inequality between the feminine and masculine aspects of God. Yet the Father had been born of the Mother, and she was worshipped as the First Principle, the Originator.

Therefore, when the males of the human androgyne on Earth felt the bond with their female counterparts slacken, they also felt a certain disorientating movement away from Source: something that they had never experienced before. To remedy this problem, by ordination of God, the females offered the males what has come to be called the 'Dew-Cup'.

The Dew-Cup was a manifestation connected to the ever-giving cup of the womb – the 'utterer' or 'uterus' of the Divine Word. It contained an ethereal substance called the 'living waters', which was sweet and fragrant, like nectar, and which correlated to a form of high-vibrational gold – gold that was pure spirit. The idea of ambrosia as a golden fluid that fed the Gods on Olympus is preserved in our mythology as a far-distant memory of the Dew-Cup.

The substance within it was indeed a kind of spiritual gold. It kept the men connected to Divine Source, to God, just as the Grail kept the Earth connected to the heart of God. (Women were naturally so connected.) The Grail forces were in the Dew-Cup. The essence it contained was a different application of the same energy.

A notion seized Annum, the male aspect of Anu, that this necessity to drink from the Dew-Cup meant that, somehow, males were inferior to their feminine counterpart. His notion was entirely spurious, of course, as the perfect balance between Mother-Father God is the essential dynamic which fuels creation. But, once it had taken hold, the notion grew into jealousy and rage. He began to drink from the Dew-Cup – which was always an offering of love and self-giving from the heart of Antu, his feminine aspect – with secret resentment, even with disgust, although what was offered to him was absolute in its purity and of the highest essence of God.

Other males from the Anunnaki assembly joined him in his surreptitious mutterings. They too began to reject the Dew-Cup and, when by necessity they were forced to accept it because of the painful dispossession they felt within when they deprived themselves of it, they ingested its contents with contempt and wrath. Soon they had hatched a plan.

By now, the project of Earthly humanity was well underway. The females who were to be impregnated with the sperm donors of the enhanced community would shortly be selected.

A terrible betrayal was planned.

Although the conspirators were compelled to allow the impregnations to go ahead, they arranged that a horrifying process comprising both scientific and esoteric sabotage would be applied to the genetic engineering procedures employed for the manipulation of the relevant sperm and ova. (The sperm was from members of the enhanced community, the ova from selected mothers of the ordinary community who had now entered into the physical plane of Earth.)

This horrible process was really akin to black magic. It would ensure that, instead of the consequent development of all the beautiful, god-like attributes intended as a gift for the little embryos, these attributes would retrograde into monstrous qualities. The resultant children would grow up to roam the world more like avenging demons than gods. That would certainly throw awry the plan for evolution on Earth, precisely the destructive deed that was the conspirators' great aim.

The second aspect of the conspirators' plot was that the Dew-Cup would be rejected outright and banned, and a new substance – monatomic gold – created so that the head and heart centres of the males could be 'renewed' via its potency. This monatomic gold would be created with dark alchemical procedures that forced its atoms into reverse-spin. The cosmic dance of love between the masculine and feminine components of its atoms would be overturned and replaced with a male-dominant dance pattern, which would throw the androgynous balance out of kilter yet more.

In other words, pure wisdom-consciousness from the heart of God, contained in the 'living waters' within the Dew-Cup, was to be replaced with artificial, manufactured poison concocted from distorted physical gold. The natural or God-attuned components within the gold that were unalterable even via the manipulations of the conspirators would ensure that head and heart centres were kept open and operative, just as the Dew-Cup did – but at a terrible cost. When it was ingested, the components within it that had succumbed to distortion would set to work within the human system like a drug.

With the contaminated gold – which in its formulation reduced to a fine white powder akin to flour so that bread cakes could be made from it – a rubescent fluid, also created from gold by dark alchemy, would be offered to the males as ceremonial wine. This time, it was a form of glass, made from the same distorted gold, which was melted into a fluid.

Within the fluid shone a light. But it was a false light. Its hypnotic, alluring attraction would feed the higher consciousness of humanity with lies. It would enter the head centre via the eye, through the pupil, as the actual fluid would enter the masculine system via the mouth. But the 'pupil' would learn a knowledge that enslaved the soul to a dark and cruel master.

The bread and the wine – the false communion.

But an even more heinous part of their plan was its third aspect – the conspirators' coup de grâce.

To separate men conclusively from their androgynous feminine counterparts, the final move of the conspirators was actually to cut off the Grail from the Earth. They knew that it connected them, as well as the planet, to the Great Mother, who, although she was one with the Father, was recognised as the Divine Originator and First Principle.

They also knew that, until they severed the Grail – and thus their conscious connection within their heart-centres to the Great Mother – they would never be able to separate entirely from their feminine androgynous selves. However much they abused and undermined this female aspect, their androgynous feminine aspect would always prevent them from breaking free and fulfilling in entirety whatever outrage and blasphemy they felt inclined to commit.

This three-part plan was eventually put into action. When the enhanced community was born to the Earth, it was indeed a race of spiritual and ethical monsters which had to be banished from the planet to prevent total carnage to the point where the ordinary human community was exterminated. It was locked away into a misty, dreaming dimension separated from Earth, with very little scope for expression. There it will remain, imprisoned and disempowered, until a way can safely be opened for these poor souls, abused and manipulated into monstrosity, to find their way back to the heart of God.

Their leader, however, with a lot of help from the conspirators, discovered a way to slip between dimensions and maintain some contact with the Earthly realms. The conspirators brought him on board with them and, in fact, got him to do their dirty work for them – it was he who delivered the blow that severed the Grail.

His name was Marduk and he had one aim – to re-establish his people upon the Earth once again, where they could all indulge in appetites and lusts that only the physical body and the physical domain could truly satisfy. Nevertheless, his people had vast intellects of high complexity, for only the machinations of the mind can impose suffering that scales the peaks of endless structures of cruelty.

However, there was something that Marduk didn't know. The conspirators, with King Annum at their head, had no intention of allowing Marduk's race (the Naphidem or the corrupted 'enhanced community' on Earth) to survive. They hated Earth and God's physical experiment. They wanted to get rid of physicality forever – not just Earth but the entire physical dimension.

Something of which they were chafingly aware was that the universe was lawful – it operated via clear rules. One of the laws that infuriated them most was that they could not just destroy Earth and her Earthly communities outright. For that to happen, those communities had to invite disaster on themselves by breaking certain codes and ethics of life to the point of no return.

So their plan was to get Marduk and his clan back to Earth, allow them to enslave its people and violate all codes of conduct that ever existed, and then sit back and enjoy the spectacle as the Earth was destroyed by karmic forces – forces they thought they stood above, apart from a few little glitches such as the one previously outlined. Physical humans, physical Naphidem, physical Earth – all gone forever as a result, and the higher realms of the universe theirs to conquer and dominate.

They had begun to see what they thought was the real God as an illusory mirror-reflection of themselves – entirely male, psychopathically scornful of the feminine principle, intent on military takeover, and ready to deck them out with the spoils of war as a reward for continually waging it.

And so there were two plots. One was the plot of overall destruction by King Annum and certain corrupt members of the Anunnaki Council. The second plot, which would fulfil the first, was the Naphidem plot, whereby the Naphidem schemed to get themselves back on Earth and into physical bodies. The Naphidem thought that the Council was helping them because it hated God, as they did, and wished to move against Her by flouting Her will and freeing those She had dispossessed: themselves. It had no idea about the first plot of total and final devastation which included them in its obliterating aims.

Meanwhile, what was Antu, the feminine counterpart of Annum, doing all this time?

She had fled to Iona to seek the counsel of God; for Iona, akin to the Grail forces that she facilitated, was an entirely feminine entity; and within her heart and upon her peak was a temple to Mother God – the most powerful place on Earth.

CHAPTER 8

THE SIGN OF THE DOVE

Antu sought refuge for her broken heart in the temple on Iona.
There Mother God comforted her, Mother God who was known
as Tiâmat, or a name akin to it, in those distant days. She spoke through a
great mystical presence of facilitation, one of surpassing spiritual beauty
and mystery who was indeed the one known as her Divine Daughter.

The name Tiâmat has many meanings, one of which is 'sea-serpent'.
This designation came from the language of Nibiru, for the Nibiruans
knew that their form, the form of the serpent, was deeply sacred. It was a
symbol of the wave-forms of energy coursing throughout the universe,
and was in particular allied to the secret of the forces of light, of the
emanations of our sun, the countless stars, and the great central sun of
the cosmos.

The serpent was linked with the sea in Mother God's name,
because the name and the symbol of the sea ('mer') is synonymous
with 'love' or 'beloved', and because the sea is the cradle of life from
which everything emerged.

When creation began, it was released from the heart of the Mother
in a flow of teardrops – her innermost essence, as our own deepest tears
are an expression of our profoundest depths. This teardrop, this 'salt
water' or 'bitter water', from which the name Mary is derived, contained
the impulses of creation and became the primal waters. It is why Mary
Magdalene is associated with flowing tears; not because she was a
penitent sinner, but because she was associated with the Great Mother,
with the primordial dynamic of creation, contained and nurtured in a
teardrop from the heart of God.

The teardrop is a mystical concept of creation; but from this mystical
concept arise all the chemical and biological and physiological processes,
in perfect scientific sequence and accuracy of application, which the
history of evolution comprises.

The Nibiruan form, based on the wondrous symbol of the serpent or
dragon, signifies the name Tiâmat in its entirety, because the Nibiruans
were sea-serpents. There was a human shape to these sea-serpents:

a shape that informs humanity throughout the cosmos and is that of a star. It translates as something similar to our own structure of form, although essentially it has nothing to do with our simian inheritance.

Nibiru, like Earth, is 70 per cent water, but is much bigger than Earth, so its seas are vaster than ours. Nevertheless, as human sea-serpents, the Nibiruans built monumental underwater cities and groves of breathtaking beauty upon their ocean floors. Underwater cities beneath huge lakes that could not be drowned land-structures are spoken of as still existing on Earth, built by the Nibiruans, who are an amphibious race. Close to Iona in the early days of the Earth, such a sacred lake existed, with wonders at its depths.

Tiâmat revealed to Queen Antu on the day that she went sobbing to the temple exactly what King Annum and his circle of conspirators intended to do. She explained with tenderness to the distraught queen that he must be allowed to carry out his wishes, because Mother-Father God had invested humanity with free will choice. However, Tiâmat informed Antu that she would not leave humanity without hope.

Tiâmat explained that Annum would seize power in his sole male right and cut Antu off from him entirely when he severed the Grail. He would depose his rightful successor, her elder son Enki who, like Antu herself, was entirely faithful to Tiâmat, and set his younger son Enlil, one of the conspirators, on the throne in his place. (Enlil was the son of Ki, Annum's second wife, whom he took to undermine Antu. These sons, of course, once the Grail had been disconnected, would no longer be even loosely androgynous.)

Yet Tiâmat would give humanity an unprecedented gift. She would infuse a crystalline matrix – an emerald tablet of exquisite purity – with all the knowledge, all the essence of higher perception, all the qualities that awoke bright-eyed in the consciousness of humanity by virtue of the Grail forces. This inconceivably precious emerald tablet would thus become keeper and guardian of the Grail.

One day, someone would be born to Earth of such perfection of soul and such radiance of spirit that the emerald tablet would be read and fully understood. This perfect soul would teach others, so that the Grail could at last be restored to Earth, and humanity's priceless inheritance returned to it. Ascension into freedom would begin. Tiâmat explained that this soul would come in the form of an androgyne, although its androgynous nature would be invisible. The soul would descend as a couple to the Earth.

Because, meanwhile, humanity would fall so deep into degradation and confusion, it would need a time of preparation and cleansing before the Grail could again be given to it via the emerald tablet. So Tiâmat would also similarly infuse a sapphire tablet, to be given to the Earth people before the emerald tablet was found and read. Its knowledge would be dispensed and absorbed prior to the discovery of the emerald tablet, to make ready for its coming.

Eventually, all would be well again on Earth. The Golden Age would return, but with this promise: that when it came once more, humanity would know even greater glories, would ascend to higher heights, than ever before.

Antu departed from the Temple of Iona still weeping, but with hope in her heart. All the course of human history from that fateful day to this – inspired but almost always war-torn, barbaric, anguished, never truly at peace – trooped wearily in phantom form through her sorrowing vision. She went down to the sacred lake and bathed her face in its silver waters. She saw the image of a dove in their shining depths; the white bird of peace – Tiâmat's sign.

...So these are the beginnings of Iona's story of joy and sorrow – that she was the most holy mountain on Earth, the sacred peak spoken of in old texts as comprising 'the high places' where unicorns were said to wander. She stood at the point of the North Pole, under the dancing lights of the Aurora Borealis. She was guardian of the mysteries of the Holy Grail, enshrining them within her body and linking heaven with Earth. Upon her and within her lived and assembled beings of untold spiritual beauty and grace, both angelic and human. Earthly humanity thought of them as gods. And one in particular shone above all.

Iona presided over a golden age, until it crumbled into ruin because of masculine rejection of the sacred feminine principle, of Mother God. When the basest point of that rejection was reached and the Grail was severed, Iona that was the peak of Mount Heredom was decapitated in a terrible act of barbaric destruction, and her lovely head was flung, first as an embedment into the surrounding land mass, and thereafter into the sea.

The paradise over which she once reigned had long since been engulfed by the waves when Mount Heredom was finally beheaded. It sank as if weighted down into the ocean by tears both human and Divine. It froze over and partly disappeared at the time that the Earth was overrun with monsters. Their barbarism and degeneracy caused the angels and the God Race to depart from Earth, because the carnage of the monster race dramatically lowered the planet's vibrational frequency. This outcome had been part of the corrupt assembly's plan from the very beginning.

The enhanced community managed to remain in Eden, although they re-established Paradise on Earth at the point of the Fertile Crescent in the East, which incorporated ancient Mesopotamia, Canaan and Egypt. Yet Iona (Mount Heredom), until her later beheading, remained 'the mountain of assembly in the far north', where angels and members of the God Race could still touch down temporarily to offer inspiration, healing and guidance.

On her re-emergence after the sinking of Polaris, her site had changed from the North Pole to a position farther south, though still very northerly – a site most interesting, as we shall see. Her climate to some degree was seasonally icy and snowbound compared to that of Polaris, but she remained nonetheless a place of profound holiness and mystery.

At the point where Eden and Iona merged, there stood a temple: the most sacred place in Eden. It was the hidden temple of Tiâmat, the temple Antu visited to carry her grief into the presence of God. In later days, access to it was blocked and, eventually, the corrupt assembly ensured that the God Race and the angels were prevented from touching down even transiently in Eden. Yet the secret temple is still there, hidden in the heart of Iona...

After the sinking of Polaris, the continent partly re-emerged, and became Hyperborea, the most northerly region of the vast continent of Atlantic, before sinking again and shifting to become part of the land mass of Europe and then, eventually, the British Isles.

Until the severing of the Grail, the mystical mountain of Iona remained intact, although it had shifted from its original location directly above the North Pole when it re-emerged after the sinking of Polaris.

It is 70,000 years since the Grail was cut off from the Earth; but Polaris sank many millions of years ago; so the stretch of human history upon our planet is much longer than we currently realise. The history of Iona herself spans an almost inconceivable expanse of time. Even before she became a mountain she was a radiant point, a star mirroring stars, upon the surface of the Earth and also before the Earth was formed: the twinkle in God's eye prior to its birth!

Considering her astonishing history, it can perhaps be understood why there is a legend on Iona of darkest treachery, of Black Angus, said to be a seal because the seals were seen by the islanders as a primordial, interchangeably human, race. They were known as the sea people.

The idea of a people allied to the sea, not as mariners but as actual inhabitants of it, seems to have lived on as a wraith of story within the mythology of Iona; for it was the king of the sea people, the serpentine race from Nibiru, who was responsible for perpetrating the crime against Iona and against the world.

Perhaps this deep link between the sea and the human spirit has connected human and seal folk, especially the seals of the Scottish Western Isles, in a way beyond our understanding. I have certainly seen a grey seal listening intently to a Hebridean girl singing in a boat with a rapt expression as if moved by deep human feeling.

Fiona reveals the almost mystical relationship between the islanders of Iona and the Seal People in one of her reminiscences:

'My friend had a little book of his mother's which contained, in a neat hand, copies of Gaelic songs...I recall an iorram that had hardly a word in it, but was only a series of barbaric cries, sometimes full of lament (hò-ro-aroo-aròne, ho-ro, ah-hòne, ah-hòne!) which was the Iona fishermen's song (or charm) to entice seals to come near.'

Black Angus is the figure of myth who, according to the story, committed one of the most heinous acts of betrayal ever known in the annals of history: the act of Judas Escariot. Certainly the world has staggered under the burden of the Judas betrayal – that of taking the decision to win submission by the sword first, with the intention of instituting spiritual truth afterwards – seemingly since the history we know of began.

Judas did not understand (or preferred to block) the teaching of his master: that the carnal law must be entirely rejected to prevent it from remaining a self-perpetuating cycle; for, if you apply the carnal law, you immediately give it authority and must therefore suffer the carnal law. Nevertheless, it seemed Judas loved Jesus as much as the other disciples. Evidence from sources contemporaneous with the time suggests that he thought he could force Jesus's hand by his action – that he believed once Jesus saw that the soldiers were about to seize him, then the Messiah would sound the call to the many factions waiting in Jerusalem that night to begin a united terrorist uprising across the land.

Judas thought his master would have no choice but to sound that call in order to save himself – and he was desperate for Jesus to save himself, not only for the sake of the overall mission but also simply because of the love he had for him. The pieces of silver were not an enticement, but just a terrible reminder of what his action had been worth once his plan had failed, which ultimately led to his suicide.

In Judas's mind, the scriptures had promised that the Messiah would free the Jewish people and their homeland from tyranny – currently the Romans. A military ideal filled his mind. But Jesus knew that the Romans were followers of 'the prince of this world', and that you do not play his game to defeat him. The failings of Judas are the endemic failings of Earth's planetary community today.

The great Judas betrayal that has overtaken the world was initiated by, and led on from, the falling from grace of King Annum and the group he led. Ever since, untempered masculine influence and the military ideal that might is right has held sway.

But the original perpetrator according to Ionean legend was not Judas, but a human sea-creature of both water and land who bore a localised name and a black heart, and who mystically married his essence with Judas as part of a dark continuum from one age to another. King Annum, father of Enlil, the son who inherited his traits, came under the full sway of the adversarial forces, of the Shadow; and the story of Black Angus is known on Iona's shores, not by the name of its subject, but by another, deeper-knowing name – the Dark Nameless One.

To further make the point, the story links Black Angus with Lilith, an 'enhanced' or goddess-woman of primordial times who was associated with the era when humankind, led by Annum and corrupt members of the Anunnaki Council, first turned on their mother Tiâmat and dubbed her an evil serpent, a child-eater (because the 'living waters' in the Dew-Cup were connected to the tides of the womb) and a night-hag. Lilith is portrayed as all of these; and indeed worked with surreptitious devotion to serve Tiâmat even though humanity, both enhanced and ordinary, had turned its face from Her.

Lilith's connection was with Adam and the bringing forth of the new humanity on Earth, not Judas. But she is linked with the degenerate Nibiruan king, as both Iona's hidden history, and Iona's ancient stories, attest. She did indeed marry, not Adam, but King Annum's son Enlil, who was as evilly-inclined as his father. She married him, and she left him, in order to help and bless humanity, whom her husband wished to destroy. And, like Black Angus, Enlil agonised over his loss and his search for her is never-ending – although he would abuse her if he found her.

There is more of Iona's story to unfold. First, it is timely to think of Queen Antu's vision as she gazed into the depths of the sacred lake in which Iona was reflected, a lake which would re-emerge and enter into the great mythological cycle of Avalon. For this lake, as in the future, was the shining gateway to a feminine dimension in which dwelt the Great Queen of Earth's destiny and her exalted sisters, and into whose heart Antu would eventually be enfolded.

When this Great Queen, sister in spirit to Antu, released the spectral form of the dove in the reflective depths of the lake, Antu felt its image rise in her heart as the Dove of the Paraclete, the feminine essence of God, or, in Fiona's words, 'the Dove of the Eternal'.

'Iona' means 'dove', and it also means something else. It means many things; but all the meanings of its name are a musical variation on this one theme: the Dove of the Holy Spirit, the Dove of the Eternal Mother.

CHAPTER 9

THE NAME OF NAMES

There is shifting, shimmering magic in Iona's name. Lyrical and many-splendoured, it is, in Fiona's words, 'a talisman of spiritual beauty'. Before we continue with Iona's story, we would do well to study her name, for her secret shines within it.

'Strange, that to this day none knows with surety the derivation or original significance of the name Iona,' Fiona remarks in her book on the isle. I believe that we can, however, glean such knowledge by allowing the name itself to speak to us.

Iona, Fiona informs us from her considerable research and even greater store of inherited knowledge, was once known as the Isle of the Druids (Dhruiddhnean), given to the island by the Shenachies or bardic storytellers of the Gaels. A certain brotherhood, the outer and earthly rendition of it reflecting a heavenly order, has always existed on Iona.

Once, as we have seen, the angels and the God Race who first comprised this brotherhood actually lived upon Iona. Since the time of her decapitation, earthly brethren have taken their place, inheriting and giving forth the Bright Knowledge, as the teachings of the heavenly brotherhood were known amongst the Druids. For centuries, Iona became a seat of learning that was formally recognised as the finest in Europe: a university of light.

There have been failings, of course. Certain misinterpretations of Iona's knowledge occurred, as was almost inevitable in our fallen and disinherited world. But there have also been radiant examples of excellence who kept Iona's magic and secrets alive. Many Druids were among them, for the Druids were an exalted brotherhood, not the barbaric sorcerers that Roman propaganda proclaimed.

Iona was also known as 'the Isle of Birds'. Every one of the Scottish islands is a habitation for numerous sea birds, so the designation is unlikely to have derived from observation of any singularity in this respect, because there is none. But Iona is legendary throughout the centuries for the sighting of angels 'surpassing white, with white wings like the swan of the wave'. There is a traditional link between birds, birdsong, and angels, apparent in many old stories of the Hebrides. It seems that Iona's white, swan-winged angels, seen by so many throughout the years, have given rise to this evocative naming. And there is a whisper of a hint that Iona was sometimes referred to, if only informally, as the 'Isle of Angels'.

'Isle of Saints' is another interpretation given to the name Iona. (II-shona, 'the Isle of Saints', pronounced in Gaelic Iona, as the letters 'sh' at the beginning of a word are invariably mute.) Kings, holy men and martyrs have been buried here. Its sands are the dust of monarchs of Scotland and the kings of Norway as well as the sanctified bones of the blessed, for the island was once under Norwegian rule.

Columba stands foremost among the saints, although St Bride or Bridget is spoken of as having once dwelt here. A much older belief traces her back to Brigid, chief deity among the Druids, from whom the Bright Knowledge issued. ('Brigid' was pronounced 'Breet', and her name bore the meaning that the word 'bright' has for us today.) St Mary Magdalene is also said to lie buried upon Iona, but that is a symbolic myth rather than a literal one.

There is one story that seems to be numbered amongst Iona's 'made-up' myths, rather than those which evolved naturally from her dreaming bedrock as in the nature of the story of Black Angus and the story of the fairy peoples who were compelled to travel back to the North Pole. It is of the time when Columba set sail in search of Iona.

In Fiona's words: 'When Columba and his few followers were sailing northward from the isle of Oronsay, in quest, it is said, of this sacred island of the Druids, suddenly one of the monks cried "Sud i!" (? siod e!) "Yonder it!" With sudden exaltation Columba exclaimed, "Mar sud bithe I, goir thear II": "Be it so, and let it be called I" (I or EE).'

Fiona goes on to confirm that this is an unsupported legend, and in any case accounts for a single syllable only. Yet any legend that persists on the sacred soil of Iona seems in some degree to bear a message. I and EE are respectively the English and Gaelic pronunciations for 'eye', and indeed are primitive renditions of the word.

Iona was known as 'the Eye of God' in her most distant days. She was associated with the sacred word 'ayin', meaning both vision and the admittance of light. 'Ayin' was a mystical title also meaning 'eye', but in a deeply esoteric rendering of that meaning. It was linked with the taking up of office of the Divine Couple (they who admitted the light and bestowed vision, becoming the designated Vehicle of Light for a planetary civilisation).

Its full rendition was 'qayin' or 'queen', because it was always the queen who took up office first, relaying the light from God to her kingly counterpart. Therefore, the queen and king became God's 'eye', admitting light into themselves and the human community that they served.

When Iona was the peak of the sacred mountain of assembly in the north (a divine trust she still holds, although secretly, and in waiting), her 'eye' was both within her, and upon her summit. This was the true structure that admitted the light of God.

Since Iona or Mount Heredom was decapitated, the symbol that was her being has been taken from her and corrupted. Her beautiful, self-giving feminine force – the force of the Grail, the light of God – has been purposefully degraded into a force that generates materialism – money, possessions and selfish power. It has become the eye within the pyramid or triangle, emblazoned on US dollar bills. It has become mammon.

This does not mean that the USA are more culpable than anyone else, of course; but they do hold a high percentage of worldly power, and within the worldwide structures of that power lurks, still, the deadly group from the Anunnaki assembly which plots our destruction. Marduk is there too, at its centre, striving to get the Naphidem back to Earth.

The two – the assembly, and Marduk who heads the Naphidem – work together in tandem, Marduk all the while kept in ignorance of just what the final solution is for our Earth and its people, including the Naphidem, although he sometimes suspects something is afoot and becomes uneasy. The two groups manipulate from an etheric level, and they are behind sinister operations occurring in high finance, politics and consequent political manoeuvres, and the decrees of the decision-makers of social and state organisation.

Countless centuries ago, Iona was known as Ioua, or the Isle of the Moon. This designation seems to celebrate Iona's essential femininity, although, because of their inherent knowledge of Brigid, goddess of fire and celestial lights and the golden sun, Celtic mysticism associated the sun with a female deity, whilst the deity of the moon was perceived as masculine. Nevertheless, in many aspects of ancient Celtic religious understanding, Brigid, queen of lights, is mistress of the stars and moon as well as the sun. At any rate, the oldest intimations of Iona's myths make reference to a time when the island was dedicated to moon veneration, and a woman, queen and goddess of the isle, was worshipped.

Yet within these misty intimations and recollections, Iona's secret history glimmers again, because the sacred fluid in the Dew-Cup, the personal essence of the Grail – just as the Grail is a Divine Woman and simultaneously a universal force of connection to God – was celebrated as a lunar fluid.

The light of Tiâmat, Mother God, could only be brought to the children of Earth via water, through reflection, because its supernal brilliance would otherwise be too great for us to bear or understand. And the mistress of the tides and the supreme symbol of celestial reflection is the moon.

Iona, keeper of the Grail and temple of the Divine Daughter who personifies the Grail and its forces, is of the essence of the moon's spiritual reality; and a dedication of Iona to the moon after the Dolorous Blow fell (for that is what the severing of the Grail is called in the Arthurian mythos and by the Knights Templar, the brotherhood allied to the Divine Woman) pays honour and homage to Iona's secret.

Fiona relates an intriguing story of these old memories of Iona that still endured in her own time. It tells of a man who, so sadly, seemed half-ashamed of his Gaelic language and the secret traditions he cherished in his heart and in the noble blood of his race:

'Three years ago I was sailing on one of the sea-lochs of Argyll. My only companion was the boatman, and incidentally I happened to speak of some skerries (a group of sea-set rocks) off the Ross of Mull...and learned with surprise that my companion knew them well, and was not only an Iona man, but had lived on the island till he was twenty. I asked him about his people, and when he found that I knew them he became more confidential. But he professed a strange ignorance of all concerning Iona. There was an old Iona iorram, or boat-song, I was anxious to have: he had never heard of it. Still more did I desire some rendering or even some lines of an ancient chant of whose existence I knew, but had never heard recited, even fragmentarily. He did not know of it: he "did not know Gaelic"; that is, he remembered only a little of it. Well, no, he added, perhaps he did remember some, "but only just to talk to fishermen an' the like".

'Suddenly a squall came down out of the hills. The loch blackened. In a moment a froth of angry foam drove in upon us, but the boat righted, and we flew before the blast, as though an arrow shot by the wind.

'I noticed a startling change in my companion. His blue eyes were wide and luminous; his lips twitched; his hands trembled. Suddenly he stooped slightly, laughed, cried some words I did not catch, and abruptly broke into a fierce and strange sea-chant. It was no other than the old Iona rann I had so vainly sought! Some memory had awakened in the man, perhaps in part from what I had said – with the old spell of the sea, the old cry of the wind.

'Then he ceased abruptly, he relapsed, and with a sheepish exclamation and awkward movement shrank beside me. Alas, I could recall only a few lines; and I failed in every effort to persuade him to repeat the rann. But I had heard enough to excite me, for again and again he had called or alluded to Iona by its pre-Columban name of Ioua, and once at least I was sure, from the words, that the chant was also to Ioua the Moon.

'That night, however, he promised to tell me on the morrow all he could remember of the old Ioua chant. On the morrow, alas, he had to leave unexpectedly...and before his return, three days later, I was gone. I have not seen him again, but it is to him I am indebted for the loan of an ancient manuscript map of Iona, a copy of which I made and have by me still.

'It was an heirloom: by his own account had been in his family, in Iona, for seven generations, "an' it's Himself knows how much more". He had been to the island the summer before, because of his father's death, and had brought this coarsely painted and rudely framed map away with him. He told me too, that night, how the oldest folk on the island – "some three or four o' them anyway; them as has the Gaelic" – had the old Iona chant in their minds. As a boy he had heard it at many a winter ceilidh. "Ay, ay, for sure, Iona was called Ioua in them old ancient days."

'On one other occasion I have heard the name Ioua used by a fisherman...before the peat-glow, while he was narrating a story of a Princess of Spain who married the King of Ireland's son, he spoke incidentally of their being wrecked on Iona, "that was then called Ioua, ay, an' that for one hundred and two hundred and three hundred years and thrice a hundred on the top o' that before it was Icolmkill ('the Isle of the Church [interchangeably 'Cell'] of Columba')...and a Mr Cameron, the minister of Brodick, in Arran, had the manuscript of an old Iona (or Hebridean) iorram, in the refrain of which Ioua was used throughout. Conclusively, St Adamnan, ninth Abbot of Iona, writing at the end of the 7th century, invariably calls the island Ioua or the Iouan Island' – the Island of the Moon.

For Fiona, the change from Ioua to Iona is explained by the coming of Columba to the island, upon which the Isle of the Moon became the Isle of the Saints (II-shona, with a silent 'sh', as forecited). However, Fiona tells of a sea-god, Shony, on whose behalf she cast little offerings into the sea-loch by which her family lived when she was a child, in hopes that he would appear.

Shony was not benign, and his way was to clutch boats by the keel, drown the sailors, and make a death-necklace of their teeth. 'Once he netted a young girl who was swimming in a loch, and when she would not give him her love he tied her to a rock, and to this day her long brown hair may be seen floating in the shallow green wave at the ebb of the tide' is another of the old stories Fiona relates of him. She also relates a more whimsical reminiscence:

'I was amused not long ago to hear a little girl singing, as she ran wading through the foam of a troubled sunlit sea, as it broke on those wonderful white sands of Iona –

"Shanny, Shanny, Shanny,
Catch my feet and tickle my toes!
And if you can, Shanny, Shanny, Shanny,
I'll go with you where no-one knows!"'

The lethal ogre had transformed into a creature of merry mischief who might playfully tease a child. There must be many such traditional stories that circulate among the Scottish isles...And yet there certainly was an ogre in human form who had once walked the Elysian fields of tranquil Iona, whose wish was to sink and drown all earthly humanity, and who is on record on ancient Mesopotamian tablets as having been denounced by the Anunnaki assembly for committing the crime of rape.

Shony might be remembered in the name II-Shona; there is the ghost of such a possibility. But it would only represent yet another dimension to Iona's name, because she certainly was known as the Isle of the Saints after Columba had sailed to her shores; it was the Gaelic name inscribed on the map that the Iona boatman had lent to Fiona.

However, it is not the Sacred Isle of the Druids, or the Isle of Birds, or the Isle of Angels, or the Isle of the Moon, or the Isle of the Church of Columba, or yet the Isle of Saints, or even the Isle of Shony, which is the true and eternal designation belonging to Iona.

That eternal designation was something Fiona barely touched upon; something of whose resonance and mystery, whose tsunami of meaning, she could never have guessed; and yet, without outwardly realising these connections, she did know; but only as a dream and a sorrow, and an articulate sigh upon the breast of the wind.

The true meaning of Iona's name – without discounting the many dimensions lent to her by all her associations – a name vouchsafed to her from the beginning of her life as an isle which began long before the coming of John the Baptist and St John the Evangelist, is the Isle of John.

CHAPTER 10

THE DOVE OF THE ETERNAL

From where did this name, 'the Isle of John', originate, and why is it so important?

Fiona writes:

'I do not know on what authority, but an anonymous Gaelic writer, in an account of Iona in 1771, alludes to the probability that Christianity was introduced there before St Columba's advent, and that the island was already dedicated to the Apostle St John, "for it was originally called I'Eoin, i.e. the Isle of John, whence Iona."'

Yet, Iona means 'the dove'. The name Columba ('the dove') was assumed by the saint as a declaration of his renunciation of his former life as a warrior – whereby he had been known as 'the Wolf' – and his assumption of a life of holiness dedicated to the Holy Spirit or the Paraclete, which today we would also allude to as the Divine Feminine.

The Holy Spirit is symbolised by the dove, and the name Columba, meaning 'dove', is identical with the Hebrew name Jonah, pronounced 'Iona', which also means 'dove'. 'Jonah' is a form of 'John'; and although 'John' is quoted as meaning 'gift of God' in the Bible, it also means 'dove', as its earlier form is 'Jonah' – 'dove'. However, this 'dove' – John – would most certainly be God's gift to stricken humanity, as we shall discover.

And so we can see a correlation between Columba, the saint of Iona who revered the spirit of the Sacred Feminine; Jonah, the man who was swallowed by a great creature of the sea (as if by Tiâmat) and re-emerged a changed man – as 'the Dove' in his love and mystical apperception of the Holy Spirit, newly perceiving that Father God came forth from Her; between John the Baptist, who baptised his followers in an enactment of the rites of Isis so that through the feminine 'living waters' they were initiated into the mysteries of the Holy Spirit, and whose ministrations summoned the mystical dove; and between John the Beloved Apostle, to whom Jesus said on the Cross, "Behold thy mother", meaning his own, who would be mother to John after his death or ascension. To his mother, Jesus said, "Behold thy son". There is an ocean-depth of meaning in these words.

Jesus reached beyond the mundane when he spoke. There was a divine twinship between Jesus and John (not a biological one). They were twin souls. Jesus personified the Christ, the son of God-the-Mother-Father, whilst John personified Father God.

The reason why Jesus gave John into Mary the Mother's keeping as he was dying on the Cross signifies a great mystery: that in spiritual understanding, Mother God bore Father God from her profoundest point, from her heart. Although there is absolute equilibrium between them, Father God came forth from the Great Mother. In an ineffable sense, He was Her Son, as the enigmatic Gnostic texts proclaim.

That is the true understanding of God, which John symbolised; and there is an unspeakably gargantuan difference between this understanding of God, and the understanding that prevails worldwide today.

It makes no difference whether or not religion is part of an individual's life. The conditioning is there; the mind-set was established in stone over 70,000 years ago. And, despite much progress and promise, especially over the last century, it remains intact and unchanged.

It constitutes a patriarchy that is a usurpation. The unease at its roots will always manifest cruelty, destruction and terror as if from an arsonist's fire smouldering among them; and civilisations will only ever advance so far before utterly destroying themselves, or being destroyed by forces whose barbarity is a reflection of, and a magnet responding to, the barbarity it nurses in its heart.

From a human point of view, Jesus was avowing his deep twinship with John to the outer world when he spoke on the Cross to his mother and his spiritual twin. He was consigning it to his teachings. He also addressed, through his own mother, his Eternal Mother – Mother God.

As his life slipped from him, he was preparing, not only for the next great step of the Resurrection, but also for another one that would come after it. For the Grail was the great resurrective force, and, in receiving with complete, sacrificial acceptance the death-blow of Longinus, who pierced his side with a spear or lance, Jesus was able to do what no-one else could have done: masterfully reverse the Dolorous Blow, and thereby reconnect the forces of the Grail to Earth to achieve the Resurrection – not only for himself, but for all.

This reconnection took place in a very particular way, through the coming again of a spirit and presence who was personified in the reincarnation of the Great Queen previously mentioned. Her coming again was made possible by Jesus, her father; and by Mary Magdalene, her mother. Her name, as their daughter, was Sara-Tamar.

This mighty reconnection would one day become universal. The Grail would rise and flourish as before. It would be the crowning gift of Jesus and Mary Magdalene, the Divine androgyne, the Divine couple, who came to Earth to rescue us from all the confusion and manipulation of the adversarial forces. The Holy Grail is part and parcel of their teachings – teachings most beautifully rendered, and given in the spirit of simplicity for all to share.

But it is also the gift of John; God's gift to humanity (the Grail and the restoration of the Grail) could only be given in its entirety through John, 'God's gift'. The Grail is a wholly feminine force; but until the enlightenment of John catches fire across the world – that the Father was born from the Mother and is of her essence – the teachings of the Christ cannot be fully comprehended, and the mystery of the Divine Woman, the Grail, will remain hidden from us.

And on Iona the world's hope rests, for it is here, at this most sanctified point, that the John enlightenment is destined to come to fruition and universally reconnect struggling, sorrowing, mind-darkened humanity with God's gift – the Holy Grail.

The Temple of John came into being with Enki, the son of the Divine androgyne who kept faith with Tiâmat. 'Sion' is the Celtic word for 'John', and Mount Sion in Jerusalem (Mount John) is a reflection of Iona ('John'), for all the stations of the Grail are marked by these 'Mounts of John'.

The name Sion (in contradistinction to 'Zion') is also an indication of Mary Magdalene, the feminine nature of heaven and the 'new Jerusalem' of precious stones that John saw in his revelatory vision. John is so intimately linked with the Sacred Feminine and with Mother God that the Celts united their meaning in the name Sion.

Before the universal reconnection could happen, however, Sara-Tamar had to be born to the Earth. Plans had already been laid for the many tasks ahead that the reconnection would comprise. Now, Jesus,

Mary Magdalene and John would advance together towards their unified destiny. Within her, Mary Magdalene, sorrowing at the foot of the cross and giving of her utmost to sustain her heart's beloved as he fought his final battle, already carried the key.

CHAPTER 11

THE DOVE OF IONA

The story of John, which is aeons old, and the story of what happened after the Crucifixion, are intimately linked, and one fulfils the other. Before proceeding with the nuts-and-bolts story, however, we should give ear to Iona. For she knows all these secrets and, furthermore, she knows their deeper meaning, which is their ultimate treasure. And if we do not grasp the deeper meaning of the story, it will not provide the revelation of the truth that shall set us free.

It is a story that could only ever be told at the very last minute, at that cusp of the moment when, as a planetary civilisation, we had attained the inner strength to overcome. An untimely telling, before we had gained such strength, would only have resulted in terror and despair and played straight into the hands of our deceivers.

We have reached the ripe moment. There is absolutely no need to fear. Fortifications of our own spiritual development as a global family rise on every side to support us, and our victory is assured.

Fiona begins to reveal these secrets, this deeper meaning, as she tells us of the mystical dove of Iona, the Dove of the Eternal – the dove of the enlightened John consciousness:

"'The Dove of the Eternal.' It was from the lips of an old priest of the Hebrides that I first heard these words. I was a child, and asked him if it was a white dove, such as I had seen fanning the sunglow in Icolmkill.

"Yes," he told me, "the Dove is white, and it was beloved of Colum, and is of you, little one, and of me."

"Then it is not dead?"

"It is not dead."

'I was in a more wild and rocky isle than Iona then, and when I went into a solitary place close by my home it was to a stony wilderness so desolate that in many moods I could not bear it. But that day, though there were no sheep lying beside boulders as grey and still, nor whinnying goats: and though I could hear nothing but the soft, swift, slipping feet of the wind among rocks and grass and a noise of the tide crawling up from a shore hidden behind crags (beloved of swallows for the small honey-flies which feed upon the thyme): still, on that day, I was not ill at ease, nor in any way disquieted. But before me I saw a white rock-dove, and followed it gladly. It flew circling among the crags, and once I thought it had flown seaward; but it came again, and alit on a boulder.

'I went upon my knees, and prayed to it, and, as nearly as I can remember, in these words:

"O Dove of the Eternal, I want to love you, and you to love me: and if you live on Iona, I want you to show me, when I go there again, the place where Colum the Holy talked with an angel. And I want to live as long as you, Dove' (I remember thinking this might seem disrespectful, and that I added hurriedly and apologetically), 'Dove of the Eternal.'"

That evening I told Father Ivor what I had done. He did not laugh at me. He took me on his knee and stroked my hair, and for a long time was so silent that I thought he was dreaming. He put me gently from him, and kneeled at the chair, and made this simple prayer which I have never forgotten: "O Dove of the Eternal, grant the little one's prayer."

That is a long while ago now, and I have sojourned since in Iona, and there and elsewhere known the wild doves of thought and dream. But I have not, though I have yearned, seen again the White Dove that Colum so loved. For long I thought it must have left Iona and Barra too, when Father Ivor died.

'Yet I have not forgotten that it is not dead. "I want to live as long as you," was my child's plea: and the words of the old priest, knowing and believing were, "O Dove of the Eternal, grant the little one's prayer."'

It is the heart of the child, the heart of simplicity and humility, which will light our way. It is the wisdom in the heart of the child that we are bidden to follow. The Dove of the Eternal, whose home was on Iona, came to the child Fiona in a rocky, barren, desolate place, to bring her the vision that the winter was past and gone, and the time of flowers and singing-birds was preparing to come to the Earth. I heard these verses from the *Song of Solomon* when I read her story:

> 'O my dove, that art in the clefts of the rock,
> in the secret places of the stairs;
> let me see thy countenance, let me hear thy voice;
> for sweet is thy voice,
> and thy countenance is comely.'

And the dove replying...

> 'My beloved spake, and said unto me,
> Rise up, my love, my fair one, and come away.
> For, lo, the winter is past,
> the rain is over and gone;
> the flowers appear on the earth;
> and the voice of the turtle-dove is heard in our land.'

It is a prophecy of beauty and hope, and fills the heart with the peace that is on Iona; Iona, where the Stairway of the Kings clambers up among the clefts of the rock, from which the Dove of the Eternal blesses simple prayers with miracles, and, with promises beyond all earthly loveliness, lights the star of future days that are coming to this Earth.

The second story of the Dove of the Eternal on Iona (there are three, in the best Druidical tradition) is a story, we might say, of the John-man, who knows the truth, and embraces it wholeheartedly in times of great spiritual danger. For throughout history, these John-men, including Zoroaster's priests, the Magi, John the Baptist's followers (Jesus was a little different to a John-man, though utterly twinned with him and working in the great temple tradition of John), the Cathars, the Knights Templar, and many, many others, have preserved and passed on their truth. Like Iona's other legends, this story is sacred, and tells of an actual encounter.

'I recall one whom I knew, a fisherman of the little green island (of Iona): and I tell this story of Coll here, for it is to me more than the story of a dreaming islander.

'One night, lying upon the hillock that is called Cnoc-nan-Aingeal, because it is here that St Colum was wont to hold converse with an angel out of heaven, he watched the moonlight move like a slow fin through the sea: and in his heart were desires as infinite as the waves of the sea...

'And while he lay and dreamed, his thoughts idly adrift as a net in deep waters, he closed his eyes, muttering the Gaelic words of an old line:

'In the Isle of Dreams God shall yet fulfill Himself anew.

'Hearing a footfall, he stirred. A man stood beside him. He did not know the man, who was young, and had eyes dark as hill-tarns, with hair light and soft as thistledown; and moved light as a shadow, delicately treading the grass as the wind treads it. In his hair he had twined the fantastic leaf of the horn-poppy. The islander did not move or speak: it was as though a spell were upon him.

"God be with you," he said at last, uttering the common salutation.

"And with you, Coll mac Coll," answered the stranger. Coll looked at him. Who was this man, with the sea-poppy in his hair, who, unknown, knew him by name? He had heard of one whom he did not wish to meet, the Green Harper: also of a grey man of the sea whom islesmen seldom alluded to by name: again, there was the Amadan Dhu...but at that name Coll made the sign of the cross, and remembering what Father Allan had told him in South Uist, muttered a holy exorcism of the Trinity.

'The man smiled.

"You need have no fear, Coll mac Coll," he said quietly.

"You that know my name so well are welcome, but if you in your turn would tell me your name I should be glad."

"I have no name that I can tell you," answered the stranger gravely; "but I am not of those who are unfriendly. And because you can see me and speak to me, I will help you to whatsoever you may wish."

'Coll laughed.

"Neither you nor any man can do that. For now that I have neither father nor mother, nor brother nor sister, and my lass too is dead, I wish neither for sheep nor cattle, nor for new nets and a fine boat, nor a big house, nor as much money as MacCailein Mòr has in the bank at Inveraora."

"What then do you wish for, Coll mac Coll?"

"I do not wish for what cannot be, or I would wish to see again the dear face of Morag, my lass. But I wish for all the glory and wonder and power there is in the world, and to have it all at my feet, and to know everything that the Holy Father himself knows, and have kings coming to me as the crofters come to MacCailein Mòr's factor."

"You can have that, Coll mac Coll," said the Green Harper, and he waved a withe of hazel he had in his hand.

"What is that for?" said Coll.

"It is to open a door that is in the air. And now, Coll, if that is your wish of all wishes, and you will give up all other wishes for that wish, you can have the sovereignty of the world. Ay, and more than that: you shall have the sun like a golden jewel in the hollow of your right hand, and all the stars as pearls in your left, and have the moon as a white shining opal above your brows, with all knowledge behind the sun, within the moon, and beyond the stars."

'Coll's face shone. He stood, waiting. Just then he heard a familiar sound in the dusk. The tears came into his eyes.

"Give me instead," he cried, "give me a warm breast-feather from that grey dove of the woods that is winging home to her young."

'He looked as one moon-dazed. None stood beside him. He was alone. Was it a dream, he wondered? But a weight was lifted from his heart. Peace fell upon him as dew on grey pastures. Slowly he walked homeward.

'Once, glancing back, he saw a white figure upon the knoll, with a face noble and beautiful. Was it Colum himself come again, he mused, or that white angel with whom the Saint was wont to discourse, and who brought him intimacies of God? Or was it but the wave-fire of his dreaming mind, as unreal as that mirage of flame which the wind of the south makes upon the wandering hearths of the sea?'

Here, the tenderness and purity of the Holy Spirit, the Divine Feminine, reaches Coll's heart and connects him with its loving wisdom to prevent him from taking his final, lethal step into the choice of ultimate material dominion via worldly power, possessions and forbidden knowledge. It may sound absurd to introduce the theme of a poor islander attaining world domination, even within the annals of what is only folk history. But Coll's encounter was not idle or fanciful.

World domination is exactly what carnal law and the lords of the elements seek throughout all physical expression of life. It is the driving force – the colonising compulsion – within every kingdom of nature. Viruses do it, bacteria does it, plants do it, insects do it, animals and birds do it: and would succeed – except for that balancing, sustaining impulse of spirit which breathes and weaves throughout nature and which is her own higher essence that, bringing all into harmony, ultimately forbids it.

Humans share the takeover impulse too, of course, in just as great a measure; but our brief is that we ourselves, in obedience to the heart as a conscious choice, have to learn to step back from it and decisively refuse it, just as Coll did.

And so there is nothing fantastical about his story, although it seems to be drawn directly from fantasy. Every individual soul, at some point along their winding karmic road, has to take the test. If the individual fails, then nations have to take it; worlds – entire planetary civilisations – have to take it. The root of the Nazi tragedy is recorded in Goethe's Faust in plain sight, for all to see and recognise this fundamental truth of the test. When they fail the test, the outcome is always catastrophic. Our own world has felt the terrible ructions of such a catastrophe many times.

But on Iona, Coll, spiritual descendant of Columba, the Dove, the John-man, was caught up in the essence of the Holy Spirit as she flew, and passed his test with honour.

Fiona's final story of the Dove of Iona is about Iona's promise of the future and her radiant spiritual reality. The story comprises a dream Fiona had after falling asleep whilst gazing at Iona from Lunga, a neighbouring island that looks directly onto Iona, the Holy Isle. When Fiona relates her dreams, it is worth paying close attention.

'In Lunga there is a hill called Cnoc Cruit or Dun Cruit, and thence one may see, as in a vast illuminated missal whose pages are of deep blue with bindings of azure and pale gold, innumerable green isles and peaks and hills of the hue of wild plum.

'When last I was there it was a day of cloudless June. There was not a sound but the hum of the wild bee foraging in the long garths of white clover, and the continual sighing of a wave. Listening, I thought I heard a harper playing in the hollow of the hill. It may have been the bees heavy with the wine of honey, but I was content with my fancy and fell asleep, and dreamed that a harper came out of the hill, at first so small that he seemed like the green stalk of a lily, and had hands like daisies, and then so great that I saw his breath darkening the waves far out on the Hebrid sea.

'He played, till I saw the stars fall in a ceaseless, dazzling rain upon Iona. A wind blew that rain away, and out of the wave that had been Iona I saw thousands upon thousands of white doves rise from the foam and fly down the four great highways of the wind.

'When I woke, there was no-one near. Iona lay like an emerald under the wild-plum bloom of the Mull mountains. The bees stumbled through the clover; a heron stood silver-grey upon a grey-blue stone; the continual wave was, as before, as one wave, and with the same hushed sighing.'

The doves of Iona that flew away on the four highways of the wind were, I believe, a dream-prophecy of the Holy Spirit, the Divine Feminine, which will one day wing out from Iona to bring the benediction of the Holy Grail and its peace and healing across the world.

And that this little isle lay as an emerald in azure within Fiona's waking vision is also prophetic, because although all the Hebridean islands are green amidst the blue of sky and sea, Fiona saw Iona as an emerald directly after waking from her dream of the Green Piper, he that came to Coll to test and bless his strength as a John-man.

Iona once knew all the wonders hidden and secured within the depths of the emerald tablet, and she will know them again, for her knowledge is only sleeping. The 'dazzle of stars' that Fiona saw in her dream is connected with the miracle of this knowledge, for it came to us from the stars, from the heart of God, whose passage to us is through the Divine fire of the stars and the star that shines in our heart: an eternal flame.

As the Green Harper suggests, and as even his name suggests, there is a certain test to be applied and passed regarding the emerald tablet, because as soon as Earth was given the true emerald tablet, a false one arose via the abuse of that template. The Green Harper is the servant of the emerald tablet and the dispenser of that crucial test. Discernment between the false and the true emerald tablet is the greatest challenge of our age, and of all the ages that have passed since it came into being.

Yet there exists every assurance, every confirmation, that Iona's magic is intact and pure and cannot be contaminated. The Green Harper affirms it with the gift of his dream. Fiona's book on Iona, which she entitled *The Isle of Dreams*, proclaims it on every page. Iona herself beats with the pulse of its certainty; her rhythms of tide and wind and the outbreathing of her essence sigh and sing and whisper of it. In the Isle of Dreams God shall yet fulfill Himself anew.

Iona will wake from her enraptured dream to become humanity's House of Inheritance once again.

CHAPTER 12

IN THE COURT OF ENLIL

How to tell John's story, in just a few chapters? It began many, many millions of years ago, whilst the profoundest, most dense physical level of life (the one we occupy today) was being brought forth on our Earth, mother to this plane of physicality that had never been summoned into existence before in the history of creation.

The actual cosmic physical sphere was birthed at the point of what scientists call the Big Bang (the initiatory moment); but its physicality was not so dense as that of today. It had to develop. At the appointed moment, our solar system, and of course within it planet Earth, was born.

Human beings were here on Earth almost from the beginning of her life as a sphere, but they lived and built their civilisations in an ethereal dimension. They were waiting for their earthly, animal body to be made ready for them, for only through its facilitation could they fully enter the material plane.

That densely physical plane was being nurtured and developed, and sown with Dragon essence (the dinosaurs), for this was a vital part of God's plan of ascension for our Earth and her humanity. The dragon and the bird of ascension are one. We might think of the great god Quetzalcoatl with regard to this mystery – the great bird-serpent or 'plumed serpent' who shared so many characteristics with Christ – with Jesus and Mary Magdalene, who lead us ever towards the Holy Grail and ascension. Quetzalcoatl is the Phoenix, the Firebird – the dragon-bird.

It is also edifying to ponder the fact that preserved soft tissue of a dinosaur has been discovered for the first time recently, and that this tissue sample strongly indicates that the dinosaurs were feathered. The tiny forelegs of the Tyrannosaurus Rex were not, it seems, inadequate little limbs, but the ligatures of great wings. In other words, the dinosaurs were giant, lumbering flightless birds waiting for refinement, for flight, freedom and rapturous song. The dinosaurs were God's imagination literalising itself into the physical dimension so that Her-His spiritual creation could, in their body, mind, soul and spirit, follow the trail the dinosaurs blazed in matter.

Meanwhile, back on Earth in those far-distant days and even long before, the arriving groups of human beings became the humanity of our planet, and their ethereal bodies were wrought on to reflect the beauty and perfection of what, one day, physical earthly humanity would become. They still retained the characteristics of their original star race to some degree within those earthly (though ethereal) human forms, for these six groups of humanity had assembled on Earth from other star systems, except the black and white serpent race from Nibiru, the twelfth planet of our own solar system.

Queen Antu and King Annum, the Divine couple overlighting both the enhanced and ordinary communities gathered on Earth, had two sons, Enki and Enlil. All were androgynous in those far-off times; but, as their androgynous state was to be overridden, it will be easier to speak of them in terms natural to today.

Becoming jealous and resentful of receiving the Dew-Cup from Antu (which was a vital ceremony that also took place throughout both the enhanced and ordinary communities on Earth), Annum with his conspirators devised the plot already examined, and brought forth the monstrous Naphidem via corrupt genetic engineering, secretly applied.

Afterwards, even though the Naphidem were gathered together and restrained in an ethereal dimension locked away securely from Earth, the beautiful Nephilim, the God race, were forced to leave our planet because its vibrational essence was lowered to the point where they could not stay.

The enhanced community relocated away from Polaris (the continent around the North Pole) to an Eden linked to the Fertile Crescent, although, despite a slight shift in her position, Iona (Mount Heredom) remained intact and was still the purest point of connection on Earth to the heavenly realms. From Mount Heredom, it was possible to ascend to the stars, to reach higher and beyond the ethereal dimension of Eden, for Mount Heredom still protected and dispensed the forces of the Holy Grail.

It was at this time that King Annum, who had bigger fish to fry beyond our solar system but who wished to keep Earth strictly under his control, by force disinherited his son Enki, who should have assumed his father's position, and supplanted him with his younger son Enlil. This was unlawful, because the inheritance of sovereignty was matrilineal, and Ki's son should not have inherited.

King Annum had, by brutal measures, detached himself from his androgynous bond with Antu as far as he could. He did this because Antu was faithful in her love and service to Tiâmat, whom Annum now despised and refused to recognise as God because she was feminine in essence. God, Annum decided, would from now on be understood as a severed masculine deity, a statement of the outright rejection of the feminine. He actually thought he could separate Father God from the Great Mother!

The final severing of Antu from Annum would come with the severing of the Grail, upon which the direct androgynous human bond would be lost to Earth's planetary civilisation. Annum wanted Enlil in charge, because his plans would never come to fruition through Enki, the rightful heir. As mentioned, Enki loved and served Tiâmat as devotedly as did Antu, his mother.

And so the court of Enlil was established, unspeakably different from the enlightened court where once Annum and Antu, as the androgyne Anu, had dispensed wisdom and the radiance of Divine spirit over all the Earth.

Enlil's court retained the trappings of democracy and high ideals, but was surreptitiously geared towards control, dominion and the cruel manipulation of ordinary humanity who lived beyond the circumference of the enhanced community. This community, once advanced brethren whose heartfelt purpose was to serve and accelerate the progress of ordinary humanity, started to become a self-serving elite.

With the disempowerment of Enki, the Grail was finally severed, and Mount Heredom was decapitated in the fulfilment of that atrocity. Her head was embedded in the soil of what is now Scotland: part of Hyperborea, most of which had sunk beneath the waves with Atlantis, whose northernmost shores Hyperborea constituted. Later, Iona broke away from this embedment to become the little island that she is today... an isle in waiting.

Upon the severing of the Grail, Tiâmat created the emerald tablet as a sacred trust and repository of the Grail secrets and essence, and gave it into Enki and Antu's care.

It was spoken of as holding within its crystalline matrix 'all that Earth was destined to know, and all that could ever be known upon Earth'. By no means was it a collection of catalogued, encyclopaedic information, but the key to a state of being which is the perfect expression of the godlike entity that the human being is destined to become; greater even, and greater by far, than the enhanced community.

Because of Enlil's status, however, the emerald tablet also had to enter into his co-guardianship. There was nothing that either Annum or Enlil could do about the creation and presence of the emerald tablet. It was inviolable and could not be destroyed, and an unseen authority which they could not disobey kept it in place within a shrine at the centre of the court.

Under Divine guidance, Enki was instructed that he must infiltrate Annum's group of conspirators in order to save the Earth and her people. He married his sister, Nin-khursag and, in a relationship difficult to understand from our point of view today, Nin-khursag also married Enlil. She did this in an attempt to maintain balance and connectedness within both men, who were suffering from the loss of their androgynous bond.

Enki proved to be her star pupil and attained highest honours; Enlil elected to be a hopeless case. Nevertheless, Nin-khursag's intervention was crucial, because she was able to lessen and distract Enlil's dire influence and, in many cases, simply play for time, which often swung the balance in favour of Nin-khursag's and Enki's great mission – the rescue of earthly humanity from Annum, Enlil and their circle of conspirators.

An important point to make clear is that Enki is indeed John. He was also known as Uan, because he and Nin-khursag replaced Anu as the Divine couple once Annum had fallen from grace, and the name of the original Divine couple, or, more accurately, androgyne, was associated with him (Uan-Anu). In later days, this name became known in earthly transcription as Oannes, the Fish-Man, and, later still, Johannes or John.

There was something a little different about the Divine Couple Nin-khursag and Enki from that of Antu and Annum. Not only were the former not androgynous, but they now needed very powerfully and clearly to reflect Divine Father in relationship to Divine Mother, because this true relationship had become so obscured and corrupt in human perception. This was why Enki chose to represent himself as the Fish-Man. The fish, or spermatozoa, swimming in the supernal waters of the Mother, the All, was a symbol of the Mother and Father as one, and showed that the Father was contained within the Mother.

Later, when the ultimate Divine Couple arrived (for Jesus and Mary Magdalene were souls more advanced even than the devoted Enki and Nin-khursag, being of the supreme God Race, the Nephilim, and the highest even among the Nephilim), they were able to receive, here on Earth, the influences of Divine Daughter and Divine Son (the Christ being) in fullest measure.

Even so, the human perception of God was still very much off kilter, and it was necessary for John to incarnate with Jesus to continue to heal that shattered human understanding, as well as for Jesus and Mary to reveal the ineffable wonders of the Christ being in the heavens, of whom we are all a part as daughters and sons of God. The magical flame in the heart, with which wonders can be wrought, is a spark of the essence of the Christ being that dwells within us.

Jesus and John were twin souls, although they did not incarnate as earthly twins. The 'Didymus' (twin) confusion also arose because two babies were born in the cave-stable of the Nativity – Mary Magdalene and Jesus, 12 inclusive (or 11) days apart, by two Marys, Mother Mary and Mary Jacob (later known as Mary Cleophas), her cousin.

The baby Mary Magdalene, the Alpha, came first; Jesus, the Omega, her second cousin, came last. This was kept secret for the sake of the girl child, because she needed protection. She must live, for she was destined to bring forth the ultimate fruition of their enterprise.

John was born later, as her younger brother, Lazarus. He received the titular name 'John' after he was brought back to life by Mary and Jesus (for Mary always worked secretly with Jesus to bring about miracles) and underwent an initiation connected with the Grail that, a thousand years later, the priests or perfecti of the enigmatic Cathars of the 'Nation of 8' (the nation of the Grail) would also undergo, and thereby become initiated into the Johannine mysteries.

So, before the story of Enki or John can properly begin, another point should be made: that Enki, although he was John, also manifested his essence throughout many 'John-men' of history. There was one supreme spiritual son of Enki, however, who is the crux of the story and who will lead us to Rosslyn, the Grail Chapel, Iona's 'twin'.

Because the Father was brought forth from the Mother, manifestation is not the direct process for Him as it is for Her, the Great Manifester. In order to manifest, the Father needs the help of the angelic hierarchy, which emanates from the feminine forces. Therefore, one of the great angels that sustain creation descended to Earth to enable the Father to manifest through Enki, and through all the John-men.

The John-men all share this angelic quality; they look angelic and indeed are connected directly with the angels. It was a secret Leonardo Da Vinci knew when he painted John the Baptist (he of the pointing finger symbolising ascension) and John the Beloved Disciple, angelic and androgynous. It is the Father's demonstration of his source within the heart of the Mother, from which the angels emanate. John the Beloved had this angelic quality, and was full of fun and laughter, as the angels are. It is this disciple who plays such a crucial part in the story of the Holy Grail.

From the point where Enki is divinely guided to penetrate the circle of conspirators with disguised intention, we can begin to trace the story of John as it intertwines with the story of the human race, and discover the state of play that this story shows us is in place today.

CHAPTER 13

THE STORY BEGINS

Enki played his part magnificently in the sinister court of Enlil. He fooled his father, King Annum, his brother Enlil, and their circle of conspirators, into thinking that he was one of them, although both his father and brother remained suspicious of him to some degree. They did not suspect a counter-plot (although they would discover the truth later), but they did regard Enki as something of a loose cannon and were never quite sure what he was up to or how far he could be trusted.

Only a very small group within the conspiratorial ring, however, was ever privy to all the secret plans of Annum and Enlil; and they decided to keep Enki firmly outside this inner core.

The rest of the enhanced community, the remainder of the Anunnaki assembly who were good-willed and goodhearted but, as time went on, became increasingly manipulated, loved Enki and Nin-khursag and grieved over their disinheritance, even though a majority had voted to carry Annum's motion that Enlil should be set up as acting king. Annum had succeeded due to his very plausible persuasions plus a certain subtle influence of command which, as a member of the Divine Couple, he should never have abused.

Enlil now headed the assembly on his father's behalf, as Annum's exploits continued to take him further abroad into the cosmos. Enlil's problem was that, although the Grail had been cut off from the Earth, some residual energies remained that, faint though they were, could yet be used by earthly humanity to penetrate the heavy veil of spiritual darkness and confusion which had fallen over the world. This posed a threat to his plans of degradation, enslavement and eventual elimination for physical humankind.

He also needed to bring down the all-important mantle that shielded the Earth from harmful cosmic influences, as Annum was now in a position to fight the battle for Earth from beyond the planet and was relying on his chosen son's ingenuity in assisting him.

The mantle was a ring of ice, formed from purest water of exquisite crystalline structure, which crowned the highest point of Earth's stratosphere. It was Tiâmat's ring of gentle reflective water through which poured the supernal light of the cosmos, protecting us from a directness for which we were not yet ready, and also from negative emanations, because the Shadow had come into being with Creation to teach discernment and choice.

It was God's plan that the Shadow should come into play via certain checks and balances and should never be allowed to run amok. It was Annum's plan to directly contravene this law.

A part of the mantle had already been destroyed through Annum's ceremonies of distortion with his conspirators involving the Naphidem, and via their development of malignant weaponry. However, much of it was still intact. It created a subtle light play within the sunrays and brought into being many lovely colours which are now lost to us.

Enlil was inspired by a stroke of genius which constituted the following plot: through the holes in the mantle and via powerful ceremonies, release as much Naphidem influence (which stoked up bad passions and produced rabble mentality) into the societies on Earth as possible; complain to the Anunnaki assembly that humankind was evidently not learning its spiritual lessons and needed something to make it stop and think; get the assembly to agree to a global inundation which would be far worse than it had understood he meant to inflict; drown most of humanity and Earth's physical biology by melting the mantle: bull's-eye.

This very astute course of action was quickly implemented. Enlil's suggestion was passed in the assembly, although Nin-khursag stormed out of the meeting in a rage, foreseeing what was to come. The Council took no notice of her, as the insight and judgement of women were already heavily undermined. The vote had taken place without giving ear to her objections.

Nin-khursag relayed to Enki what Tiâmat had revealed to her about Enlil's plan. They went to her secret temple, where she advised Enki not to break Anunnaki law by directly reporting the business of the Council to the earthly communities, but instead to whisper to the reeds of a river which flowed by the royal residence of a certain king and queen, spiritually attuned people who would listen in their dreams to the spirit voice that drifted to them across the waters in the night.

This was how Zi-u-sudra (the biblical Noah) and his queen, both highly accomplished in the scientific arts, came to build the great ark that carried their household, certain animals, and the seeds and embryos of 'living things', as Enki had directed, to safety, whilst a great swathe of the world perished. The British mainland as it is today was created by that disaster; it broke away from the rest of Hyperborea, which was swallowed and overcome by a massive tsunami so that eventually Britain stood alone as an island.

The rainbow appeared above the ark, the true covenant of God as it had once appeared long ago, just before the Grail was severed, when Tiâmat had revealed her plans to Enki and Nin-khursag.

She had told them then that the secret temple in which they worshipped her (as Mother-Father God) was to be aligned to a high sphere of heaven, higher than the Eden in which the enhanced community dwelt in the ethereal dimension of Earth. It was to be known as the Sphere of John, or Sharon (the same name: Sha-ron being the androgynous version of the name John), and it would connect with the Earth via Mount Heredom and the other stations of the Grail, although it was a celestial region more refined than any of the Earth planes. It was to be the new Shambalah.

It would link with the great angel who manifested the Father, and it would be an inner sanctum for the Earth of the true knowledge and understanding of God: that the Mother and Father are one, that the Father is of the All which is the Mother, and that their child, the Divine Daughter-Son, although an ineffable being in the heavens, is also a spark within each member of humanity. That Divine spark is destined to bring such light to the soul as to enable it, if it will make the free-will choice, to step through the mirror of creation and become a fully conscious son or daughter of God in his or her own right.

This is the glorious destiny that Annum and Enlil and their followers desire so desperately to veil from us, imagining delusionally that they can change the rules of the universe, and become its masters. The sanctified Sphere of John was destined to comprise the vast temple which would, via harmonious understanding, lead humanity back to the heart of God, and ultimately result in the restoration of the Grail to planet Earth.

Once the Grail was reconnected, the Sphere of John would be enabled to descend to Earth, and a golden age, of a shining splendour even more radiant than that of the first, would begin.

Tiâmat further told them that, because of the Naphidem horror, the structure of the human soul was to be changed. Every ensouled creation has an inner geometrical structure, and ours, long ago, was akin to a tall obelisk or a tower with a peak at its topmost point, like a slender cone.

After the Grail was cut off from us, we had built such towers in actuality upon the Earth, topped with what the Sumerians called the 'highward fire-stone', made by alchemical processes, which ignited with spiritual force when certain techniques were enacted within the towers: techniques that caused the fire-stone to light up with self-generated radiance. This process enabled the enhanced community to travel down to earth from Eden, and the ordinary community to ascend to Eden, for a considerable number of years after the Grail was lost, although ascension beyond Eden was now impossible. It was just such a use of the remnant of the Grail forces that was a thorn in the side of Enlil.

From now on, Tiâmat told them, the human soul was to evolve within the structure of a pyramid, so that the massive, four-square base that supported ascension sturdily from every side could not so easily be set upon and toppled in the way that, first the conspirators, and then the Naphidem, had been assaulted and toppled by dark forces directed against them and into them.

These pyramids, when built in physicality upon the Earth, as they would be both before and after the flood, would give access to Eden, just as the former obelisks had. Because of their strength and ingenuity, the new inner pyramidal design of the human soul would be robust enough to support a further four-square design.

This design was God's plan to build into the structure of the human soul, the aptitude, the preparedness, the necessary wiring and power-sockets, so to speak, to take on board the full stature and might of the emerald tablet, once its light-encrypted knowledge and encoded realisations had been read and understood and the essential key to them had been supplied.

After the application of this key, it would simply be a matter of developing and honing the soul by direct and simple process to the point where the full power and essence of the emerald tablet could be absorbed to perfection, individually, by each and every human being who would accept it.

Iona would still have to be reawakened. That act was part of the key. Nevertheless, once Iona was reconnected, and the Grail forces flooded back to Earth via the God-light in the human heart, the Holy Grail could never be severed again by malignant intent. We would have it active within us to a point much more potent than ever before, and nothing could take it away. If the Shadow tried to shatter Iona once more, the Grail within us would protect her and automatically restore her. It would be an indwelling power of the human heart that nothing could overturn.

To fulfil this plan, God had directed Enki and Nin-khursag to develop, via their skill in the science of genetics, three pairs of human beings who would receive sequentially one quarter of this dynamic new patterning each, until the point had been reached where the third couple, having received the third quarter, would prepare the way for the whole of humanity to receive the fourth quarter en masse.

As humanity received that fourth and final quarter, they would automatically come into the inheritance of the ability to receive the whole of the emerald tablet once the key had been provided.

In this way, our all-loving and forgiving Mother-Father would protect us forever from the depredations of the Shadow. No longer would it be able to encroach by wholesale deceit and manipulation, as it does so pervasively today.

Zi-u-sudra and his queen were the first pair of human beings, refined by genetic engineering (which was a spiritual as well as a scientific process overlit by the Holy Spirit, just as life is today), to receive the aptitude within them for receipt of the first quarter of the emerald tablet.

These four quarters of the emerald tablet enshrine within them what are known as the Four Hallows of the Grail. Their spiritual essence is to be found on Iona, and the human heart can intuit them and draw sustenance from them, even though the Grail has not yet been restored to us. Fiona, whose words unfailingly summon the presence of Iona and evoke the holy isle's spiritual moods, can reveal them for our delight.

CHAPTER 14

THE FOUR HALLOWS OF THE GRAIL UPON IONA

It might be easier to understand fully the promises of the Grail if its Four Hallows, or four gifts, are thrown into stark relief by their mirror reflection in negative mode: for the Four Horsemen of Doom from Scripture comprise the four Grail gifts in reverse. They are what Enlil, the slave of the Shadow, would have us reap instead of our rightful inheritance.

The Four Horsemen of Doom are those who bring War, Famine, Plague and Death.

The Four Hallows of the Grail comprise the sure and certain promise of Peace, Abundance, Healing and Immortality.

The Four Horsemen have nothing to do with Iona and the spirit that breathes through her and over her and will give us the breath of Life if we will open to her – 'the Iona that, if we will it so, is a mirror of your heart and of mine' as Fiona so succinctly expresses it. Within Iona's mirror dwell only the reflections of her sanctity. And Iona's sanctity is the Holy Grail and her Four Hallows.

Peace, perhaps, is the easiest quality to perceive straightaway on Iona. There are many places, natural shrines, where she harbours it and dispenses it so that it is all-encompassing. And her legends tell of it.

Fiona speaks again of the Divine Woman whose coming is linked to Iona, for she embodies the prophecy of peace:

'From one man only, on Iona itself, I have heard any allusion to the prophecy as to the Saviour who shall yet come: and he in part was obscure, and confused the advent of Mary into the spiritual world with the possible coming again to Earth of Mary, as another Redeemer, or with a descending of the Divine Womanhood upon the human heart as an universal spirit descending upon awaiting souls. But in intimate remembrance I recall the words and faith of one or two whom I loved well. Nor must I forget that my old nurse, Barabal, used to sing a strange 'oran', to the effect that when St Bride came again, it would be to bind the hair and wash the feet of the Bride of Christ.

'One of those to whom I allude was a young Hebridean priest: and he told me once how, "as our forefathers and elders believed and still believe, that Holy Spirit shall come again which once was born among us as the Son of God, but, then, shall be the daughter of God. The Divine Spirit shall come again as a Woman. Then for the first time the world will know peace."

'And when I asked him if it were not prophesied that the Woman is to be born in Iona, he said that if this prophecy had been made, it was doubtless of an Iona that was symbolic, but that this was a matter of no moment, for She would rise suddenly in many hearts, and have her habitation among dreams and hopes.

'The other who spoke to me of this Woman who is to save was an old fisherman of a remote island of the Hebrides, and one to whom I owe more than to any other spiritual influence in my childhood, for it was he who opened to me the three gates of Beauty.

'Once this old man, Seumas Macleod, took me with him to a lonely haven in the rocks, and held me on his knee as we sat watching the sun sink and the moon climb out of the eastern wave. I saw no-one, but abruptly he rose and put me from him, and bowed his grey head as he knelt before one who suddenly was standing in that place. I asked eagerly who it was. He told me that it was an Angel.

'Later, I learned (I remember my disappointment that the beautiful vision was not winged with great white wings) that the Angel was one soft flame of pure white, and that below the soles of his feet were curling scarlet flames.

'He had come in answer to the old man's prayer. He had come to say that we could not see the Divine One whom we awaited. "But you will yet see that Holy Beauty," said the Angel, and Seumas believed, and I too believed, and believe. He took my hand, and I knelt beside him, and he bade me repeat the words he said. And that was how I first prayed to Her who shall yet be the Balm of the World.'

These are astonishing words, especially from Presbyterian Scotland at the turn of the 19th century, yet so beautifully wrought within the flowing text of the book that they pass almost unnoticed. Who were these 'forefathers and elders'? On returning to Iona's story, a guess will be hazarded.

For now, we might look over to Skye, visible from Iona, and reflect that the island's name derives from a great queen who held court there, and who was so advanced in the prowess of warriorship that young men from nearby and far off would travel to her court to learn from her the arts of combat and weaponry. She was a most noble queen, yet not a woman of peace; but on her island there are the remains of a temple to a mysterious feminine deity whose secrets have never been uncovered.

Who was this feminine deity? No temple to her worship was ever erected upon Iona; but that is because the entire mountain that constituted Iona was once her temple; and it is why Iona's essence is unmistakably feminine.

In the East, she was called Anaitis; but she did not come from the East. She was first known to the world as she who dwelt within the sacred mountain of Heredom. By the side of the mountain lay a sacred lake; and that, too, was her domain.

Everywhere, the sanctity of her memory was purposely despoiled and trodden underfoot. The grace and shining light of her legends remain, but a dark underbelly has been artificially obtruded onto them. One of the clearest indications of this is given in Gustav Meyrink's novel, *The Angel of the West Window*.

The angel of the title is an agent of the false emerald tablet, and depicts what the rites of Anaitis became due to its influence, culminating in the horrible ritual of Taghairm, where cats were tortured in unspeakable ways so that their fear and agony would eventually give rise to the manifestation of a giant black cat, a goddess of the infernal regions who was summoned as an oracle.

Not surprisingly, these obscene rituals first began in the vicinity of Scotland, for it was in the precise location of the decapitated holy mountain that the adversarial forces sought to do their worst in stoking up fear and loathing of the Sacred Feminine. They used and abused the feminine psychic forces within the cat soul to fulfill their aim, and these abominable practices spread into many cultures, except for Egypt and other civilisations that preserved ancient truths within their doctrines. Even in these lands, the veneration and protection of cats suffered from a markedly schizophrenic aspect.

There was also a secret cult within the Temple of Mithras, the bull god of war and warriors, which involved a lurid and disturbing worship of the feminine principle that culminated in the self-castration of its adherents. Its point was clear. Perversion, enervation and castration, in fact an irretrievable descent into degenerate madness, were the inevitable results of worshipping the Divine Feminine.

Let us turn decisively away from these deceptive evil mirrors to the truth of 'Anaitis'.

She was a goddess of fertility, of creation and the Earth's flowering and fruitfulness, associated with both water and fire, who was worshipped in Persia, Canaan, Egypt, Anatolia (which is considered to have derived its name from her) and other lands of the Near and Middle East. Her sacred sites were marked by fire sanctuaries and a source of fresh water, such as a running brook, a spring, a well or a fountain.

She was a goddess of highest knowledge, of the Bright Knowledge, for she shepherded the light of God through the mantle of purest water around Earth's brow down to the mantle of cosmic heat and fire at Earth's heart, from where its spiritual measure could then rise safely to bless the Earth.

Why is it that her eastern name is known in the British Isles, especially in Scotland? Certainly, the male and female genes (J2 and J1b1 respectively) which characterise Semitic-speaking people, are particularly concentrated in Scotland, although they arrived by different routes, the first from the eastern Mediterranean and the second by way of the Black Sea and Norway.

It is possible that the Pictish tribes – a small, dark, fiery race – may have comprised such a Near-Eastern people, or, at least, from an alternative viewpoint of history, a Near-Eastern people that had interbred with northern natives. They would no doubt have brought their religious devotions with them, and the name Anaitis or Anit thus become localised. In Mesopotamia, most tellingly, the same goddess was known as Antu.

Within the temples of Anaitis stood an image of the goddess, which was ritually carried during certain ceremonies to the nearby brook or spring within her sacred enclosure and immersed in the water. This rite is reminiscent of the statues of Mary Magdalene and of her 'servant' Sara, which are similarly baptised each year during Christian ceremonies in the south of France, where Mary Magdalene, Sara and many of the disciples were said to have docked after setting sail from the shores of Alexandria in a boat without rudder or sails.

From such ancient rites the term 'merry (Mary) maid' or 'mermaid' derives, the name Mary meaning 'bitter water' or 'salt water' – the sea; the statues of Mary and Sara are ceremonially submerged in the sea, reminiscent of Isis; for Isis was the great goddess who introduced the ritual of baptism to the world. And, magically, there is a mermaid of Iona, with whose song Fiona was familiar.

Yet the name for Anaitis that has passed through British folklore, and which may be much older than we can imagine and her original name, is Ain or Ani, which also has a reflection in the Near East, as though perhaps the influences surrounding her name are bilateral and it was not simply imported from the East; Mary Magdalene was Mary of Bethany or Beth-Ani – 'House of Ani'. And the author Laurence Gardner has shown that Mary Magdalene is of a bloodline that reaches back to that of Enki; Enki who was Antu's first son.

There are 65 sites throughout Scotland where Anaitis is believed to have been worshipped. Was she Antu?

I believe that deep, primordial soul memories of Antu were preserved in the worship of Anaitis, and that those who tried to blacken her memory are those who have always sought humanity's degeneration and destruction. And yet Antu was the spiritual daughter of a Divine queen, a queen so mysterious that we can only catch elusive glimpses of her: the Great Queen to whom allusion has been made in earlier chapters. And it is this queen who has always dwelt in the deepest heart of humanity.

Without her presence in our world, the Grail could never have come into being. For, veritably, she is the Holy Grail.

Her name and memory were passed down as the Morrigan, Great Queen, Great One, Great Tower of Light, the All. And in the word 'mountain' we have 'the Mount of Ain', her sacred home. The name Magdalene is a titular designation bearing the same meanings, for Mary was not Mary of Magdala, as sometimes cited. This town was called Tarichea in her day, and became Magdala ('tower') when a tower was erected there 70 years or so after her time. Mary was: Mary, the Magdalene (or Morrigan), Great Queen, Great One, Great Tower of Light, the All.

And herein we see that the initiating Mother and Daughter (Ain and Antu) are barely distinguishable from one another and were remembered together, as one, in the name 'Anaitis'. As mentioned, it was because of Ain that Antu was able to come to Earth with Annum and in herself make the spiritual link with God that was the Grail. Ain was the androgyne Anu's spiritual stairway down to Earth.

It was because of Ain's presence here on Earth that the secret temple could exist in which Tiâmat could speak so directly to Antu, to Enki and Nin-khursag, and, before they fell from grace, to Annum and Enlil and other members of the Anunnaki Council. For when they spoke to Tiâmat, they spoke to her through Ain. Again, on a higher octave, Divine Mother and Daughter (Tiâmat and Ain) were barely distinguishable from one another.

This meant that, whilst Antu and Annum were queen and king upon Iona in the early days of the world (after the coming of the Naphidem they relocated to the Fertile Crescent in the Near and Middle East), Ain was always the Great Queen within the sacred mountain, whom Antu reflected: the mystic Queen, the most holy Queen, a drop of Tiâmat's veritable essence on Earth, the primordial and originating Mother. All the titles relating to Ain (and to Mary Magdalene and Antu) sing of this Mother, who is remembered despite every attempt to degrade and disinherit Her.

The Morrigan is known in Celtic and Norse culture as the dread Hag of War – another terrible distortion. Whoever the Hag of War may be, she is not the Divine one that was truly called Morrigan.

Another name for her was Derdekea – the Divine Drop, known in Persian culture, which was Enki's culture, as we shall see. She was, indeed, a drop of the essence of the Great Mother – of Tiâmat, come down to root the Grail into the body of the Earth for us, and to hold forth its miraculous cup in our hearts.

So let us go to the place of peace upon Iona, although there are many places of peace there, and contemplate some of the mysteries of the Divine Woman, to whom Fiona and Seumas Macleod prayed in their haven of the rocks.

And we might think, too, of Leonardo's painting of the *Virgin of the Rocks*. He was making a bawdy and humorous point with his painting, and it had a defiant message for the Pope; but it also makes an exquisite statement in that it envisions the Divine Woman, bathed in a light found nowhere on Earth but at this sacred spot.

The sea floods in through the great grotto of the rocks; and the place is Iona.

CHAPTER 15

GREEN CHILDREN

A place of Peace upon Iona, the first of the Four Hallows of the Grail, is conjured by Fiona's words:

'There is a spot on Iona that has always had a strange enchantment for me. Behind the ruined walls of the Columban church, the slopes rise, and the one isolated hill of Iona is, there, a steep and sudden wilderness. It is commonly called Dûn-I (Doon-ee), for at the summit in old days was an island fortress; but the Gaelic name of the whole of this uplifted shoulder of the isle is Slibh Meanach...There, through the boggy pastures, where the huge-horned shaggy cattle stared at me, and up through the ling and roitch, I climbed...

'As I write, here on the hill-slope of Dûn-I, the sound of the furtive sea is as the sighing in a shell. I am alone between sea and sky, for there is no other on this bouldered height, nothing visible but a single blue shadow that slowly sails the hillside. The bleating of lambs and ewes, the lowing of kine, these come up from the Machar (the sandy, rock-frontiered plane of duneland on the west side of Iona, exposed to the Atlantic); these ascend as the very smoke of sound.

'All round the island there is a continuous breathing; deeper and more prolonged on the west, where the open sea is; but audible everywhere. The seals on Soa are even now putting their breasts against the running tide...In the sunblaze, the waters of the Sound dance their blue bodies and swirl their flashing white hair o' foam; and, as I look, they seem to me like children of the wind and the sunshine, leaping and running in these flowing pastures, with a laughter as sweet against the ears as the voices of children at play.

'The joy of life vibrates everywhere. Yet, an Isle of Dream Iona is indeed. I would that the birds of Angus Ogue might, for once, be changed, not, as fabled, into the kisses of love, but into doves of peace, that they might fly into the green world, and nest there in many hearts, in many minds, crooning their incommunicable song of joy and hope.'

In spirit, sit upon this high point of Iona, the capstone of the ancient and beautiful Mount Heredom, of a sanctity so vast that it is unimaginable, and enter into the magic of the holy isle. Here, many secrets will be revealed. It is the eye of the isle, and its vision is both inward and outward.

There is a major pilgrimage route leading from Iona to Glen Lyon on the mainland, soft with blue and violet shadow, upon which you can gaze with the mind's eye. At the entrance to Glen Lyon stands the Fortingall yew, reputed to be over five thousand years old and the most ancient tree in the world. Excavations at Glastonbury show that Joseph of Arimathea brought dried-out yew saplings with him from the Holy Land, and that these have a reputation for magically springing to life, even though apparently desiccated. The yew is the queen among trees that hold the magic of the Sacred Feminine, the tree-wisdom of the boreal forests which connects with the knowledge of the Grail. The Queen of Iona, the Divine Woman, whispers her knowledge through the medium of this great Fortingall yew, and here on Iona you can attune the inner ear to its murmurings.

Interestingly, the name Iova means 'Yew Island' and is one of the numerous associations linked with Iona's many-faceted name. Certainly the yew, which stands as portal to Glen Lyon and the pilgrimage route to Iona, is linked directly to her deeper significance.

There is a beautiful and mystical phenomenon, happening in our time and replete with intimations of what is to come, which has recently been discovered by Janis Fry and Allen Meredith, authors of *The God Tree*.

To their astonishment, they found a most exquisite 'golden bough', burgeoning forth with delicate filigree foliage, growing directly from the trunk of an ancient yew. It seems that this is the famous 'golden bough' of legend, manifesting in earthly reality for the first time. Since then, other yew-trees have brought forth the same miracle.

The golden bough is a wonder that in myth must be presented to Proserpina, the queen of the underworld (the worlds within) before the hero, who in Roman myth is the Trojan warrior Aeneas, can make entry; once within, the golden bough must be held aloft to gain admittance into the Elysian fields, the heaven worlds. Significantly, the hero's mother, the goddess Venus, sends two white doves to help her son find the golden bough.

Venus is considered to be the feminine planet of our solar system which is especially blessed by Divine Mother so that the Venusian community and that of Earth can grow together into the light. Although her people are much more advanced than us and are of course an ethereal people, they assist us in our struggle, unseen and unknown. Venus is the only planet of our solar system to spin sunwise or clockwise, the 'positive revolution'. Once, long ago, planet Earth spun sunwise, and one day, some time after Iona is reconnected, she will do so again.

Glen Lyon used to be known as 'the Desert glen' because of its association with the monks called the Culdees. They came with Columba to Iona, arising jointly from the Essenes (among them the Desert Prophets) and the Druids, truly one within the circle of east and west.

A special order within them was known as the mysterious 'Sons of the Valley', whose hidden seat was upon Iona. They were custodians and mentors to the famous Knights Templar and were an inner order of the Temple of John. They were the 'forefathers and elders' who prophesied the coming of a Divine Woman upon Iona referred to by the young Hebridean priest discussed in the previous chapter. A secret brotherhood has always existed within Iona's hidden dimensions, which links with a very strange tale that yet makes perfect sense.

Of this brotherhood was St Martin, two St Martins it seems, for there are two versions of St Martin's Cross on Iona, one an ancient high cross known as Cròis Mhartuinn (Martin's Cross), and the other, the Great Cross of Iona, of massive red granite, which commemorates the French (originally Hungarian) St Martin of Tours, a significant keeper of the Grail secrets.

It is the other St Martin, who actually belonged to the island, about whom there is a mystery. A tale hundreds of years old is told of two green children who emerged from the mouth of a cavern in Suffolk, a girl and a boy. After they had learned to speak English (their own dialect was incomprehensible), they explained that they lived in a country underground, lit by a gentle twilight. They had emerged into our world inadvertently after getting lost and wandering in a cavern they had never seen before.

The boy died, but the girl thrived, and gradually lost her green colour. She said that all the people in her country were green-skinned, and that it was called St Martin's Land. They practised a Christianity which seemed to give equal status to women, as she was markedly assertive and uninhibited in her conduct. The story was authenticated by two men, Ralph of Coggeshall and William of Newbridge, the former of whom was acquainted with the knight who gave the children refuge, the other being a monk of good standing.

It is an odd tale, and seems to corroborate the existence of an underground community, and perhaps of a certain John Martinus, who was born on Iona and was of the secret brotherhood. It has been said that John Martinus was the son of Mary Magdalene and Jesus, but that does not align with the story of Iona and the Divine couple as it has been revealed to me. Yet certainly there is a shroud of mystery about him.

The story of the green children, of a world underground, might seem possible under Iona's sea-spell. The strange history of John Martinus and Iona, with its possible link to the mystery of the green children, will later be revealed.

From Dûn-I ('the Dwelling-Place of the Eye' in esoteric translation) we can look out again in dream to the mystic Fortingall yew, and see there in Fortingall a pile of stones in triangular formation. From here, a Scottish dowser, David Cowan, has perceived a key ley line running to a cleft standing stone of megalithic rock in Glen Lyon called 'the praying hands of Mary', and from there, where there are also the ruins of an ancient temple to Anaitis, it runs to Fingal's Cave on the Isle of Staffa, the wondrous cavern of magnetic basalt rock with which the hero Fionn is associated and where he is said to have been initiated into his life of heroism and magical feats.

The mouth of Fingal's Cave opens onto Iona; and in fact the same dowser traced another ley line passing out of the mouth of Fingal's Cave to run through the Abbey on Iona, as though what the sacred stones and the sacred yew at Fortingall, and the monolith and the temple in Glen Lyon give out to Fingal's Cave, returns in state to Iona.

Triangles or pyramids, the yew, the praying hands of Mary, the temple to Anaitis, caverns, even magnetism – all are feminine symbols. Their concentrated focus is on the House of Prayer upon Iona. On still nights, enchanting music, as of fairyland, has been heard issuing from the mouth of Fingal's Cave and drifting across Iona, forming another strand of the tapestry of her peace.

What is the mystery at the heart of that peace? It is, I believe, that long, long ago, as forecited, a mysterious queen dwelt within Mount

Heredom, and she in herself was the sacred inheritance that Mount Heredom housed. Her essence was a gift to all humanity, for this Great Queen, this Tower of Light, was a drop of the Primordial All, a drop of Mother God who had given herself to the Earth and to her Earth children that they might become gods.

So holy was this queen, of such mysterious essence, that only the mightiest angels and initiates of the highest degree among the God Race, all of them Shining Ones, came into her presence, and yet she blessed all on Earth, even the humblest atom. She was the personification of the living khu, most essential, mysterious, holy, and entirely feminine essence.

When moves were made against her, because of jealousy and misunderstanding, Mount Heredom was submerged, but yet emerged again intact from the waves. A new land formed itself around the holy mountain, snowier and stormier than the former paradise of Polaris, but yet a land of grandeur and beauty. It became known as Hyperborea, that fabled land of the far north that shone under the light of the dancing Aurora.

Now the Great Queen, to protect her domain and her God-appointed task, brought forth her androgynous self so that there was, most anciently, a king of the high places, sovereign lord of Hyperborea, noble in his graces and span of soul, whose spirit bore its God-light in fullness of beauty and beneficence and with a brightness of purity that was wondered at even among the God Race.

This king was known as Ar-Thor, Giant of Albion (giant in his soul-stature, although he stood taller than other men), great guardian of Britain. His reign was one of dedicated service, self-sacrific, and love.

Beside him sat his beloved queen, the Holy One of Heredom, she who bore the source and origin of all things within her. Because of her ineffable presence, the beautiful soul-worlds within the finer ethers of the Earth were an open door to all her people. She reigned with Ar-Thor, but in spite of her dazzling majesty she let the planetary community see that she and her king were in perfect equilibrium, and that there was no inequality between them.

In this blessed age of the king and queen of Mount Heredom, the Great Queen and her King were able to admit high initiates from the physical sphere into their presence, where formerly only angels and beings of pure spirit could be admitted. The king and queen dwelt upon the Earth, and were known throughout the world; yet their dwelling-place was also a higher sphere than that of Earth, and indeed had its dimensions upon a more exalted plane than Eden, where rulers of a lower degree plotted against them.

The reign of the king and queen of Heredom came after Annum had dispossessed Antu his wife and Enki his rightful son and heir, and had left the Earth for the wider cosmos. Even so, there had always been this ineffable queen within Mount Heredom, unseen, higher in spiritual status even than Annum and Antu. They had their dwelling in Eden, linked with Mount Heredom; whereas the Great Queen and her king resided within the mountain and within a domain that was loftier than Eden.

The Grail was duly severed, and the Great Queen was banished from the Earth. Her king was not entirely separated from her, by stint of his own spiritual strength. They continued to overlight the Earth from their higher dimension, although they were not linked to it, or even to each other, as they had been. They became known in ancient Egypt as Isis and Osiris.

Osiris was known as the 'once and future king', as records of antiquity attest. What is not so well-known, and yet is Earth's hope, is that Isis was known as the 'once and future queen'.

And if we can cast our net of vision far, far back into the past, we might on retrieval see it leap with the catch of an extraordinary intimation: that Osiris did indeed come again to this world, first as Joseph of Arimathea, with his shepherd's crook that flowered when it was thrust into the sacred land of Glastonbury, and then again as Arthur, giant of Albion, king and guardian of Britain, the mystic isle.

The Giants' Causeway, on the east coast of Ireland, can be seen from Iona. It is thought that once an isthmus of land joined Ireland to the Isle of Staffa, and that the Isle of Staffa was similarly joined to Iona; and that the Great Queen and Ar-Thor, the Giant of Albion, sent their influences to Ireland through Fingal's Cave and down the Giants' Causeway into Ireland's heart.

For a great mystery is enshrined there that can be read in Ireland's beautiful myths, involving Sara-Tamar, the daughter of Jesus and Mary

Magdalene who was and is in herself the Holy Grail. Perhaps we might envision her walking, walking in sacred ceremony, down that causeway at the age of 21, from her dûn in Ireland to Iona, to its seat or its heart, ready to take on the mantle of her life's ultimate destiny.

Indeed, Ireland had to be prepared for long ages to receive Sara-Tamar, the Holy Grail, daughter and only child of Mary Magdalene and Jesus, who once was the Giant of Albion's (Ar-Thor's) queen.

His life as Arthur was a replay on a smaller scale of his reign as Ar-Thor, purposely enacted at the lowest realm of Earth life (the physical domain) so that the Great Queen and her King could influence and interact with ordinary mortals but, also, consequently subject to the limitations and confusions of that domain. Sadly, Arthur fell into the hands of deceivers who put his deeper memory to sleep, and the Grail could not be restored to the Earth; for that, of course, was the purpose of his reign.

Isis (Ain, the Divine Woman) came again, as Sara-Tamar, the daughter of Mary Magdalene and Jesus, under the guardianship of Joseph of Arimathea, and then as the first wife of Arthur (not Guinevere). In the first instance, Sara-Tamar was left to die of starvation in a Roman prison, although she ascended and left nothing of her body behind. The Grail was not restored because she was not allowed to come into the full fruition of her womanhood and so reconnect its powers, as was partially the case in her later incarnation as Arthur's true queen.

Nevertheless, the essential deed, which was to return her, Derdekea or Ain, the Drop of Divinity, to Earth in physical human form, had been achieved when she came as Sara-Tamar in AD 33. The seed had been sown and the terrible severance of the Grail overcome, if not yet healed and restored.

As Arthur's queen she was banished. She continued to live in the soul realm of the Earth, devastated and heartbroken but not vanquished, ever trying to lift the blindness from the eyes of Arthur, who had sent her away after listening to monks from Alexandria purporting to be Christian, but who were in fact agents of the Shadow from 'dark Egypt' (the negative aspect of Egyptian culture, known as 'the body', or materialism).

But the peace of Dûn-I shall have the last word regarding this tragic history. Fiona speaks of two prophecies, one of them her own:

'It is so hard to believe that what has fallen may arise. Yet we have perpetual symbols; the tree, that the winds of autumn ravage and the spring restores; the trodden weed, that in April awakes white and fragrant; the swallow, that in the south remembers the north. We forget the ebbing wave that from the sea-depths comes again: the Day, shod with sunrise while his head is crowned with stars.

'But many, I fear, have little faith that Iona can again, as a new influence, minister to the spiritual need of the world. These would have it that her sole ministry lies now in remembrance; in the memory of what Iona was and did. Once ruined, that cannot be again which was. That is the common belief.

'More far-seeing the vision of the old Gael, who prophesied that Iona would never wholly cease to be 'the lamp of faith', but would in the end shine forth as gloriously as of yore, and that, after dark days, a new hope would go hence into the world. But before that (and he prophesied when the island was in its greatness):

"Before this happens,
Iona will be as it was,
Without the voice of a monk,
Under the dung of cows."

'A more polished later version [with a different emphasis], though attributed to Columba, runs:

"In Iona that is my heart's desire,
Iona that is my love,
the lowing of cows shall yet replace
the voices of monks:
but before the end is come,
Iona shall again be as it was."

'And truly enough the little island was for long given over to the sea-wind...that of old was "this our little sea-bounded Garden of Eden." But now that Iona has been "as it was", the other and greater change may yet be...'

The old Erse-speaking Gael, and Columba, and Fiona herself, can see through the mists that time and sorrow and the girdle of sea have wrought. Somehow they remember Iona's feminine essence, the Divine Woman she served and shielded, and the king of kings who came to Earth by virtue of her presence.

Long ago the people of the isles remembered Anaitis or Antu, and through her they remembered Ain, the Divine Woman; just as, not as a memory but as a literality, Mary Magdalene, of that same line, brought forth Sara-Tamar, who was the Divine Woman of the ancient past – Ain, the Great Queen of the Mount, of the High Places; and who will come again, miraculously, more than miraculously, in our own time.

Remembering that magical evening when, in the haven of the rocks, she was with Seumas Macleod and the angel came to him, and how they afterwards prayed to Her, the Divine Woman who shall yet be the Balm of the World, Fiona writes:

'And since then I have learned, and do see, that not only prophecies and hopes, and desires unclothed yet in word or thought, foretell Her coming, but already a multitude of spirits are in the gardens of the soul, and are sowing seed and calling upon the wind of the south; and that everywhere are watching eyes and uplifted hands, and signs which cannot be mistaken, in many lands, in many peoples, in many minds; and, in the heaven itself that the soul sees, the surpassing signature.'

CHAPTER 16

THE DIVINE FORGES

In search of the symbolic places of Immortality and Healing on Iona, we can follow Fiona to the Fountain of Youth and to the Divine Forges, for both are to be found on the little holy isle.

'In Iona, while yet a child, I set out one evening to find the Divine Forges. A Gaelic sermon, preached on the shoreside by an earnest man going poor and homeless through the west, had been my ministrant in these words. The 'revivalist' had spoken of God as one who would hammer the evil out of the soul and weld it to good, as a blacksmith at his anvil: and suddenly, with a dramatic gesture, he cried: "This little island of Iona is this anvil; God is your blacksmith: but oh, poor people, who among you knows the narrow way to the Divine Forges?"'

The idea links immediately with Enki, or John; for in esoteric circles he is referred to as 'the first Mr Smith'. Enki was known as the Great Artificer, and he gathered around him a Craftworkers' Guild of devotees.

His craftworkers were drawn from both the enhanced and ordinary communities. In one sense, they were taught the simple craft of life, as Jesus and Mary taught it in their mission on Earth. In another, they were instructed in the highest esoteric arts. They were taught to build with the 'hands' of their soul and spirit. They learned many wonders by applying exalted scientific principles, which are always spiritual in nature and produce miracles.

The concept of the Divine Forges is Enki-inspired, except that his teachings would have us think not so much of evil as of evolution and growth. He was and is known as the Architect of Truth. He shows us how to build, in the deepest, holiest sense of the word as well as its practical application. He is a metal-worker, a forger, a mason, an artisan; he is also angelically inspired, and an alchemist of the noblest degree. His message to us is that we are building ourselves – building our own temple so that it is fit for the little spark of God-essence within us to fill it and so become a towering flame – a God in its own right.

Today, Uri Geller, by bending metal and causing seeds to sprout in his hand, shows evidence of the ancient Mesopotamian bloodline that Enki instructed and indeed initiated and entered, first by genetic manipulation (numbered amongst his 'building' skills), and then directly, by fathering a son. These skills, of course, are for all; his Craftworkers demonstrate them for our example and encouragement.

Enlil, too, inherited the same skills, a gift from Divine Father. They were an outworking of the inspirations of Divine Mother. The two brothers should have worked together to build an Earth of wonder and joy; but he chose to turn his skills to dark and sinister designs, ever increasing in their hideous intent. Annum, of course, had followed the same abysmal path ahead of his son. Annum and Enlil have their Mordor-like Forges; but they are certainly not Divine and just as certainly cannot be found on Iona!

Climbing Dûn-I after listening to this inspired sermon by the wandering preacher, Fiona stopped by the Fountain of Youth, also known as the Pool of Healing:

'Hidden under a wave of heath and boulder, near the broken rocks, is a little pool. From generation to generation this has been known, and frequented, as the Fountain of Youth. Although half-concealed beneath an overhanging rock, to this small, black-brown tarn that is also called the Pool of Healing, pilgrims of every generation, for hundreds of years, have come.

'Solitary, these; not only because the pilgrim to the Fount of Eternal Youth must fare hither alone, and at dawn, so as to touch the healing water the moment the first sunray quickens it – but solitary, also, because those who go in quest of this Fount of Youth are the dreamers and the Children of Dream, and few come now to this lonely place.

'If anywhere, I thought that from there I might see the Divine Forges, or at least might discover a hidden way, because of the power of that water, touched on the eyelids at sunlift, at sunset, or at the rising of the moon.

'From where I stood I could see the people still gathered upon the dunes by the shore, and the tall, ungainly figure of the preacher. In the narrow strait were two boats, one being rowed across to Fionnaphort, and the other, with a dun sail burning flame-brown, hanging like a bird's wing against Glas Eilean, on the tideway to the promontory of Earraid.

'Was the preacher still talking of the Divine Forges, I wondered; or were the men and women in the ferry hurrying across to the Ross of

Mull to look for them among the inland hills? And the Earraid men in the fishing-smack: were they sailing to see if they lay hidden in the wilderness of rocks, where the muffled barking of the seals made the loneliness more wild and remote?

'I wetted my eyelids, as I had so often done before (and not always vainly, though whether vision came from the water, or from a more quenchless spring within, I know not), and looked into the little pool. Alas! I could see nothing but the reflection of a star, too obscured by light as yet for me to see in the sky, and, for a moment, the shadow of a gull's wing as the bird flew by far overhead.

'I was too young then to be content with the symbols of coincidence, or I might have thought that the shadow of a wing from Heaven, and the light of a star out of the East, were enough indication. But, as it was, I turned and walked idly northward, and went down the side of Dun Bhuirg. Still seeking a way to the Divine Forges, I skirted the shore and crossed the sandy plain of the Machar, and mounted the upland district known as Sliav Starr (the Hill of Noises), and walked to a place, to me sacred.

'This was a deserted green airidh between great rocks. From here I could look across the extreme western part of Iona, to where it shelved precipitously around the little Port-a-churaich, the Haven of the Coracle, the spot where St Columba landed when he came to the island.

'I knew every foot of ground here, as every cave along the wave-worn shore. How often I had wandered in these solitudes, to see the great spout of water rise through the grass from the caverns beneath, forced upward when tide and wind harried the sea-flocks from the north; or to look across the ocean to the cliffs of Antrim, from the Carn cul Ri Eirinn, the Cairn of the Hermit King of Ireland, about whom I had woven many a romance.

'I was tired, and fell asleep. Perhaps the Druid of a neighbouring mound, or the lonely Irish King, or Colum himself (whose own Mound of the Outlook was near), or one of his angels who ministered to him, watched, and shepherded my dreams to the desired fold. At least I dreamed, and thus:

'The skies to the west beyond the seas were not built of flushed clouds, but of transparent flame. These flames rose in solemn stillness above a vast forge, whose anvil was the shining breast of the sea. Three great Spirits stood by it, and one lifted a soul out of the deep shadow that was below; and one with his hands forged the soul of its dross and welded it anew; and the third breathed upon it, so that it was winged and beautiful.

'Suddenly the glory-cloud waned, and I saw the multitude of the stars. Each star was the gate of a long, shining road. Many – a countless number – travelled these roads. Far off I saw white walls, built of the pale gold and ivory of sunrise. There again I saw the three Spirits, standing and waiting. So these, I thought, were not the walls of Heaven, but the Divine Forges.

'That was my dream. When I awoke, the curlews were crying under the stars.

'When I reached the shadowy glebe, behind the manse by the sea, I saw the preacher walking there by himself, and doubtless praying. I told him I had seen the Divine Forges, and twice; and in crude, childish words told how I had seen them.

"It is not a dream," he said.

'I know now what he meant.'

When I had read the text of Fiona's dream, the three Spirits seemed to stand clearly revealed. The Fisher of Souls who stood over the anvil of the sea – the Mother – were Jesus and Mary Magdalene; the Forger and Welder was Enki, he who is known as John; the Holy Spirit or the Holy Breath was the Divine Woman, Ain or Sara-Tamar, blessed Holy Grail. The forge itself was Brigid, the aspect of the Mother who shines behind the sun with a supernal light, and gives forth the Bright Knowledge.

There are legends of all five upon Iona, and also of Mary, the Mother.

Joseph of Arimathea is said to have come here too, bringing Jesus as a boy. All were teachers; all belonged to ancient secret brotherhoods of the Bright Knowledge; they each dedicated their lives to lift us into it, like Osiris shepherding his brilliant imperishable stars into the heights of heaven.

The place of abundance, of plenty and fertility, upon Iona, has been spoken of as the aforementioned Port-a-churaich, the Haven of the Coracle, which is the little bay where Columba first brought his boat into harbour after setting out from Ireland to dedicate his life to the Holy Spirit, his Dove of the Eternal.

What Columba brought to the isle and to the world is undoubtedly of the richest abundance. The Spouting Cave, too, with its sudden and startling uprush of energy that sends a fountain into the heavens, and its strange fabled creature, the Mar-Tarbh, 'dread creature of the sea' that swims at full tide and is said to guard treasure in the cave's deep fastnesses, is associated with fertility and seeding and plenty, if also with the teeth and spiritual challenge of these gifts; although within the whisper of Iona's future promise, the Mar-Tarbh becomes an angel.

But I would reveal to pilgrims a place that was one of Fiona's favourite haunts and which held a strange enchantment for her: a spell of beauty and of the mysteries of love; because the Hallow of Abundance is always associated with the Sacred Marriage.

'Down the north side of Dûn Bhuirg there lies a thyme-covered mound that had for me a most singular fascination. It is a place to this day called Dûn Mananain. Here, a friend who told me many things, a Gaelic farmer named Macarthur, had related once a fantastic legend about a god of the sea. Manaun (Manannan) was his name, and he lived in the times when Iona was part of the kingdom of the Suderöer.

'Whenever he willed he was like the sea, and that is not wonderful, for he was born of the sea. Thus his body was made of a green wave. His hair was of wrack and tangle, glistening with spray; his robe was of windy foam; his feet, of white sand. That is, when he was with his own, or when he willed; otherwise, he was as men are.

'He loved a woman of the south so beautiful that she was named Dèarsadh-na-Ghréine (Sunshine). He captured her and brought her to Iona in September, when it is the month of peace. For one month she was happy: when the wet gales from the west set in, she pined for her own land: yet in the dream-days of November, she smiled so often that Manaun hoped; but when Winter was come, her lover saw that she could not live. So he changed her into a seal.

"You shall be a sleeping woman by day," he said, "and sleep in my dûn here on Iona: and by night, when the dews fall, you shall be a seal, and shall hear me calling to you from a wave, and shall come out and meet me."

'They have mortal offspring, it is said.'

'That summer I had been thrilled to the inmost life by coming suddenly, by moonlight, on a seal moving across the last sand-dune between this place and the bay called Port Ban. A strange voice, too, I heard upon the sea. True, I saw no white arms upthrown, as the seal plunged into the long wave that swept the shore; and it was a grey skua that wailed above me, winging inland; yet had I not had a vision of the miracle?'

It is a story of a love so deep that it changes the body, and of the free-handed giving of the spirit that transforms the sorrow and despair of life into liberty and immortality, as in the story of the Resurrection. But whereas today the Four Hallows of the Grail upon Iona have their being in whispers, glimmers, intimations and the telling of old tales, the day is surely fast advancing when these blessings of peace, healing, abundance and immortality will enter into the actuality of our lives like the homing dove flying to her nest.

Such is the promise of the ages: that the Golden Age will come again when the door to Shambalah opens – and the accurate translation of that ancient prophecy reads: when Iona awakens.

CHAPTER 17

THE STORY OF JOHN

We left Enki (John) with Zi-u-sudra, explaining to the earthly king, after he had survived the great flood, that he and his queen represented the first quarter of the emerald tablet in the preparation for its receipt into humanity's consciousness.

The royal family and their household were urged by Enki and Nin-khursag to 'go forth and multiply' so that the vast swathes of humanity who had perished in the flood could eventually return again to Earth in order to be able to complete their cycles of reincarnation – a crucially necessary process in the building and preparation of their own personal soul temple, and in the proper establishment of the Earth as a world of joy and exalted evolution for the whole of humanity.

The readiness for the first quarter of the emerald tablet to descend into human consciousness would be passed on through their own DNA, but also through what is known as the Sheldrake method. Rupert Sheldrake, a research scientist, has proven conclusively that if a skill is taught comprehensively to an animal within a group, then simultaneously the entire group is gifted with that same aptitude.

The subtle programming for the receipt of the emerald tablet was especially adapted to be passed on in such a way. Enki and Nin-khursag had done their work well. By this remarkable method of subconscious telegraphing and subsequent absorption, therefore, every human being on Earth would benefit from the special conditioning and divine processing that the souls of Zi-u-sudra and his queen had received as a gift and blessing from God.

The king and queen went on to establish the remarkable civilisation of ancient Mesopotamia, which arose like a magnificent beacon as if from nowhere. There were many other remnants of mighty civilisations after the flood, of course; but Mesopotamia was the world leader of the time.

As in ages past, Enki and Nin-khursag were on hand to teach the arts of civilisation to humanity. They were educators and mentors. Enki became known as 'the First Gentleman' and 'the Wise Knight' at this time. He instructed men to behave with grace and courtesy, and to honour and respect women unconditionally. He initiated true knighthood, which in its intended state was the perfect rendition of the all-loving Father, who acknowledged his source within the Mother and who bowed his knee to the wisdom and authority of the heart rather than to the power of might and will.

The true knight's military stance was always as protector and defender, never as aggressor or conqueror.

All this absolutely infuriated Enlil, of course. But as Enki took pains to hide his part in it from Enlil, and presented himself as nothing more than a facilitator for ensuring that humanity survived and was fit to serve the purposes of the enhanced community, there was little he could do.

Enlil had pretended all along that the flood was only for the 'good' of humanity (to bring it up short in its chaotic course), and had made all sorts of excuses for the fact that the inundation was monumentally worse than the uncorrupt members of the Council had ever suspected it would be. He could hardly show his true hand by banning Enki's activities and thereby risk revealing his real agenda. At this point there was still a possibility that he and his circle could be overthrown.

Meanwhile, Enki and Nin-khursag busily devoted themselves to their God-given task, which was to educate and spiritualise humanity, and to engineer the next couple to receive the second part of the emerald tablet.

This couple was the king Ga-nadin-ur and his queen, truly unsung heroes of history. They were the halfway house of Tiâmat's grand scheme, which challenged the dark forces so keenly that the Shadow peaked in its attempts to bring all to the point of disintegration.

It was Ga-nadin-ur who first wore the silver scales of knightly armour, not as a metallic suit, as later knights would who sought to honour the shining silver scales of the fish or the Fish-Man – the Wise Knight who was Enki – by wearing chain mail. The royal couple wore robes of serpent skin; but they were produced by Enki's consummate skill in conjuring matter, and were not acquired by killing serpents.

The king's story is a sad one. He and his queen inherited rulership many generations after Zi-u-sudra and his wife alighted from the ark. They were direct descendants of this royal line, and established the historic metropolis of Ur as a city state.

Those who received the graces of the preparation for the emerald tablet lived greatly extended lives, and so Zi-u-sudra was still living when Ga-nadin-ur became king. The latter was therefore Zi-u-sudra's vassal, although Zi-u-sudra, Ga-nadin-ur's overlord, was a benevolent man who respected the importance of Ur and its dynasty.

King Ga-nadin-ur and his wife had one child, a daughter filled with spiritual grace. As the king and queen represented the halfway point of preparation for the assumption of the emerald tablet, it was necessary for a manifestation of Divine Mother and Divine Daughter to be brought forth. This had happened at the foundation of the enterprise, when Antu and Nin-khursag had initiated it and Enki and Nin-khursag had set to work on it.

Now it was to happen again through the medium of this beautiful princess, who would in time bring forth her own daughter, a member of the soul group of the Divine Woman. It would happen for the third and last time when Mary Magdalene and Sara-Tamar came to Earth, for the Divine Woman was a pyramidal expression of Being with the emerald tablet as her four-square base, and Sara-Tamar was her fulfilment. When Sara-Tamar arrived, the Divine Woman had come back to Earth and the brutal severance was overcome.

The name of Ga-nadin-ur's daughter was the Princess Gra-al.

It is difficult to comprehend that she came from the stars; that as we ourselves cluster on planets, Gra-al was of the essence of the imperishable stars. She was not of a community whose being resonated with the supernal light of a star, although such communities certainly exist. She was a supernal star, of the light that shines behind the stars, in her own right, although we are all one and our life is part of a community, from the highest to the lowest. Yet in her beinghood, in her womanhood, Gra-al was indeed of the essence of the purest light of creation.

It is so hard to grasp such realities from our earthly perspective, for if we were to think of Gra-al as a star such as we see in the night sky, the thought would clearly be absurd; yet that spiritual light that shines behind the stars, the magnificence and magnitude of such mysterious light and its ineffable source – she was of such light. We are all of that light; but in the way that a candle-flame is of the same essence as the sun. In spiritual expression, Gra-al was a sun.

Though she was humble and radiated an exquisite spiritual silence as she went about her life, this exceptional young woman came to the attention of Enlil. Though he despised the earthlings, he felt intuitively that he really had to bag this one for the furtherance of his schemes.

First of all, her intense spiritual light must be corrupted. He could think of no better man for the job than the negatively illustrious Marduk, leader of the Naphidem. Accordingly, he arranged an alliance and called the king and queen into his presence in Eden. There he told them of his marriage plans for their daughter.

At first, the royal couple were delighted. They did not have a complete understanding of the machinations of the conspirators, as Tiâmat had decided it would be better for their peace of mind if they remained in partial ignorance of Enlil's schemes. They believed, therefore, that their daughter had been chosen by a great prince, one of the God people (the enhanced community). However, they worshipped in the secret temple of Tiâmat, linked to the Sphere of John (associated with the true Father); and they followed the guidance of the temple faithfully.

It was to the inner sanctum of this temple that Enki and Nin-khursag now led them, where Tiâmat spoke to them through Nin-khursag, who shared a heart-connection with the banished Ain. They were instructed that Marduk, although the royal couple had heard rumours of him as a great prince of the enhanced community, was in fact an unimaginably dangerous monster who wished to spiritually devour the princess.

The only solution, Tiâmat explained, was for Gra-al to flee the court. She must go to ancient Hyperborea (or its remains) to marry a king who was her twin flame, and to remain with him in secret for the rest of her life. The king and queen would never see their daughter again; but if she remained within the precincts of Ur, her fate would be one of endless suffering and horror.

With the help of Enki, the heartbroken couple spirited their daughter away immediately. A Hyperborean brotherhood, posing as merchant travellers, escorted her by night out of the country. She married her king, and gave birth to Brigid in a great cave complex beneath Glastonbury Tor where the king held secret court. (By this time, Iona had long been decapitated.) There, she and her child were tenderly shielded all their lives.

Enlil could not work out where she had fled. Incensed, in a towering inferno of rage he attempted to storm the Earth by bringing the Naphidem straight down the Ur ziggurat, which held a remnant of the Grail forces (Ur being one of its great stations). As far as he was concerned, he was going to put his plan into action right here, right now, without any further pussyfooting delays.

Ga-nadin-ur and his queen stood against that almighty army. They fought a battle of wills, of pure evil, of supernatural mayhem. Terrible destruction was wrought. I have been given the vision of this almighty John-man, true knight in Enki's service in shining silver scales, many times, and nothing is so similar as Gandalf in the mines of Moriah crying out "You-shall-not-pass!" to the Balrog! Although the incident in its telling has echoes of a popular film, the situation was one of deadly seriousness. If the Naphidem had 'passed', our world would not have survived.

Ur was destroyed in the conflagration, and ructions shook the Earth; but with the help of Enki and Nin-khursag, the Naphidem were driven back, and the wormhole that had partially opened was sealed and secured against their invasion. Ga-nadin-ur and his queen had stood firm; but they were injured and devastated in their innermost selves, and it took long, long cycles of time for them to be completely healed and made whole again.

Their outstanding sacrifice was maligned as an assault on Earth and Eden. Ga-nadin-ur had been practising the black arts, Enlil told the Council, and had tried to bring the Naphidem back down to Earth. It had taken all Enlil's strength and resolve to force them back into their allotted dimension and protect the planet. Ga-nadin-ur's kingdom had been swept away in the furore, and Ur lay in ruins. Well, it served him right; and never, never again, vowed Enlil in an orgy of fake self-righteousness, would Anunnaki genes be spliced with those of the ordinary community on the surface of the Earth. Just look what happened when it was permitted!

Shocked to the core by the 'wickedness' and 'disobedience' of Ga-nadin-ur, the Council quietly agreed. His kingship was declared a failure and consigned to history. Enki and Nin-khursag, sharing glances across the great table of state, sought to muster their strength for their next move. At least Princess Gra-al, undiscoverable in her Hyperborean sanctuary, was safe with her king, and was by this time already with child.

CHAPTER 18

CRUNCH TIME

What were Enki and Nin-khursag to do? The situation was desperate. Gra-al had arrived; Brigid had arrived. The halfway point had been reached. The New Woman and the New Man were ready to be brought forth, they who would be processed with the aptitude to receive three-quarters of the emerald tablet. The endeavour must be fulfilled, or all their struggles and successes to date would be as nothing. And, far beyond the confines of one little solar system, the fate of all creation hung in the balance.

If the obtaining dire situation were not resolved and reversed, creation itself could not continue. Humanity, as it was represented on our Earth, so tiny but so significant, must turn the tide with its own hands, of its own will, listening to its heart and summoning all its spiritual strength and faith.

Otherwise, the creature God had made would be judged to be fundamentally inadequate to the task of becoming Godlike. And if it could not become Godlike, it would become something unconscionably different. The only solution to the power of such a nightmare would be to withdraw creation from existence. The enormity of their success or failure weighed on Enki and Nin-khursag with an appalling cosmic vastness.

It was at this point that the spirit within Enki arose. Inspired by his dynamic sister-wife, Nin-khursag, with whom he had discussed his plans and practised his piece, he gave the performance of his life.

Privately, outside the great assembly hall, he sought an audience with Enlil. The Council had, once again, just refused to pass Enki's motion to give the earthlings another chance to receive enhanced community genes to help them to live their lives with greater facility. Enki and Nin-khursag, leading a clandestine coterie who helped the ordinary communities to fulfill their aims and to aspire to greater things, were already doing everything in their power to advance these human societies and souls dwelling on the physical plane; but the embryo manipulation that was needed before the third emerald tablet couple could be brought forth required conditions that were only available in Eden.

Enki could hide what he and Nin-khursag were actually doing inside the sacred Creation Chamber that was enshrined there (called the House of Winds, relating to the Holy Breath or Spirit), but he could not disguise the fact that he needed to enter that sanctified space and make use of its every facility in order to get on with the job.

Enki, who is named on ancient clay tablets simultaneously as 'the trickster god' and as 'Enki the Wise' because of his skill in dealing with Enlil, began to talk to his brother in persuasive terms. Carefully bearing in mind the lies and deceptions Enlil had imposed to create illusions as to how history had unfolded, Enki said to him that he could understand Enlil's reservations about giving enhanced community genes and alchemical genetic manipulations to the earthlings.

After all, Zi-u-sudra had been unable to keep his people under control and Ga-nadin-ur's rebelliousness had been shocking and unprecedented. He could see that these kings had absolutely failed the Anunnaki and their aims and objectives. However, Enki said, he had been studying the matter, and Nin-khursag and he thought they could see where they had gone wrong. They just needed to introduce an influence into the applied genes that would ensure submission and robot-like obedience.

This done, Enlil could be certain that no more disturbing uprisings would take place, and of course the great advantage was that the earthlings could be put to the use of the Anunnaki much more efficiently and effectively than they could be without an enhanced community upgrading.

Enlil thought about Enki's proposition. He had no desire to indulge Enki, quite the opposite, but he was in a difficult situation. Both Marduk and the conspirators needed huge amounts of gold and other precious metals to be made available to them very quickly. Marduk was experimenting with gold's anti-gravitational aspects to get the Naphidem back down to Earth, and he himself needed vast stores, not only to create the white powder en masse, but also to further develop a range of weapons of total destruction he had been working on lately, to say nothing of an ingenious device he hoped to perfect, which will be discussed later.

There was also another urgent need for gold. The planet Nibiru had taken a direct hit in its spiritual and soul spheres, manifesting in practical reality, from Annum's and Enlil's wickedness and barbarity, especially in the instance of it that had severed the Grail. Annum was intimately linked to Nibiru, its conditions and its destiny, because he was a member of its Divine Couple, or its Christ. What happened within his soul directly impacted on Nibiru, and the result of Annum's soul deterioration was that Nibiru had become very cold. The Nibiruans were perishing.

Enlil, of course, refused to acknowledge that his home planet's difficulties were in any way connected to his own and his father's actions. He knew deep within himself that what was happening there was simply an outworking of ineluctable spiritual law, although he refused to listen to the voice of wisdom in his heart. As far as his blindness and stubbornness were concerned, the icy temperatures on Nibiru were the result of interference from the she-devil Tiâmat, and of course in his mind, he and Annum and their allies were set to change all that and disempower her completely.

Nevertheless, the only immediate solution to Nibiru's problems was to atomise gold and use the introduction of it into the planet's atmosphere to create heat. And the only way to come by the vast quantities of gold required was for the earthlings to locate it and mine it.

At the moment, earthly human societies were still recovering from the impact of the flood and the further destruction and disintegration caused by Ga-nadin-ur's battle with the Naphidem. The idea of applying a good dose of efficient machine-like organising qualities to the earthlings, and an even bigger dose of submission and robotic compliance on top, appealed to Enlil considerably. Realistically, Enki's plan was the only way to secure his gold. Enlil gave his consent.

Enki went away rejoicing. The New Woman and the New Man could now be brought forth.

They would be known as Adam and Eve.

CHAPTER 19

THE DEW-CUP

In the House of Winds, Nin-khursag and Enki toiled unremittingly. Angelic entities worked alongside them, and above them brooded the great angel that linked them to Tiâmat: to Mother-Father God.

Eve was created first. So that the baby could be given a special dispensation regarding the Dew-Cup, Nin-khursag, Mistress of the Dew-Cup, took an unprecedented step. She travelled down the Ur ziggurat, transforming her etheric atoms into physical atoms as she did so: a procedure which all the enhanced community undertook when they visited Earth. In the time of the Grail, it was instantaneous and could be achieved anywhere. Now, with only the fading remnants of the Grail available (which would never die away completely), the process was difficult and could only be undertaken at the point of the Grail stations.

In a temple at the foot of the ziggurat, Nin-khursag gave physical birth to Eve. Thus Eve was her surrogate daughter. And because of this, Eve was born specially prepared, in a way that no earthly woman had been previously, to dispense the Dew-Cup to Adam, who was created after Eve. This meant that Eve had been invested with the highest essence of that Divine substance which normally passed from God to the Mistress of the Dew-Cup herself, who was the prime goddess among the Anunnaki.

The prime goddess was Antu; but Antu, in a ceremony of devotion to Tiâmat, had bequeathed the Dew-Cup to her daughter, Nin-khursag. She had undertaken this self-sacrifice because she herself was circumscribed in her freedom by her cold, cruel, tyrannical spouse, Annum. Therefore she could not work for the good of humanity as powerfully as Nin-khursag could, who enjoyed much more liberty, simply due to the indifference of Annum and Enlil towards her.

In order for Tiâmat's concealed pyramid soul-construction plan and Grail plan to go ahead, the feminine input on Earth was vital. And so Antu, of her own free will and via secret ritual, made Nin-khursag Mistress of the Dew-Cup, even though by doing so she would be made much more susceptible and vulnerable to Annum's violations.

Adam was born to Nin-khursag in exactly the same way as Eve. Enki's donated sperm had fertilised two ova from two separate earthly women, which as embryos had undergone scientific and spiritual processes in the House of Winds; and Nin-khursag had given physical birth in the physical realm to the two resultant babies. She was surrogate mother to both. Enki was their father.

Secretly, in hidden temples, Nin-khursag and Enki instructed the children and infused them with their spiritual light and devotion. They were taught about Tiâmat and about the True Father, and that their power was the force of Divine love. Eve, through her birth and development, earthed the three-quarters stage of the emerald tablet deep into the planet, so that it was there within the etheric dimensions of the heart of collective humanity and within the heart of the Earth.

Adam and Eve together, via their birth and what they carried within them, perfected the pyramidal design of the human soul that Tiâmat had constructed for the protection of all her children of Earth. It came into perfected operational form through them. Complete and fully functioning, everyone on Earth was absorbed into it and benefited from it. In this sense, Adam and Eve were the originating man and woman, as the pyramidal design of our souls first came into being in its final stage with and through them. With this soul-pyramid safely in place, the scene was set for all of us eventually to receive the fourth and final part of the emerald tablet.

Adam entered deeply into the mysteries of Tiâmat's secret temple under Enki's tuition and Nin-khursag's guiding presence. He was taught therein how to understand and worship the True Father, the Father who was of the Mother, who shared perfect equality with her, who acknowledged his presence within her, and who bowed his knee in reverence to the supreme command of the heart.

The True Father, whilst radiating and inspiring the full range of qualities that comprise perfected manhood, was unimaginably different to the false Father whom Annum and Enlil concocted from the basest elements in their nature, fuelled by jealously and rage, and whom Enlil eventually became. Interestingly, on Iona he was always known as 'the Haughty Father'. It was clearly understood that he was far from benevolent, and that he was certainly not the One God!

However, there was more work to be done. A bloodline, present and functional in every way upon the lowest earthly plane (the plane of dense physicality) had been brought into being, by Tiâmat's decree. It was God's gift of mercy and forgiveness to humankind. They had severed the Grail; for their sake, a substitute must be provided until it could be restored.

The substitute was the special bloodline. Descending to Earth via this bloodline, as if via the Grail, would come souls of exalted degree who would help humanity, and who could touch down by no other means than the bloodline. It would facilitate the descent of such souls because of its high vibrational resonance.

It would not be perfect. Souls with feet of clay would also be able to slip down its ladder from time to time; and of course it did not change the fact that human spirituality is never the servant of inheritance and DNA, but their transcendent master. This is an eternal truth; but there was unavoidably an inbuilt possibility that the existence of the bloodline might appear to muddy the waters a little in humanity's correct perception of that central truth.

There would be ways of misunderstanding the bloodline that would put humanity into acute soul danger, as expressed by Zionism, the Nazi doctrine, and generally the ignorance which is racism, with its disturbing manifestation today relating to 'lizard people'! Nevertheless, it was the only substitute available, and so it was vital that it should be put in place.

It had begun with Zi-u-sudra and his queen. Nin-khursag had properly instigated it by bearing earthly children in the normal way on Earth. Now it was Enki's turn to further establish the bloodline and cement it firmly into place in our world.

Therefore, when Eve had attained womanhood, Enki impregnated her directly. This impregnation was rendered by means of holy ceremony, attended by angels, and was not a normal coupling of passion and desire. Only a virgin mother could conceive a child in this way; but 'virgin' must be understood in its proper context, which is not that of a woman without sexual experience but a woman within whose chakras (points aligned with the spine and upon the head that connect the body directly with the spiritual worlds) shines the perfect celestial light – 'the seven lamps of Heaven'. Such a woman or a man is a vehicle of perfect sanctity.

To undertake this special ceremony of conception, the male partner, too, must be virgin, although the success of the ceremony is somewhat more dependent on the mother's perfect light. Nevertheless, the rule applies to both partners equally.

Eve gave birth to Cain, Enki's son. 'Cain' is a rendition of 'quayin' or 'ayin' (the Eye of God: the mystical title also applied to Iona). Within this 'ayin' name of Cain, there exists the sacred name of Ain. Cain, in his exalted masculinity, carried forward the noble teachings of the True Father: that the True Father was contained in the All which is the Mother and is sourced in her. His name expressed this truth and teaching flawlessly. Cain also inherited from his Anunnaki father the rituals and skills, both spiritual and physical, of Master Craftsmanship.

Eve withdrew into the temple of Ur under Nin-khursag's instruction, because she had to prepare for her great mission. This was set to come into full manifestation very shortly. It involved the offering of the Dew-Cup to Adam, which, on his willing receipt of it, would ensure that the Divine essence within the Cup gave all earthly men access to it directly from that point onwards, without the need any more for it to be passed to the male in practical actuality by the female. In other words, the facility would pass within, and there would be no further outward dependency.

However, the clear understanding of this situation is that the male would continue to receive a Divine essence from the female, but it would be something he drew on from within his own consciousness. It would be recognised as the voice in the heart which is Love, which is Pure Reason, which is God. Receiving it in this way, men would therefore no longer suffer the dangerous disorientation that laid them low if they failed to receive the Dew-Cup in practicality.

However, if they refused to listen to the Sacred Feminine within, which is connected to women and womanhood and venerates the Star Fire within them, then they would of course become very disorientated in their soul and spiritual development. And, as all rests on spiritual principles and not persons, obviously women could also become disconnected from their sacred source and thus become equally disorientated, without the ability to nourish themselves or apply such nourishment to men.

Nevertheless, the establishment of three-quarters of the readiness to receive the emerald tablet within the human soul (which brought with it a natural infusing of three-quarters of the tablet's virtues to a certain degree of restricted potency), together with the completion of the pyramidal design for the soul-structure of humanity, did, in this deep inner sense, reconnect the androgynous link that had been severed with the Grail. Yet it would depend on the individual conscience as to whether it properly availed itself of this source of spiritual nourishment or not.

This, then, was the great gift of progression that would be given to humanity with the offering of the Dew-Cup to Adam. After the event, no male could be cut off completely from the Sacred Feminine. A certain reconnection would take place, yet with unavoidable qualifications.

To entirely eradicate this connection, and any possibility of its restoration, was Enlil's one aim. He had no knowledge of what was going on. He was ignorant of how Enki had 'betrayed' him in the House of Winds, where his genetic engineering, although transplanting a certain enhanced recovery impulse within earthly human genes as agreed, had also included many more interesting aspects that Enlil would have judged pure blasphemy. (His delusion that he was God was quite advanced by now.)

Yet something kept whispering to him, and he had a feeling he could barely articulate. He now extended the law he had first made in the Anunnaki Council – that enhanced women could no longer feed enhanced men with their Dew-Cup essence – to include Earth also. His distorted gold in the form of white powder was already being used by enhanced men, and Enlil had laid plans to feed this sinister substance to leaders of the earthly communities as well.

He suddenly had a psychic impulse that this must come into force at once, and therefore banned the ingestion of blood even for earthlings; for it is important to understand that the essence within the Dew-Cup was akin to menstrual blood. On Earth, an order of High Priestesses, collectively called the Scarlet Women (and around whom Enlil constructed a web of derogatory 'whore' mythology, as was his wont), ministered their purified menstrual blood to men.

The Scarlet Women were revered, and were those women selected to receive the special dispensation of the Dew-Cup essence from on high: from Nin-Khursag (formerly from Antu), who was linked so intimately to Tiâmat and who received the Dew-Cup essence directly from Her.

The great edict therefore went out from the king in Eden. No blood was to be ingested under any circumstances. Enlil didn't mean, of course, the edict explained carefully, that people were to become vegetarian. (Cruelty towards animals, and their slaughter, was a huge factor in producing dire vibrations on Earth and in humankind which enabled Enlil to control and manipulate the earthly populace.) The king only meant that he claimed the blood of life as his own; his subjects could keep the meat. But no blood of any kind was to be taken internally, at any time, for any reason whatsoever.

He issued this law, but the whispering voice would not stop. In his disquiet, he summoned Adam into his presence in Eden.

CHAPTER 20

IN THE COURT OF ENLIL

Adam came to the court with his queen, Eve, whom Enlil always ignored. Eve had married Adam, and they now had two sons of their own, Abel and Seth, who were being brought up with Cain in the royal household.

Adam was a deeply respected king, the most authoritative on Earth, whom his people were glad to support and follow. After his great initiation in accepting the essence within the Dew-Cup, Adam would become the first fully graduated priest-king, newly invested with the spiritual authority gifted to him by Eve. All of this, of course, was kept carefully hidden from Enlil and those in sympathy with him.

Adam was given Enlil's edict personally, on pain of death. To further boost the likelihood of Adam's obedience, just in case the earthly king was planning any secret flouting of Enlil's will that he thought he could permanently conceal, Enlil told Adam that if he did imbibe Eve's blood, then he would die. With this double insurance, Enlil felt certain he would be safe.

But in fact the imbibing of Eve's blood, the sacred essence in the Dew-Cup, by Adam, went ahead anyway, within the temple of Ur, on the specified day (a day which corresponded, about six thousand years ago, with our current Friday 22nd of July, now Mary Magdalene's feast day). The event was called 'partaking of the Fruit of the Tree'.

Two Trees are connected to Tiâmat and conduct her forces back and forth to her creation through their system of 'roots, stem, branches and leaves'. The Trees are family trees, and they are the Tree of Life and the Tree of the Knowledge of Good and Evil (Wisdom, Discernment, Intuition).

They are really one tree with one root, but with two stems. They are pivotal expressions of Divine Intelligence, of the consciousness of God. They are rooted into Earth and into heaven. Every earthly tree reflects and upholds this profoundly mysterious truth: that it is a sacred expression on Earth, in nature, of the truth and beauty of the Lineage Tree.

111

The expression of the ramification of bloodlines, of the human family, dwells within the inner mystery and the outer form of the tree. The spiritual counterpart of this blood, whose physical expression is that of the living waters – the blood-essence of the Dew-Cup – within us all, connects us to God-consciousness, the source and the root of all bloodlines. We are one: a connected, united family; and the trees of the natural world show us every moment that this is so.

The idea of the 'apple' as the fruit of the Tree of the Knowledge of Good and Evil can be understood if an apple is sliced in half to expose its core. It is a perfect delineation of female genitalia, the temple of the blood-essence in the Dew-Cup. And the apple is of the family of the rose, symbol of the Divine Feminine, and therefore of the Holy Blood: the menstrual blood or the 'living waters'.

It is easy to imagine how much Enlil hated the two Trees, and this one in particular! He saw that this 'abhorrent' Tree was responsible for the other one (vile, loathsome, physical Life); and to end the abominable expression of the latter, it was imperative to cut off and deny facilitation to the former.

The 'partaking of the Fruit of the Tree' was overseen by Nin-khursag, who presided at the ceremony. And the next time that Adam and Eve were routinely called into Enlil's presence in Eden, it was evident to the royal couple that something was very much amiss.

To begin with, Eden looked different to the way it had before they both undertook the ceremony. They could feel and sense the presence of evil, the presence of decay. It was as if a glamour were lifted from their eyes. And they began to see Enlil as a dark, writhing, hideous serpent.

They were used to witnessing Enki and Nin-khursag take on their beautiful, undulating, serpentine form, throughout which an exquisite, antiphonal music seemed to sound. Adam and Eve delighted in such magical, beautiful manifestations of their mentors. But the serpent form that Enlil was exhibiting was truly horrific. And they could see this giant snake of petrifying nightmare materialising itself over his normal form (in line with the form of earthly humanity) even though they were at some distance from the court and had not yet entered its precincts.

Nin-khursag and Enki realised that they could not hope to achieve what they had thought might be possible – that the royal couple would be able to behave as if everything was normal in front of Enlil. They were far too traumatised by what their truth-seeing eyes were disclosing to them. So Enki and his wife hurried them to Tiâmat's temple, the Temple of John, hidden in Eden's secret depths.

Here, they hoped to shield Adam and Eve until they regained their composure; but, before they could do so, Enlil came walking through Eden's evening shades, calling on them to appear.

The Anunnaki king knew they were nearby; he felt it. In his reception room in his palace he had sensed it. And he could not understand why they did not appear before him. It was unprecedented behaviour! He became so restless and uneasy that he went in search of them.

Being in Eden, the secret temple of Tiâmat was easily hidden in an Edenic dimension, one of the many beauteous 'gardens' of Eden. It was therefore invisible. But, as Enlil approached, Adam began to experience sheer terror. Enlil's promised judgement of death seemed about to fall upon him, and he was terrified of this approaching giant black snake, careering along as if engulfed in menacing shadow.

As his terror intensified, the vibration of the higher Edenic dimension which concealed them was lowered, and thus lost its veil of invisibility, until Enlil could actually see the secret temple and its occupants. He was able to intuit what had happened at once, especially as Eve stood before him unbowed, with no fear.

Her hair looked strange, as if an exquisite filigree network of fine roots was connecting her to heaven. Even as he erupted, Enlil made a mental note to issue an edict that women should keep their offensive heads covered at all times when in the presence of the superior sex.

Entering into one of his volcanic rages, Enlil tried over and over again to blast Adam and Eve to death on the spot. But they were one as never before, united and strengthened by the essence of the Dew-Cup in its full expression, which Nin-khursag had gradually been passing to and building tenderly within Eve, until the moment when it could be given in love to Adam, her half-brother and spouse.

Adam and Eve did not fall. They were inviolate. Nin-khursag and Enki swiftly escorted them down the ziggurat to the cellars of the Ur temple, where they all took refuge. Even as they fled down the ziggurat, they could feel the first terrible vibrations of the devastation that was to come.

Enlil's rage was cosmic. He destroyed the revealed temple of Tiâmat in Eden, simultaneously reducing the Ur ziggurat to rubble. He cursed Adam and all of humanity with slavery and struggle, and promised distress in menstruation and terrible pain in childbirth to all women. He banished the royal couple, and all earthlings, from Eden forevermore, and bound them fast with his power to the earthly level alone, so that ascension to Eden via the remnant of the Grail forces was no longer possible for them.

From now on, except via the inalienable facility of meditation and one or two other very special circumstances, there was no level other than the dimension of physical Earth to which they could rise, unless through death. This is what was meant by giving them 'coats of skin', words in Genesis which simply meant that they were bound fast into the earthly sphere and could not move out of it.

Their boundary from now on was their skin. Their bodies stopped at that physical threshold, and the material plane could not be overridden. From one perspective, they were locked into it, as we all are today.

Enlil at this stage suspected nothing more of Enki than that his brother had attempted a coup, being, so Enlil thought, jealous of Enlil's acting kingship and wanting it for himself. He had recruited Adam and Eve, Enlil decided, because they were the most influential rulers on Earth. Enki's plan must have been that they would oblige him by influencing the earthlings to back him, so in pursuit of this he had obviously worked with the despised Tiâmat to empower the royal couple via the banned Dew-Cup to get them on side.

Enlil phenomenally underestimated Enki. However, Enki could not hide his opposition to Enlil and his tactics any more after the debacle in Eden. There came into existence at this time two distinct temples with two very different agendas: the temple of Enki and the temple of Enlil.

The first sought to protect, liberate and educate humankind and lead it to the heights of its spiritual and evolutional potential. The second temple was dedicated to the control and enslavement of humanity via fear, suffering and mind-control, and the wielding of total dominance and suppression regarding its spiritual and evolutional capacity.

The first temple was known among Enki and Nin-khursag's followers as the Temple of John (Enki), he who worshipped and was a representation of the True Father. It was really another name for the secret temple of Tiâmat (the Temple of Mother-Father God) which had been destroyed in Eden by Enlil. Withdrawing into the heart of the mysteries of this temple, Enki now began to work behind the scenes of life, ever-present in the human world, but inspiring his descendants and his spiritual sons more often than making personal appearances, although these did continue.

Cain was Enki's direct earthly son; and of Cain, descending from his bloodline, came Ham (in Sanskrit, 'I Am': the Holy One). Ham was not Noah's son or the brother of Shem, as the Bible relates. He belonged to a different family that shared a distant cousinship with that of Noah. Ham's story is a continuation of the story of John, and in fact Ham himself was a reincarnation of Cain. He was a supreme 'John-man', who served Enki, and therefore Nin-khursag, the Holy Grail and Tiâmat, with utter faithfulness.

CHAPTER 21

BABYLON

Enlil could not sweep away Adam and Eve's kingdom with a great flood, as he had imposed upon Zi-u-sudra's world. Nor could he lay it to waste, as had happened to Ga-nadin-ur and his queen. The strength imparted to the royal couple by the ceremony of the 'partaking of the Fruit of the Tree' protected them and their people; it protected all the world.

What Enlil could do, however, was to sow seeds of dissension between the sons of the royal household; and this he did with all his vigour and cunning. So far, Enlil had acted partly through the promptings of his psychic senses, and partly through the promptings of the demonic intelligences that propelled him. Now, however, he knew beyond doubt that Enki was in league against him; and he became even more dangerous than before.

Thankfully, he still knew nothing of Tiâmat's great plans to rescue her beloved children of Earth. He thought that Enki simply wanted to oust him for political reasons.

First on his agenda was to have Cain murdered. Cain served as High Priest in Enki's temple, so he obviously posed a threat. Enlil went to work to prevail upon Abel, Eve's second son, via flattery and bribes, to become High Priest of his own temple. He set Abel and Seth against Cain, whispering to them through subconscious agents. Cain hated them, he murmured, because Adam was their father but not his, and would kill them as soon as the opportunity arose.

The idea that Cain was jealous of Abel because God preferred Abel's offerings is a confusion. In the temple of Enlil, headed by Abel, Enlil's imperative was that animals should be sacrificed. He loved the blood and gore and the fear and anguish of the animals involved and made energetic capital out of them. In Enki's temple, only grain, honey, flowers, nuts, seeds, oil and wine were offered, as harmlessness was Enki's rule. So the offerings of either temple would not have been acceptable to the other.

It was a story that tried to explain Cain's supposed jealousy of Abel, which in fact did not exist, except in Abel's contaminated perception.

It was already established that the inheritance of kingship would, in any case, eventually pass to Cain, so it was evident that Adam made no distinction between his sons, even though he had not fathered Cain. It was much more likely that Abel was jealous of Cain, and thought he himself should inherit, as he was in fact Adam's elder son.

One day, whilst Adam and Cain were communing with Enki and with God in a rural retreat some distance from the city, the uprising Enlil had encouraged took place. Abel came with his men to kill Cain. Fortunately, Enki had advised Cain not to leave home without his bodyguard, and these men, bearing the superior weaponry of the Master Craftsman Cain, soon put the assailants to flight.

Abel was incensed and attempted to kill both Cain and Adam, whom Cain was protecting. The result was that Cain's men were forced to fight Abel to the death, as he would not retreat or surrender. Enlil had lent him one of his famous insane rages.

When Enlil appeared to Cain (a capacity he retained as far as his ethereal form was concerned, although he could no longer physicalise the atoms of his body, as had been possible when the remnants of the Grail were still in use) and demanded to know why he had not preserved his brother's life, the correctly recorded though misunderstood reply that Cain gave ("Am I my brother's keeper?") was actually a statement of frustration.

It meant, "Was I supposed to have fought my own bodyguard, as if I were one of my brother's own fighting men, to save Abel's life when he was trying to take not only mine but that of our father's as well?" For Cain had always looked upon Adam as his father, although Enki also assumed this role, but more distantly.

Despite his innocence, Cain was banished, not by Adam, but by the populace, as Enlil influenced them to believe that Cain had killed his brother purposely, and plotted to kill Adam too.

Enki placed his symbol on Cain – the powerful sign of Tiâmat – which was a cross of light within a circle of light (the 'mark of Cain'), to protect him from the bands of assassins that Enlil regularly despatched to kill him. During his banishment, Cain married Luluwa, a royal princess of the land of Nodh who was the daughter of Lilith.

Lilith, a powerful woman among the enhanced community and of the royal line, had married Enki to provide him with his second wife (a law that Enlil made absolute decreed that all men should take more than one wife), and also to assist Enki and Nin-khursag in their great project.

After Nin-khursag had given birth to Adam and Eve in secret, Enlil suddenly became suspicious of her and restricted her movements as much as he could, making it difficult for her to mother and cultivate both children. As Nin-khursag's main concern was with Eve (because of their preparations for the Dew-Cup ceremony), Lilith took over the care of Adam, providing him with all the careful nurture he needed whilst he was under the tutelage of Enki.

It was necessary for Enki's son by Eve, Cain, to marry a woman with enhanced genes in order to pass them down the bloodline, so, in time, Lilith gave birth to Luluwa in exactly the same way as Nin-khursag had given birth to Eve. This ensured that Luluwa was of the appropriate generation to marry Cain.

Afterwards, Lilith married Enlil, for exactly the same reason as Nin-khursag had become his wife – to shield Enki and to ensure that his efforts on humanity's behalf remained veiled.

Enlil eventually discovered Lilith's secret and banished her, calling her a traitor of the worst order and a demon who taught degenerate humans to drink blood. This was because she gave of her own Dew-Cup essence to Adam prior to his reception of it from Eve, to protect him from ingestion of Enlil's white powder. (Sensing his importance, Enlil tried to give it to Adam from the beginning to get him on side, well in advance of his plans for other earthly rulers to take it.)

He also called her a devourer of babies, because she assisted Nin-khursag in preparing Eve to give her purified menstrual blood, produced in the normal way for an unfertilised ovum, to Adam.

Whilst in exile, Cain and Luluwa were entrusted with a magical task. They were given the dispensation by Tiâmat to root the remnant of the Grail forces, which Enlil had blocked in Ur, anew into the sacred land on which they maintained their court.

This land would afterwards be known as Canaan; and the point where Cain and Luluwa revived the vestigial Grail energy was the spot where once it had thrived after penetrating the Earth when the Grail was first established: the site of the future Jerusalem.

Only Luluwa, guarded and supported by Cain, could fulfil this task, because she, as an earthly woman, contained within her DNA the genes of Lilith, her surrogate mother, and Enki, which linked her with Antu. She also bore the genes of Nin-khursag, Mistress of the Dew-Cup, which she had received whilst an embryo in the Creation Chamber. And so the residue of the Grail could awaken within her and pass through her into the Earth.

After Adam's death (which was not long in coming, as the great king was heartbroken over the loss of his two sons), Cain returned from exile and assumed kingship, according to Adam and Eve's wishes. The line of priest-kings (serving in the Temple of John) thus became established, which eventually produced Ham, the great descendant and spiritual son of Enki.

In time, being of the royal line, Ham became king of Ur. He requested that Shulgi, Zi-u-sudra's son, should stand in as acting king on his behalf, because Enki had a very special mission for Ham. It was associated with the title of Master Craftsman, which Enki wished to bestow on him at the earthly level.

So deeply esoteric was this title that it conferred on Ham, once he had qualified for it, the unimaginable opportunity of assisting Tiâmat in her creation. There was no greater honour on Earth than to be chosen for this role. Ham therefore needed to withdraw into the Temple of John as its High Priest to perfect his Craft on every level. Acting kingship was offered to Shulgi in particular in order to honour Zi-u-sudra, the noble old patriarch who was still alive on Earth at this time. Although Zi-u-sudra had largely retired from office, Ham, as Ga-nadin-ur had been before him, was nevertheless Zi-u-sudra's vassal.

Ham had married a mysterious woman called Neelâta-mek. She entered into the temple with him and nourished him with her wisdom and with her Star Fire (another name for the blood-essence in the Dew-Cup, given because the spiritual energy from the imperishable stars was exactly what it was).

Even though, thanks to Eve and Adam, all men could now draw on the Dew-Cup by their own facility from within, the kings of the special bloodline were still nurtured with the Star Fire from the Anunnaki goddesses (Nin-khursag and Lilith). This was carried out to ensure that their advanced perceptual centres remained pure and high-vibrational, working to their full Tiâmat-inspired resonance and capacity.

Although Neelâta-mek was not of the enhanced community (despite bearing their genes, as did her mother), she was a beacon of such spiritual magnitude that she actually excelled them in brightness. Her secret identity was Brigid, Gra-al's beloved daughter from Britain.

She was of such hallowed mysticism that her form was only ever partly physicalised, and she dwelt in heaven even whilst she was on Earth. She generally manifested in her ethereal form. Nonetheless, she and Ham had a son, Canaan, who at this time had been given the kingship of neighbouring Lagesh.

There is more to be discovered of Neelâta-mek, and the secret identity of Makeda, Queen of Sheba, when we come to her story.

Canaan was also known as King Ur-baba, and it was from him that the Arab peoples descended, for their beginnings were earlier than Ishmael, Abraham's son, although he continued and stabilised their line.

Brigid is the goddess of fire, of poetry, of spiritual ecstasy, of exalted smith-ship (practical alchemy) and the Bright Knowledge. Into the Arab peoples passed the magic of Brigid's fire and spiritual passion, and the inheritance of Ham's Master Craftsmanship. These, indeed, became the guiding principles of the East, which of course ensured that Enlil did everything in his power to disturb and disintegrate the stability of the Eastern peoples.

It is worth noting that the ancient Persians, like the British bards, wrote in verse. Prose was unknown. In Britain we do indeed share a very close kinship with Ur-baba's descendants, as Brigid was born of the old British bloodline descending from her father, the British king whose ancestor was Ar-Thor. And on Iona, Brigid was worshipped for millennia, and is even now remembered with deep reverence.

Ham was in fact black, being descended from Enki, and also from the royal Ethiopian line of his mother, Nin-banda. Brigid, like Gra-al and Nin-khursag, was white, although when she assumed physical form she appeared as a black woman because she held the point of balance between the two races. These holy women expressed principles of the sacred Light and the sacred Darkness (darkness is another form of light in its spiritual context, just as some forms of light are in fact a kind of spiritual darkness).

King Canaan (Ham's son, also known as Ur-baba) and King Shulgi (Zi-u-sudra's son, also known as Shem) were great friends, and were kinsmen, as both were descended from the great dynasty of Ur. With Shulgi's blessing and royal sanction, Canaan founded the city of Babylon (Bab-y-lon) just after 2,000 BC, building this new site of kingship so close to the ancient city of Ur as to be almost contiguous with it.

The idea was that, as Canaan doubted that his father, busy with his great projects, would ever assume sovereignty of Ur, and as kingship would pass to him, Canaan would persuade Shulgi to remain as acting king, and they would rule together over both city-states – Ur and Babylon. Canaan hoped the great cities would merge to become one.

The reason that Babylon was so important to Canaan was that the whole project had been instigated by Enki, Nin-khursag and Lilith, who directed Canaan to build a ziggurat temple at the centre of the new city, because this temple was to be the new site of the Temple of John.

Eventually, Enki hoped, Ur-Babylon would become the equivalent of the New Jerusalem that in later years would be spoken of by John in his Revelation. The ancient Ur dynasty – now appropriately enhanced by Zi-u-sudra, Ga-nadin-ur, Adam, and the hugely significant Gra-al, Brigid and Eve, all of whom bore Anunnaki genes from Nin-khursag, Enki and Lilith – would bring forth the Divine Woman (Ain, pronounced An) who, stepping down the bloodline as if descending a stairway, would reconnect the Grail in its full glory.

Tiâmat stood behind Enki and Nin-khursag in directing the Babylon project. She was ready to remove the blocked remnants of the Grail in Ur (which still remained although they had been directed anew into the site of the future Jerusalem) from the obstructed Ur ziggurat to the new, fully functional, ziggurat of Babylon, which stood virtually alongside it. Thus the double station of the Grail in the east would be as operative as it was possible to arrange, and all would be in place for the grand plan.

Such was the state of things when, one summer day, Enki and his wives descended from Eden in their ethereal forms to give Zi-u-sudra some important news. From this point, Zi-u-sudra will be given his later biblical name of Noah.

They were apprehensive regarding their mission, as they knew that their tidings would not be welcomed by the aged patriarch. They convened in a tent within which stood a simple altar. (Enki had long ago instructed his followers to set up tents, away from the bustling city, in which they could pray and commune in peace.) Noah's tent was in the gardens of the palace, as, due to his age, he preferred not to travel very far.

The time had come to explain to Noah that his own son, Shulgi (also known as Shem) would not inherit the Archonship, the title of Supreme Master Craftsman for which Ham had already entered into training. As mentioned, this title bequeathed on its bearer the unique privilege of actually working with God as an assistant in creation, albeit limited to a certain sphere and a certain planet. Nevertheless, the honour was immense.

Noah was horror-stricken. He had not expected the honour for himself, but he had expected it for his son. After all, the Earth would be a desolate, brutish, sparsely populated place if he (and his queen, whom he forgot for the moment) had not come to its rescue with the Ark!

Seeing his distress, the Anunnaki group decided to show rather than tell Noah why it was that Ham must inherit. Ham came at their call (the Temple of John had been established in the nearby Ur temple). Within the confines of the tent they 'stripped' Ham of his outer appearance so that he stood before them in his spiritual vestments, which shone with an exquisite spiritual light that illumined his heart-link to Tiâmat.

There was a facility in Ham's bloodline which crucially empowered this link. Noah, although he shared Enki and Nin-khursag's genes which had been given to him in the Creation Chamber, was not directly of their blood through birth, as was Ham. It was Ham who could wield the Archonship to its greatest capacity to serve the Temple of John, the Divine Mother-Father, and so it must be Ham, and not Shulgi, who inherited.

Noah made a great outcry, and Shulgi (Shem) came running with Japhet, Ham's brother, who had both been walking nearby, enjoying the summer peace of the palace gardens.

It seemed from Noah's vociferous lamentations that Ham had struck the venerated elder, although the two young men could hardly believe this to be the truth. However, Ham seemed to be in a strange state, so they pushed him out of the tent and took Noah to his rooms in the palace. The Anunnaki group had disappeared with Noah's outcry, as the sensitive etheric link with which they connected to the earthly realm had been severed by it.

What none of them knew was that Noah had been secretly targeted by Enlil, who had been pressing on him for some time the idea that Enki did not show him enough respect, and that, if he only came over to Enlil's side and, abandoning the Temple of Enki, became High Priest within Enlil's own temple, then Enlil would treat him with all the respect he deserved.

Conferring with Shulgi and Japhet, Noah now declared his intention to accept Enlil's offer. At this point Japhet left, because he felt impelled to warn his brother Ham of the disaster that was looming.

CHAPTER 22

DEATH RAY

Events now moved rapidly. Ham, horrified by Japhet's news, set off immediately for Babylon, where his son Canaan was directing operations for the building of the new city. Both Ham and Canaan then made for the land of Nodh (now the land of Cain, in time to become Canaan), where, due to Lilith's and Luluwa's influences, Enlil's malignancy could not follow them. Meanwhile, very sinister happenings were underway in the temple of Enlil.

Having completely changed their allegiance, Noah and Shem were busy revealing to Enlil every last detail of Tiâmat's plan. Enlil listened, stunned and outraged, as Noah revealed Tiâmat's pyramidal fortifying of the human soul, her step-by-step preparation of earthly humanity to receive the full potency of the emerald tablet, and the fulfillment of her will in the safe reception of Gra-al, Brigid and Eve to the earthly planes in order to prepare for the coming of the Divine Woman who finally would reconnect the Grail.

He reeled as he heard of Eve's triumph in linking earthly men integrally with the Star Fire, Tiâmat's reactivation of the vestigial Grail forces in Nodh (the future site of Jerusalem), her intention to redirect them into Babylon, and the establishment of the Temple of John with its secret network of allies, soon to take up residence in Babylon, the city specially built to enshrine it.

Enlil had thought that Enki's temple was no more than a contentious statement by his brother that he was still angling after the kingship; he had entertained no notion of its true purpose, which was now revealed to him – that it sought to restore the worship of the True Father sourced within the Mother – Tiâmat! (Enlil saw Tiâmat as an evil entity who told the outrageous lie that the Father was sourced within her.)

Now he knew all, Enlil's wrath was more monumental than ever before. He promised Noah that Shem (Shulgi) would have a kingship that ruled the world! And to ensure that they stayed on side, he undertook a ceremony on the spot which ousted Canaan (the king that would have ruled alongside, and officially over, Shem, who was only acting king) from all kingly authority, and established Shem's line firmly in place instead of his. Canaan would be the lowest of the low, Enlil assured them enticingly:

'Cursed be Canaan; a servant of servants shall he be to his brethren... Blessed be the Lord God of Shem, and Canaan shall be his servant.' (*Genesis* 9: 25–26)

Enlil decided that day that he must gain as much influence as possible over the land of Nodh (known as the land of Cain since Cain had settled there). In his early days, when seemingly he was a benign and beneficent soul, a helpful member of the enhanced community to the earthly community in Nodh, Enlil had gained a foothold. The people had appreciated his beneficial deeds.

They still worshipped Tiâmat secretly (due to Lilith's influence through her daughter, Queen Luluwa, although so far Enlil knew nothing of this), and they had little understanding of Enlil's opposition to her. He must capitalise on their goodwill, because now he had been apprised that the Grail would spring anew in the land of Cain.

He saw, too, with psychic vision, that Canaan would follow his illustrious ancestor Cain into that sacred land, and would try to thwart his plans from there. And so he concocted his strategy, which included gaining a strong foothold in Ur, because it seemed to be a den of vipers that bred his adversaries, and must be brought under control.

As for the emerald tablet, Enlil decided that he would consult Noah about the matter at once. Noah was a highly accomplished scientist, a genius of the first degree. And Enlil received from Noah the help he craved.

The plot was that Enlil would orchestrate an uprising in his palace, and have Marduk steal the emerald tablet. He could only do this with Noah's assistance, because the protective energy field around it ensured that it could not be stolen or harmed. It could not be removed from the palace. It was impossible for Noah to devise a way to harm it, but what he could do was allow Marduk to appear to steal it and give it into Enlil's hands for a short time.

Together, they would work their will. Some of its truth and beauty Enlil would reflect into a duplicate, false emerald tablet; but with that truth and beauty Enlil would weave lies, deceptions, allurements, false paths, false lights, false beckonings of terrible danger, so that those receiving the emanations of the hoax emerald tablet – which was the totality of human consciousness on Earth – would fall again and again into hopeless confusion and despair.

Meanwhile, Noah would hide the real emerald tablet, not in a place, but in a dimension. This dimension would actually be located within the palace, so that the impossibility of removing the emerald tablet would not have to arise as an obstacle. And he would employ all his genius to ensure that no-one would ever be able to find it.

But, of course, if the tablet was lost, people would seek it, and that might cause disquiet and rebellion, even though they would never find it. They would wonder how it could have been lost, and might suspect that some plot was being perpetrated against them by Enlil.

However, the presence of the false emerald tablet would ensure that they never searched for it, because it would not be considered as lost. Enlil would present the false emerald tablet triumphantly to the assembly, telling them that it had been recovered and could be placed in its shrine again for all to venerate. Sitting in the rightful place of the real emerald tablet would give the false tablet even more power.

Enlil, with Noah at his side, would refine and perfect his weapons of mass destruction; he had used them in the far-distant past, but they had never quite succeeded in obliterating all life, as he had hoped; and he would build a secret weapon of consummate power that no-one would ever suspect existed.

Not only that, but he would set up a secret syndicate among the earthlings, composed of a small number of lethally powerful members of the earthly community who were susceptible to the worst influences of the Naphidem, and who could be brought directly under his control. In their hands would be the reins of the history that he himself would write. If Tiâmat could plan and design and reach to embrace the future, so could he!

For now, he would confiscate Babylon, hand it over ostensibly to Shem but really to Marduk, and build a tower of his own next to the existing ziggurat at its centre.

The reason Enlil needed the tower was that the Babylonian ziggurat was useless to his malignant plans. The noble protector Ga-nadin-ur stood guard within its ethereal dimensions and would block Enlil's attempts to divert the vestigial Grail forces into channels for his own use.

These Grail forces, originally located in the Ur ziggurat, had been recently redirected by Tiâmat into the brand new Babylonian ziggurat to strengthen her Earth children's chances of escaping Enlil's lethal shadow. Although these forces could never be anything other than a weak sub-current until Sara-Tamar could be returned to Earth, Tiâmat had breathed renewed life into them as far as was possible within her Divine Plan so that they could be rooted anew in Babylon. Ur and Babylon, now both Grail-endowed and standing side by side, could then grow into deeply blessed and enlightened twin city states, which would serve as mighty towers shedding glory and freedom upon the straitened world.

It was this plan of Tiâmat's, given from the heart of her Divine love and mercy, that Enlil was determined to overthrow.

Therefore, his own plan was to build a tower next to the Babylonian ziggurat, and, with Noah's help, call the newly-released Grail forces into it so that he could thereafter use them as he wished. That of course involved returning the Naphidem back down to Earth as quickly as possible, because he was sick of shilly-shallying around whilst others stole the march on him in his great battle. As far as Enlil was concerned, tomorrow was not soon enough for his plans to come to fruition.

From this point onwards, Shulgi's name became Shem, as later recorded in the Old Testament. It was a name given to exalt (flatter) him. 'You are as the mighty shem, conveyor of the highest power and direct route to the Lord God Enlil,' it was supposed to declare. Enlil also gave Shem a hefty dose of the invidious white powder, and kept him on it, just to be sure of his man. However, in formal circles, Shulgi continued to be known by his original name.

News got out that Enlil was threatening Ham, and Ham's supporters began to gather. Driven by his impetus to triumph, Enlil massed his own supporters (those he had been able to oppress, enslave, or entice on board with promises of power, pleasure and material reward) and urged them to build his precious tower with the greatest possible speed.

He had a very narrow time frame, he knew, before the forces of light rose up on every level to stay his hand. He told his workers that they must make a superhuman effort to get the shem ready in time, for their own protection.

What they understood by this was that hostile armies were preparing to invade Ur (Babylon was really an extension of the old city), and that somehow Enlil would safeguard them from death and dispersal by means of the tower. What Enlil understood by it was that he needed to get the Naphidem down the tower and back to Earth before he was prevented from doing so.

Enlil had changed the name of Babylon ('the Temple of the True Father') to Babel (Bab-El, 'Father El', after himself, El Shaddai or El Elyon). Afterwards, he allowed the original name to be resumed as a sneering joke. However, the edifice he was urging his workers to build was, of course, the Tower of Babel. It had a ziggurat design, but Enlil had reversed its energies. Instead of carrying upwards, they conducted downwards. He called it a 'shem', which was certainly a misnomer.

The day came at last when Enlil could act. Leading the Naphidem down the 'shem' in a euphoric frenzy, he sent forth a ray from one of his weapons of mental confusion so that the citizens of Ur-Babylon fell into disarray and bewilderment and could not really work out what was happening. Their right, feminine-orientated brain was affected, and their language-centres became disordered.

They sent forth an impassioned prayer to the Most High God (a title to which Enlil pretended). However, Enki, Nin-khursag, Lilith, and Ga-nadin-ur were standing by. With the help of the ministers of the temple of John, they were able to penetrate the haze caused by the white powder (utilised for the mind-confusion weapon) and direct the people's prayerful appeal straight to Tiâmat.

Because her gift of free will to her children would not be countermanded, Tiâmat could now act without destroying the purpose and principle of her creation. She brought down the shem and propelled the Naphidem, shrieking with indignation, back into their own dimension, re-sealing it as she did so.

Enlil's rage was like the pounding of giant demonic drums. He opened the gates of Ur, and the teeming masses that had assembled outside, demanding an explanation as to why their beloved king, Canaan, had been sent into exile and the mighty city of Ur taken over, poured within. A rabble accompanied them, and Naphidemic influences still present in the atmosphere turned all to conflagration and blood-lust.

Enlil let loose his weaponry in an orgy of destruction. Texts from the time bewail the terrible scenes and the passing of Ur.

'Ur is destroyed, bitter is its lament.' 'The sacred dynasty from the temple they exiled.' 'The country's blood now fills its holes like hot bronze in a mould. Bodies dissolve like fat in the sun. Our temple is destroyed. Smoke lies on our cities like a shroud.' : just a few samples of these anguished texts.

One of them, mournfully, confirms that 'The gods are abandoning us like migrating birds.' Tiâmat was obliged to shut down Eden at this time, and the 'gods' (the enhanced community) had to leave. This was because Enlil and his cronies (who had flocked behind him as he descended the shem) must not be allowed to return to it. From Eden, they could have done such damage to the Earth and her ordinary communities that the progression of life would have become virtually unsustainable. And so Tiâmat acted.

Enlil and his circle of conspirators were enclosed in an earthly but ethereal dimension, closer to earth than the Naphidem: a place of gloom and spiritual heaviness. Because of their power of reversal and science of converse alchemy, they could not be entirely contained within it; but their access to Earth was limited.

As ever, human free will decreed that those who would lend an ear to them, and abide by their sinister maxims, could do so. Unfortunately, this meant that Enlil could remain operative upon the Earth. An inviolable denial of his powers would have contravened free will, which would in turn have stultified the purposeful flow of creation.

The first thing Enlil did was to move Babylon further north-west, well out of the way of the conjoined ruined cities, so that it lay between the banks of the Tigris and Euphrates rivers. This gave him a certain enhanced power over it, even though it was placed under Marduk's rule, because Enlil's place of potency in the ethers (similar to the 'seat' of an ancient family) was the point of convergence of these two great rivers.

During the cataclysm in Ur, King Shem had died in the arms of a close friend, a kinsman from the Royal House of Ur who had remained loyal to him throughout, although he was formerly also a friend of King Canaan's.

His name was Avram, and he would later be known as Abraham.

CHAPTER 23

EGYPT'S TWIN BROTHER

From this point on, the story of John (Enki) and the story of Ham fuse and become one; for Enki, Ham's ancestor and spiritual son, dedicated his life wholly to the service of Tiâmat; and Ham dedicated his life with similar devotion to Enki and to Tiâmat. Enki, or John, as was his titular designation (meaning 'gift of God', pertaining to the Grail), stayed ever by Ham's side, inspiring and supporting his great mission; for Ham's mission was John's, and at the deepest level of being they were and are one.

Ham was ever the supreme 'John-man' on Earth, the John-man being a man who serves the True Father, Father God; and in so doing, loves and reveres Mother-God and looks to her heart-centred wisdom to set the standard in life.

Ham, or John, became an Avesa, one who does not leave the Earth but passes directly from body to body. His was the true identity behind many historical figures; and when he became John the Baptist, and then on his beheading passed into Lazarus (who had to die for four days whilst the transition was made!), to become John the Beloved, Jesus said of him in answer to Peter's question as to what John would do for his lord (for the Christ spirit within Jesus): "If I will that he tarry till I come [the Second Coming], what is that to thee?"

The disciples thought Jesus meant that John would not die, but John himself points out that Jesus did not say that he would not die, but only that he would tarry until the Second Coming (*John* 21:21–24). In fact, the arrival of John the Beloved through Lazarus marks a momentous event: the time when Ham fused entirely with the soul of Enki, and Enki came to Earth via a miracle. We might say that the deepest jewel of Ham's soul was called forth, and that this deepest jewel was Enki, who was always Ham's deeper self.

Only Mary Magdalene and Jesus could bring about this profound miracle of calling forth; and it required the span of four days for Enki and Ham to conjoin themselves in preparation, hosted by Lazarus, who was also a strand of that great soul that comprised Enki/Ham.

Now that Enki and Ham were truly and indivisibly one, Jesus was able to greet Enki/Ham as his twin soul. The idea of the twin pillars upholding the reign of the Divine Light on Earth was expressed in the beginnings of the rise of Ur and Babylon together (destroyed by Enlil), the later rise of Canaan and Egypt (the former brought down by Enlil, the other contaminated by him), and even in New York's former Twin Towers, demolished by a hidden influence attempting to initiate World War III and the end of hope for humanity – a scenario that will never happen. These eternal twin towers are symbolised in the Twin Pillars that are the mainstay of Solomon's temple.

One day, the twin towers will arise to fulfill their destiny at last in the Middle East and become beacons of civilisation that will comprise a doubly fortified lighthouse for all the world.

To return to our story: Enlil's first move was to secure Avram and to take him into the land of Cain, because it was imperative that he should spread Enlil's influence there. The country was protected, and Enlil could not force entry. He needed an ambassador, a conductor; and he was determined that Avram should be his man. He presented Avram with the false emerald tablet, in Enlil's possession because he had progressed down the shem with it held aloft, although he had engaged its deceptive powers to make it invisible.

To shield the knowledge from him that it was falsified, Enlil claimed that Avram had been given what had been due to pass to Ham and Canaan, because Avram had been found more worthy. Therefore, to mark this great honour, Enlil renamed Avram Abraham – he who held the mystical knowledge of Ham, Master Craftsman and Archon of the Tenth Age of Capricorn (that which is coming).

Shortly afterwards, Enlil arranged for Abraham to win a military victory in rescuing his kinsman Lot from capture by the forces of invading kings. He routed them and, to celebrate this victory, he was made a Priest-King within Enlil's temple by the great priest Melchisedek of Salem (Jerusalem), a mighty and noble soul who had been inveigled into accepting the false communion bread and wine, and so had fallen to some degree into Enlil's power. He was the designated guardian to the forces of the Grail in Jerusalem, elect of Tiâmat and blessed by Enki, being the supreme head (under Enki) of Enki's Master Craftsmen.

He served an angelic order; and Enlil had been obliged to fight long and hard to gain a slight foothold in his soul.

Melchisedek dispensed the false communion to Abraham, and the curtain came down over Abraham's deeper vision and wisdom. The priestly line of kingship had now been transferred from Ham and Canaan to Abraham, although in actuality Ham and Canaan continued to retain it.

Noah, grieving for Shem, was satisfied with this move, because Abraham was a descendant of the great patriarch, who had initiated the line of the kings of Ur. Although Abraham fell further into confusion after taking the false communion, he, like Melchisedek, remained pure of heart.

Enlil now presented himself to Abraham as 'the Most High God'; as 'El of the Mountain', for he had been blessed by Iona (Mount Heredom) and present upon her as one of her lesser kings (Ain and Ar-Thor being of higher spiritual status), until he had fallen from grace and conspired to decapitate her.

However, he liked his former title – 'Lord of the Mountain' –and held on to it. And he instructed Abraham that he must never have anything to do with Canaan, as he and his father, Ham, had 'fallen into the ways of evil'. He intimated that they had forbidden relationships with their mothers and their mothers' female relatives – a kind of orgy of mother-incest.

This was absolute nonsense, of course; it was just Enlil's way of describing what he thought of males who pledged their faithful love, honour and worship to Mother God and who held females in high esteem.

This was heartbreaking for Canaan, or Ur-baba, because Abraham had once been his good friend, as Canaan had also been Shulgi's good friend. But all attempts at reconciliation made by Canaan were rejected, and Abraham with his followers was a wanderer in the land of Cain, although he was protected by Canaan, who continued to love and respect him.

Afterwards, Ham and Canaan together, siting the new Temple of John in the land of Cain (an ancient temple had existed there for countless generations, in which Lilith and Luluwa served as High Priestesses, but due to Melchisedek's fall it had to be renewed), built an almighty civilisation. Ham called the land on which it rose up, Canaan, after his son. The country had in fact become informally known as Canaan as soon as Canaan himself had fled into it from the wrath of Enlil and established himself there.

It outshone Egypt in its many-splendoured glory, and it was more beautiful, more hallowed, the seat of greater marvels and miracles, than Egypt ever was, because it was more spiritually attuned than that towering civilisation of darkness and light.

It lasted over 400 years, until Egypt destroyed it. We know nothing of it today, because the ancient chroniclers carefully airbrushed it out of history, having been influenced to do so by Enlil, who by that time had refined many mind-influencing weapons that hit with silent, invisible rays.

There was an important reason for the obliteration of its history, involving the obfuscation of just which Joseph it was who was in power at the court of the Pharaoh when Egypt's timeline and Tiâmat's bloodline produced a highly significant king's son.

If the history of religion, and world history itself, had clearly understood that this king's son was one and the same with the identity of a certain prominent figure, Enlil and his schemes ran the risk of being unmasked. Moreover, Enlil certainly didn't want any breathtaking, wondrous testimony to a civilisation built around the Temple of John to be available for enquirers of the future to ponder over!

All that is left of its proper testimony is a missing 430-years' span in biblical chronology. I saw it, with inner vision, dying patiently, a silent dove. It knows it will come again, because it is the Dove of the Eternal, that resides on Iona. When it rises again into even greater magnificence, it will be erected by two nations that build it in brotherhood.

Whilst it existed, Enlil plotted against it, until he eventually brought it down via his usual scurrilous means of encroachment. Still its beauty persisted, and its old altars sent an incense to heaven that Enlil could not bear. His plots continued. He would not rest until he had smashed its altars and desecrated its sacred gathering-grounds, and made those temples his own.

Meanwhile, Enlil wanted to be absolutely certain of Abraham's loyalty. Noah's former allegiance to Tiâmat, and the 'disobedience' of

Adam and of Ga-nadin-ur who still stood with her, made him uneasy. He wanted proof positive that Abraham would comply with his every wish. And so he commanded Abraham to sacrifice his son Isaac.

The name Isaac means 'laughter', and it was this name that Enlil inspired Abraham to give him. He was to be Enlil's laughter, for as Abraham was compelled to make a human sacrifice, so Abraham and his followers would fall entirely under Enlil's influence, and in no time at all (relatively speaking), his plan for human extinction would come to fruition.

Mercifully, the tables were turned, because a ram, with its horns tangled in the bushes, spoke to Abraham's heart on the day that the terrible deed was to be done. Enki's spirit was within the ram. It represented the Ram knowledge, the supreme knowledge of mysticism and the workings of the cosmos that is second only to the Ham or I-Am knowledge, which is of God and is God.

Abraham was invested with the Ram knowledge (Av-ram) because of his advanced soul and his link to the Blood Royal, the bloodline which had descended from Cain and Luluwa, Enki's son and Lilith's daughter. And, with the symbolic sacrifice of the ram instead of his son, Abraham, following the guidance of Enki, who spoke to him with the words of the true God, sacrificed himself.

He laid his own Ram knowledge, the deepest, most treasured part of himself, on Enlil's altar in place of Isaac. He did not realise consciously that he did so, yet his inner will absolutely complied. He thought he heard the voice of Enlil, whom he confused with the One True God, when it was actually Enki who spoke to him.

But with this self-sacrifice, he saved the world. Human sacrifices would not be made; and, although Enlil was able to persuade many under his sway, even some of the later Hebrews, to make human sacrifices, the founding father and guiding light of the Jewish race resolutely turned from it; and an essential component of Enlil's power was overthrown and dissipated.

Isaac became God's laughter, the laughter of joy; not the laughter of bloodthirsty triumph and spite that was Enlil's. We will encounter this laughter of his in carven form when our pilgrimage to Iona takes us by way of Rosslyn Chapel.

Furious with Enki for spoiling his plans, Enlil now determined to use the enweaponed white powder in an even more deadly assault than that which he had inflicted on Ur. Noah and he had been busy refining their WMD ('weapons of mass destruction') ever since, and now, only a few decades later, the white powder was ready to cause permanent catastrophe (the blighted earth where it fell would not recover) on a much wider scale.

Enlil chose as his target the two cities of Sodom and Gomorrah. These twin cities, not too far from Ur and Babylon, were now filled with their refugees, and had become sanctuaries for the very advanced and progressive civilisation that had fled from their ruins. Philosophers, artists, free thinkers of every kind amassed here, almost all of them devotees of the Temple of John.

Enlil considered them very dangerous and undesirable, and a real threat to the principles of enslavement and imprisonment with which he sought to chain human consciousness. He also had an idea that Tiâmat had chosen them to become her new God-touched twin city-states now that Ur and the original Babylon had fallen. So he thought he would try out his super-weapon on them.

Abraham was fobbed off with stories of the wickedness of the Sodom and Gomorrah citizens, but in fact, to support this claim, Enlil had taken care to set up Naphidem influences within the cities so that a very small minority fell prey to their terrible incitements. However, Abraham insisted that there were many good people in residence there. He was finally persuaded by Enlil that there were fewer than five (Abraham's nephew Lot and his family), who would be saved, and Enlil prepared for action.

Again, Enki and Nin-khursag came to the rescue. Enki and another member of the enhanced community, under the rigours of extreme effort, managed to use the Grail remnants to physicalise their bodies and descend to the material plane for a short time, as in the old days.

The leniency that Abraham had won from Enlil regarding the people to be saved actually helped in this process, although of course Abraham remained unaware of the real situation. Enki and his colleague came to Lot's house to warn him of the impending disaster, urging him to gather together any who would be willing to escape with him. They thus flouted Enlil's 'fewer than five to be saved' regulation, which of course they were very happy to do. Unfortunately, Lot was hesitant and failed to act with promptitude on their words. When Enlil spied the developing situation, he hurriedly engineered a course of action that would ensure that only Lot's family alone (as he had promised Abraham) would in fact be saved.

The enhanced community members who had remained with Enki and Nin-khursag dwelt in an ethereal dimension closer to Earth than Eden, but much more beautiful than the one Enlil and his supporters inhabited. Led by Enki, Nin-khursag and Lilith, they had remained in such constraint because of their love for humanity and the Earth.

It was from this sphere that the two shining beings, Enki and a colleague, had descended; but Enlil saw them enter the city, and sent his Naphidem-incited mob to pound at the door of Lot's house and demand that the two 'angels' be given over to them for the purposes of homosexual gang rape.

The two 'angels' had come for a second, crucial, purpose; to disable Enlil's noxious weapon and to protect the Earth from its annihilating malignancy once it had been implemented. They had come to rescue Lot's family, and any others who would listen, as an act of mercy; but also because it was through Lot and his daughters that Tiâmat's bloodline must proceed. If the mob could drag the two shining men outside and subject them to mass beatings and rape before they could escape by reverting their bodies to an ethereal state, they would have been so traumatised as to fail in their two vital endeavours.

The baying mob was resisted, and in the morning Lot's family left. Their two shining companions instructed them not to look back, because Enlil's destructive ray engaged with human consciousness through the 'ayin' to do its work. Lot's wife did look back when she thought the party was at a safe distance, and was immediately desiccated and crystallised where she stood.

She, together with the two cities and all in them, were encrusted with salt by the two 'shining ones', as a means of safely containing the toxic emanations of the death ray. The reflective crystals in salt had the power to neutralise these toxins. Having successfully dealt with the manifest fall-out of Enlil's weapon, the earthly access of the shining ones to it made possible the weapon's complete disablement.

The two cities have been discovered at the bottom of the Dead Sea, still enshrouded in their protective layers of salt. Unfortunately (or perhaps in fact very fortunately!), because of the difficult political position between Jordan and Israel, further archaeological investigation has not so far been undertaken.

For the time being, Enlil was foiled yet again.

CHAPTER 24

THE GOLDEN CALF

Throughout history, Enki and Ham have fought for us over and over again, always rescuing us from walking blindfold over the edge of the final cliff, even though our history has been almost as tragic, tortured and blood-soaked as Enlil could have wished.

Enlil's ingenious subtlety has infected every one of our religions, every culture, every political framework, all our ideology, even the way we use our language. We seem to be heading in the right direction; and then, with consummate skill, Enlil whispers his bearings to us. And, being a global community that tends to be led by its passions and its lower mind (the intellect), we trot obediently where he beckons.

Only by establishing our consciousness firmly in the heart, through meditation, through quiet reflection, and always through love, which allows us to enter into the dynamics of the consciousness deep within the heart, can we rescue ourselves from his lethal grip. Once we have centred ourselves in the beauty and purity of heart consciousness, where our true humanity resides, Enlil is rendered powerless.

Although there are numerous stories of Enlil's deceptions and Enki's struggles on our behalf along the timeline between the severing of the Grail and today, there is one particular story to tell before we repair to Rosslyn.

It concerns a woman who has touched our destiny in living memory: Grace Cooke, the well-known medium and visionary who died in the mid years of the 20th century. (It is important to stress that this story has arisen from inner guidance alone, and does not necessarily represent the views of the White Eagle Lodge, the spiritual organisation that Grace Cooke founded with her husband in 1936.)

Grace Cooke reincarnated, after many lives lived in preparation, as Tuya, wife of Yuya, in Egypt. This brings us to the point in history wherein 430 years have been eliminated from record. Genesis ends with Jacob (given the name of Israel by the true God) settling in Egypt, his son Joseph of the Coat of Many Colours being sold into slavery by his brother Judah, being taken to the capital, wowing the pharaoh, and eventually being embalmed and buried in Egypt with full honours. Exodus then proceeds with the story of Moses, as if it occurred shortly afterwards.

In fact, over 400 years elapsed, which measured the heyday of Canaan. During that time, a veritable dynasty of 'Josephs' arose within the Egyptian palace, founded by the original Joseph who interpreted dreams and was master of other wondrous occult arts. His descendants in turn became the 'wise men' of the court, their wives the designated 'wise women'. The name of Joseph was titular, passing to the eldest son in each case as pharaohs came and went.

The wives of the inheriting Josephs were very important, because they kept the flame of The Temple of John (Uan) alive in their husbands' hearts and focus. The followers of Abraham were won back to Enki and Tiâmat at the point when Jacob had struggled all night with the angel upon Mount Bethel, for of course his vision of the ladder was a vision of the Grail, and the great competitors who had fought for his soul were Enki and Enlil.

Enki had emerged as the champion of that night-long exertion, and Jacob had been newly named as Israel ('Isis-the Sun-Father', or 'Mother-Divine Child-Father', the three aspects of the One True God, in which we note that the Mother is firmly placed first). His mission thereafter was to leave Canaan and go into Egypt, where Enlil was strongest, and beard the fallen dragon in his den.

At the time of Tuya and her husband Yuya (the latter a form of the Hebraic Yosef or Joseph), huge advances had been made in introducing the Temple of John into the Egyptian royal house. To bring this process to fruition was the radiant reason why Jacob had been inspired to leave the majesty of Canaan for the darker, more materialistic and Enlil-inspired Egypt, although it was by no means entirely, or even mainly, under Enlil's sway.

Yuya obviously had a Canaanite ancestry from the original Joseph, and his wife Tuya was also a lady of great status. She was of the direct line from Nin-khursag, and her grandfather, Tuthmosis III, was the founder of the Great White Brotherhood of the Therapeutate.

Her father was an important, Enki-inspired priest of Heliopolis, and was descended from Esau via Igrath, Esau's daughter. Igrath was the mother of Queen Sobeknefru, and it was Queen Sobeknefru who established the secret and ancient Dragon Court as a royal institution in Egypt.

Therefore, due to Esau and his daughter Igrath, Tuya also had a Canaanite ancestry, and was of the crucial line which had established the Dragon Court, the veiled but recognised organisation which was guardian of the secrets of Tiâmat.

Yuya and Tuya virtually ruled Egypt during the reign of Tuthmosis IV, because he was withdrawing into a life of spiritual contemplation guided by Tuya, the Dragon Court and the Temple of John. From the assembling of the Dragon Court had arisen a secret sisterhood, of which Tuya was a prominent member, rising to leader in her later years. She passed on her knowledge to her granddaughter, Tiye, who married Amenhotep lll.

Amenhotep adored Tiye. He followed her guidance and extolled her greatness; thus the Temple of Oannes became firmly established within the precincts of the royal court of Egypt; and it was headed by women of high spiritual degree. Tiye had charge of Nefertiti, brought to her as a baby after her mother Sitamun, Amenhotep's first wife, died soon after giving birth. She gave Nefertiti the status of Mistress of the Star Fire, conferred on Tiye by her grandmother Tuya.

Nefertiti married Amenhotep IV, Amenhotep lll's son with Tiye. They had six daughters together, and one of these, Meretaten, was the reincarnation of Tuya. Nefertiti passed on the status of Mistress of the Star Fire to her, knowing her destiny, and, wonderfully, depictions still exist from ancient Egypt of this time, wherein Nefertiti transfers the Star Fire or the Dew-Cup essence to Meretaten, and Meretaten tenderly feeds it to her father.

By Tiâmat's marvellous workings the Star Fire could now be passed on by a kiss on the lips, as in later times Mary Magdalene fed it to Jesus, who, according to the Gnostic gospels, 'kissed her often on the mouth'. The last word has disappeared from the anciently inscribed page, mysteriously torn away, but the context is clear.

Meretaten's father was, of course, the unforgettable pharaoh Akhenaten. He publicly declared his allegiance with the Temple of John, initiated the worship of the One True God (the Aten, God of Light), endorsed paintings of himself in androgyne mode, and sponsored a mystic, flowing, feminine art into Egypt's somewhat rigid culture.

Enlil, of course, was absolutely incensed. He had just about got Egypt to the point of seeking world domination when Yuya and Tuya had to come along and ruin everything. He had tried his utmost to set up this situation in Babylon, where for a time Marduk, whom Enlil had backed to the hilt for his own reasons, had made great progress in following his ideal.

But then a most wretched king had arisen by the name of Hamm-ur-abi, who appeared at first to be on his side and to make very satisfactory headway, but who afterwards circumscribed everything with the wrong sort of laws and then seemed purposely to cause the dissolution of the Babylonian empire on his death. Everyone knew, Enlil stormed to himself, that Enki the Trickster was behind it all, in cahoots with that lackey of his, Ham. Who else would Hamm-ur-abi be? This time, Enlil was going to have his rightful revenge.

Since Noah's change of allegiance, Enlil knew all about the sapphire tablet that was meant to prepare humanity for the coming of the emerald tablet. He knew that it was the sapphire tablet that was about to be dispensed to the world via Meretaten, who, with Moses, would begin a spiritual revolution that would change everything, so that when the ultimate king and queen came along to rescue the emerald tablet, the entire planet would begin its ascension. All his powers of destruction and spite were therefore trained on the elimination of the sapphire tablet.

His first job was to hurl every disaster he could at Egypt, and to influence as many people as possible through Naphidemic emanations and his own priests there. The result was that the Egyptians thought they were under attack from their angry dispossessed gods, so they ousted Akhenaten and also, soon afterwards, Smenkhkare, the pharaoh who followed him, as he was clearly of the same mind as Akhenaten.

Tiye arranged shelter for her son, Akhenaten, with his Midianite kinsfolk (all descended from Esau), led by Lord Jethro. His nephew Smenkhkare (Aaron) joined him in due course.

Akhenaten took with him his second wife, Kiya, who had already given birth to Tutankhamen (in his first years, before Akhenaten's banishment, he was known as Tutankhaten). He was left behind at court under the care of Nefertiti and Tiye. Meanwhile, Kiya was pregnant again with her second son, Moses.

Moses was smuggled into Egypt secretly, as a newborn baby. His parents knew his destiny; and the only way to enable him to be brought up in the royal household, under the care of Nefertiti and Tiye, was to hide him in the reeds of the river Nile so that Tiye could come upon him 'unexpectedly'. What really happened was that little Meretaten stood guard all night with a fiery stick to scare away predators, and Tiye came at once to claim him, as soon as the morning light touched the waters.

The story of Moses eventually delivering the Israelites from the tyranny of the pharaoh who came to power after the death of Tutankhamen and Ay (which ended the 18th Dynasty into which Moses had been born) is well known. The rest of the story is not.

Lord Jethro of the Midianites had fallen into Enlil's power and, using his influence with Moses, persuaded him to allow the creation of the white powder (atomised gold) in the alchemical laboratory of Hathor. This mystical cavern lay within the mountain that Meretaten and Moses were to climb in order to receive the sapphire tablet from Tiâmat.

This mountain was the Mountain of Hathor, a sacred place since the most ancient of days. It lay among the many mountain peaks of the Sinai Peninsula, and was famous for its numerous veins of turquoise, which was Hathor's sacred stone. It was a symbol of Tiâmat's most holy emerald and sapphire tablets blended into one, and it celebrated the Mother Goddess of the Egyptians, who was represented as a great queenly bovine with an ever-replenished flow of milk.

Enlil needed huge stocks of his white powder, because he was building an invisible ring around the Earth in place of the canopy of purest ice that Tiâmat had put in place to protect the planet, and which Enlil had melted, causing the great flood.

His ring around the Earth contained reflective crystals which were programmed to addle the mind and confuse the emotions, so that very important things looked as if they were trifles hardly worthy of note, and very unimportant things were blown up into a state of ludicrous significance. Lord Jethro was given the unholy task of preparing the monatomic gold needed for this purpose, and to have plenty on hand to feed to Moses when he came down the mountain. It was Enlil's only chance of saving his precious plan of human extermination.

Moses and Meretaten (now known by her Hebraic name, Miriam) ascended the mountain, whilst the Israelites prayed at its foot. They had created a small golden calf, not as an idol, but as a symbolic object of beauty and deep spiritual significance in veneration of the enterprise and of God. Miriam was to fall pregnant within the rites of the Sacred Marriage that she and Moses would enact upon the mountaintop; and the presence of Hathor had already entered her: the spirit of the Mother, who would greet her daughter upon the mountain peak, and vouchsafe to her children, Moses and Miriam, the precious sapphire tablet that they would give to the world.

Within Miriam was to be conceived the 'calf of Hathor', their beloved daughter, who was the Divine Woman that must be born so that the spiritual forces about to be released via the sapphire tablet could be earthed and secured. As ever, without the Divine Woman, there could be no descent, reception and grounding of this beautiful potency from God.

In order to create a magnetic point of the highest spiritual power, Miriam and Moses entered into the rites of the sacred marriage upon the mountain top. There, the spirit of Tiâmat came to them, and oversaw the conception of their daughter. She thereafter manifested the sapphire tablet as an objectification of her love, so that the couple could avail themselves of it. In that holiest of moments, Miriam received it. With a kiss that offered him the Dew-Cup, that tablet, as if it were a child, was given into the hands of Moses by Miriam. Although it was not heavy, he would bear it down the mountain.

The air was rolling with the coils of smoke that belched from the furnace raging within the Cave of Hathor as they approached the midpoint of their descent. Appearing from out of the mists stood Jethro, with the false communion wine and bread made ready.

CHAPTER 25

MIRIAM'S SORROW

To Miriam's horror, the Lord of the Midianites began to browbeat Moses. What was he thinking of, letting the women run things? Was he man or mouse? There the Children of Israel were (now also known, very temporarily, as the Children of Hathor), down below, entering into all sorts of abominable orgies whilst their proper leader (Moses) went sprinting off on some half-witted whim. It was time Moses took charge, and said what was what!

Here in his hands, continued Jethro, he held the time-honoured answer to such feminine outrage: the holy communion which the great Melchisedek had given to their noble patriarch Abraham. It had a special potency, he explained, which restored a man's dignity so that the women couldn't manage to pull the wool over his eyes. Wouldn't he take it now?

Miriam stepped forward in blazing anger. Who was Lord Jethro, she demanded, to command the Children of Israel? Were not their culture and religious traditions (the Temple of John) considerably older and more firmly established than those of the Midianites? Why did he assume such unwarranted authority?

Jethro glanced at Moses as if to say, 'I rest my case.' Enlil was with Moses at that moment, not in his heart but at his elbow, egging him on. The truth was that Moses *was* jealous of Miriam, this queenly, brilliant elder sister who had always shone like a star at court and who was Nefertiti's favourite (or so it seemed). And the Israelites clearly saw her as their leader, not him.

Moses stretched out his hand. He took the bread; he drank the wine.

The wondrous sapphire tablet, neither big nor heavy, sprang out of his retaining hand as if it were alive. In fact, his own nerve-reflexes had rejected it as soon as he had swallowed. It smashed into irretrievable pieces upon a rock. Miriam gave a great cry and ran away down the mountain, weeping.

Enlil appeared in his ethereal form among the shifting smoke wraiths. Who was he? Moses could not tell. There was certainly a weight of presence around him, but Moses thought to himself that perhaps he found it oppressive because he was more aware of its masculine force now that Miriam had gone. Was it the same presence he had felt upon the sunlit, airy mountain top? Maybe it was; and it just felt different because of all this gloom and smoke, and the tongues of flame dancing in the nearby cave of Hathor which were reddening in the gathering dusk.

Enlil gave him another sapphire tablet, not like the heavenly blue one he had dropped, but a black one, with a deep red flame in it, like an angry eye. "Put your mark on this tablet," Enlil said in velvet tones. "Carve it for me. It is a replacement stone. I will make all right." In a soothed but drugged state, Moses carved about 40 laws into the stone with a small chisel that Jethro had provided, although he was alone on the mountain with Enlil. Jethro had gone after Miriam, as he needed to contest what she would say to the waiting Israelites.

The laws that Enlil dictated to Moses were old laws, well-known in the Egyptian Negative Confession and in the annals of the Midianites. They were serviceable laws as far as they went, basic laws that had to be learnt; but they were not inspired with any new vision. They would not change anything. They were the fundaments, but not the temple. And if Enlil had his way, humanity would fail in learning even these fundaments.

Whilst Enlil dictated and Moses obediently carved, the Anunnaki king was busily up to something else. He was not really interested in what he was dictating; it was just a means of distracting Moses whilst Enlil fulfilled his real purpose. For, with the help of his blasphemous processes within the sacred Cave of Hathor, Enlil was infusing the stone tablet with a combined physical and spiritual malignancy of unprecedented proportions. Now he would be able to lead a civilisation that would rule the world!

When he had finished, Moses, with his new carven block of stone, heavier and much more unwieldy than the first that had been broken, came down the mountain glowing.

As he descended, an inexplicable rage fell on him. He deposited the black stone with its ominous red flicker in the care of Jethro, and then raged through the camp like a madman. It is even said that he killed some of the Israelites. He was consumed with a deadly urgency. No time now for the niceties of baking the white powder into bread-cakes!

With a roar he built up the fire, melted down the golden calf, and performed the reverse alchemy that reduced it to powder. The water he used for this process would stand in for the backward-spin wine. The Israelites would have both from the desecrated symbol of Hathor, which he now despised with a loathing that was a deep, innards-twisting, virulent pathology like a dark writhing snake within him.

In truth, he had been possessed by Enlil. And although it may have been inaudible, Enlil's laughter, terrible, cruel and mocking, flowed forth from him as he watched the entire cowed gathering take the white powder immersed in water.

Miriam, meanwhile, had done all she could to stop this hideous turn of events from progressing, even throwing herself in Moses' path as he made his maniacal headlong charges. He thundered to Jethro's men (none of the Israelites would have obeyed this particular command) to throw Miriam into captivity. She was the one weak link in the electrified chain-link fence of insanity that Enlil had thrown around his reason.

Jasher was Moses' royal standard-bearer, and his contemporary account, as told in the book of Jasher, makes clear that these things happened. Miriam was adored of the Israelites, he tells us. She was obeyed first, before Moses. She was called 'The Teacher', and subjugated by his rage as they were, still the people demanded of Moses that he release their beloved leader. Moses waited a week before he succumbed to their insistence.

Miriam was immediately imprisoned in the Cave of Hathor. However, she stood guard and allowed no-one to enter, preventing Moses and Jethro from accessing the white powder stocks therein so that Moses was forced to make use of the golden calf to force-feed the white powder to the Israelites.

Nearby, the sight of a statue of Queen Tiye's head with her cartouche set in its crown, her beloved grandmother who had formerly conducted the sacred rites of Hathor within the cavern, comforted her.

She contemplated the barefaced lies of Jethro. There had been no wanton orgy among the Israelites. They had, instead, performed ceremonies and orisons to bless the Sacred Marriage, the *hieros gamos*, which was being undertaken by Miriam and Moses upon the mountain top.

There, deep in the silent darkness, she wept and prayed. Tiâmat heard her; within her womb, the Divine Woman heard her. Her teardrops, falling like silver darts in the dying light of the sinister fires, held power.

As she was escorted out of the Cave of Hathor, a great rumble from the depths of the ground under their feet was heard, and the sacred Cave fell into rubble and ruin. The masses of white powder, ready and waiting in the gloom for Enlil's purposes like mounds of soft platinum gold spun by the goblin Rumpelstiltskin, would not be made available to him after all. The cave was alchemically sealed by Miriam's will.

Not only this, but that mighty, unassailable will achieved yet another glorious purpose. The same force that shook the Cave of Hathor into devastation shattered the evil stone tablet which Enlil had laced with poisons beyond comprehension. And, although Moses had partaken of those poisons, and would die a year later from their terrible encroachment, he recovered from his encounter with Enlil.

The Israelites were under Enlil's control again, but only partially. They would successfully contain Enlil's terrible death energies in a circle of human souls which protected humanity and the Earth, and they would suffer desperately throughout the centuries in that act of continual self-sacrifice.

Meanwhile, Miriam alerted Bezaleel, in Egypt, to come at once to the Israelites' camp. He was a Master Craftsman under the tutelage of Ham, and in fact Ham's spirit entered him once he began his work, for Ham and Enki, unseen, toiled with him and above him.

Together, they created the Mercy Seat, which comprised the containment and protection of Tiâmat, given as her loving gift to shield humanity from the vile energies within the casket. The integrity of the stone tablet –and therefore the intensity of its power – had been shattered by Miriam when she had destroyed the Cave of Hathor; and Tiâmat's gift of gold, brought forth by three of her most faithful and dedicated servants, Enki, Ham and Bezaleel, sealed her children of Earth from its terrible purpose.

How strange that it is known it is the Shekinah, the Light of the Mother, which is the presence that dwells within the Mercy Seat, and is the Mercy Seat. We know this story with every part of our being, except, until now, with alpha consciousness!

147

To his eternal credit, Moses did not take over the world, as he could have done, and indeed as Enlil had set him up to do, and urged him to do. If he had agreed, Enlil would have changed his atoms to a more Naphidemic vibration, and staved off the cruel incursions of the 'glow' he had received from the malignant stone on the mountain. Enlil, Marduk and Noah were refining their dark scientific arts all the time. But, as Moses refused to serve Enlil in this respect, Enlil had no further use for him, and left him to die in sickness and pain.

The unholy contents of the Ark of the Covenant were later housed in the Israelites' Holy Temple, within the Holy of Holies, to further protect humankind from its emanations. Unfortunately, a few problems arose, not the least of which was the theft of the Ark by the Philistines, who opened the casket and filed by it in procession to look inside as a ceremony of triumph! Many of them were struck down by horrific tumours and a strange sickness (akin to radiation sickness, although the poison in the black stone is far worse than nuclear fall-out). All who had been affected died.

The casket was recovered by Tamar, King David's sister, and then hidden away again. Yet sometimes the Israelites took it with them into battle, knowing they would invariably win if they did. The elemental life in the shattered stones (entirely demonic) made it rear up on such occasions, and the casket on its carrying poles swept its carriers forward towards the enemy with a force of volition that was terrifying to both sides!

Because the killings it accomplished gave increased life to the stone fragments, it eventually became impossible to contain the Ark's death energies in entirety, even within the Mercy Seat and the Holy of Holies. So, when a Jewish king arose who followed Enki and placed a symbol of Tiâmat within the Holy of Holies, the spiritual grace that this bestowed made it possible to divide the invidious contents of the casket and take a certain portion of them away for separate containment, protection and sealing.

These fragments went first to Egypt, to the isle of Elephantini, sacred to the black Mother Goddess and where the knowledge of containment of such monstrosity outside the Ark was known, for it was an ancient Jewish stronghold where a Holy Temple had been built.

Yet even for Egypt the task grew too great, and the presence of these fragments of the Ark brought ruin on the Jewish community there. So they were finally removed to a place where the shrine of the Black Mother was even stronger: Ethiopia, the birthplace of Nin-Banda, Ham's mother, whose line was sourced in Nin-khursag and which eventually produced the Queen of Sheba, Mary Magdalene, and Sara-Tamar, daughter of Jesus and Mary. This magical connection made it possible for Ham to contain the fragments successfully in his mother's homeland.

They were guarded by a succession of Ethiopian priests of Ham's line, who sacrificed their lives to shield them. Their guardians soon developed cancers and other sicknesses, and their lives were very short. The Ethiopian priest who is their guardian today has developed very pronounced cataracts which have blinded him. Thankfully, at the beginning of 2013, angelic ministrants were finally able to seal the entire Ark, both in Jerusalem and Ethiopia, and no further priests will die because they guard it.

The little chapel in which the Ethiopian fragments are guarded sits very close to the Cathedral of St Mary of Zion in Ethiopia. St Mary of Zion, in esoteric circles, is recognised as Mary Magdalene, who descended from the Ethiopian line of Nin-Banda to bear Sara-Tamar, the Divine Woman who is the spirit and force of the emerald tablet. She is its mystery personified.

The main portion of the stone, contained within Bezaleel's golden Ark is, as mentioned, still within Jerusalem, buried and sealed within the Temple Mount. Sinister forces can no longer draw upon its 'leakage', as they have done in the past, to stoke up unrest between Israel and Palestine. Human choices still have to be made regarding this situation, of course; but they can no longer be manipulated and inflamed, as before.

Miriam left in sorrow, because her bond with Moses had been broken. She went into the desert with many followers, and her beautiful, cosmic wisdom was given into the care of those who afterwards settled in the Baltic lands. The gypsies partook of her wisdom ('wanderers from Egypt', which of course defines Miriam and her people) and were predictably hounded, attacked, debased and degraded throughout the centuries at every opportunity by Enlil.

Her sanctified daughter, so beloved even in the womb, could not come to Earth because of the sad outworkings of destiny, and was stillborn to Miriam one sorrowful night in the desert.

However, the mercy of Divine Spirit is profound, and Miriam was born again as Grace Cooke, who, after many years of devoted seeking, was given through guidance an exposition of the Gospel of John. This gospel, central to the White Eagle Lodge which she founded with her husband, was the core of the wisdom of the sapphire tablet, which has now been dispensed to many millions of people across the world in numerous forms of esoteric wisdom.

Although a movement of revelation had begun before Grace Cooke came into incarnation, and many different centres of it have evolved since, it was her determination, self-sacrifice and spiritual potency which are responsible for the unfoldment and dissemination of this knowledge on a global scale. We are now fully prepared as a planetary community, thanks to her resolution, to reclaim the emerald tablet and to move forward into the assumption of the last quarter of its transformational mystery and power. Miriam was silenced; but she came again through grace, and completed her mission with high honours.

The Mountain of Hathor, called in Moses and Miriam's time Mount Serâbît, afterwards became known as Horeb, because the military general Horemheb who overtook the royal Egyptian line after the passing of the 18th Dynasty wanted to have it named after himself, it being the seat of Enlil's triumph and he being most definitely Enlil's man. Today, we know it as Mount Sinai, although there are a vast number of mountain peaks upon the Sinai Peninsula whereon it stands.

Upon Mount Sinai, to this day, there are strange, bluish stones which are marked with clear suggestions of Arabic or hieroglyphic writing. These stones occur naturally and are a mystery. They are found nowhere else on Earth but in the vicinity of Mount Sinai. Some say it is proof that this is indeed the Mountain of the Law, and that the stones are the reflections in nature of what Moses brought down from the mountain.

It is with greater truth that we might perceive these strange stones to be nature's sorrowful expression of the true sapphire tablet, lost forever on the desolate mountainside amid Miriam's tears.

But that was not the end of the story.

Above the site of the transcriptions of the emerald tablet today (their resting-place will be revealed), a strange stone head has been set, looking down upon it. It wears the hair of a woman from ancient Egypt, but you cannot see its face, because it has been gouged away.

All traces of Akhenaten, Nefertiti and Smenkhkare were defaced and smashed out of the stelas and record-keeping tablets of ancient Egypt. Portraits of Nefertiti have been discovered hanging upside down, the ultimate insult within the culture of the time to the honour of a royal woman.

This gouging out and dishonouring is so exclusive to Akhenaten's reign, and so wholesale and seemingly demented, that it is quite clear and undeniable that something abnormal was going on regarding its execution. These frantic erasures represent Enlil's rabid hatred of the Akhenaten regime and all it symbolised, but, as ever, Enlil is nothing if not canny. The spiteful scrubbings-out, defilement and eliminations were also implemented to hide the least whisper of the identity of Miriam and Moses as Akhenaten's daughter and son.

Yet, over the Grail site, hangs the defaced Egyptian head, the statement of someone long ago who knew the real story.

The head is that of Meretaten: Miriam, guardian of the Grail.

CHAPTER 26

HOLY WANDERINGS

And so we return, perhaps with some relief, to the peace and beauty of Iona, the heart's sanctuary.

The sighing of the sea and the boundless skies are all around, a perfect encirclement of serenity. It seems timely to think of other days, and to call forth Iona's memories of long ago, when, so it is said, Jesus and Mary the Mother walked here, and then Jesus with Mary Magdalene; and one other. And, of course, John.

John! It is such a simple name, yet it sounds the boundless depths of mystery. Iona is 'The Isle of John', and when as its sanctified peak she was integral with her greater body, Mount Heredom, she was the Temple of the Holy Grail. The Grail can only come again when as a planetary community we are blessed with the knowledge of John, the True Father who loves the Mother beyond imagining, as she loves him, and who honours the Sacred Feminine. It is the False Father, the phantom of Enlil, which prevents us from connecting with the Divine Woman and re-establishing the Grail.

On Iona, there is a name for Enlil: 'An Athair Uaibhreach' in the old Gaelic, meaning 'the Haughty Father'. No name could suit Enlil's cold, sneering, outrageously arrogant stance better. He thinks he is God, our Father, having become deranged; although he remains ingenious in his deadly psychopathology.

Fiona says in relation to this:

'Once on the way from Iona to Gometra, I heard a boatman speak of him thus (as An Athair Uaibhreach) and add that he might be known by his favourite curse if one met him in mortal guise – namely, 'Deireadh nan seachd Sathurn' ort': 'The end of the seven Saturdays upon you'; that is, as my friend thought, the week of the ending of the world, which shall follow the Black Friday of the last trump, and consist of seven Black Saturdays, when Death shall have his will upon the world.'

Such interpretations of biblical text are inspired directly by Enlil, and are his sweetest fantasies. Of course the Ionians did not know the full history of Enlil, but recognised him only as an evil presence in the world that brought upon them the hereditary 'Gloom'. This Gaelic Gloom was well-known and acknowledged. One day Fiona came upon a little girl sobbing heartrendingly upon the shore. When she asked what the child's trouble was, she could only gasp out, 'The Gloom; it is the Gloom.'

However, Fiona's text does provide an important revelation. Enlil was an elected lesser lord of karma before he fell from grace; a servant of Saturn, governor of Saturday (Saturn's day).

As human beings ascend the evolutionary scale, there comes a point where it is possible to undertake such an office. The great lords of karma are on a par with the highest angels and are far beyond Enlil's level of development; but he was sufficiently evolved at one time to become a lesser lord of karma. This, of course, was why he was able to impose consequences such as the great flood upon the world.

As soon as he abused his position, he was removed from it. But he remained an outlaw, a renegade, not able to alter the law of karma but definitely capable of tinkering about at its edges. His favourite trick for a long time has been to egg us on into creating bad karma for ourselves, and then hurl it at us in full spate.

He was entrusted with the beautiful influences of Saturn, for the spirit of Saturn is the karmic commander of our solar system. Nin-khursag shared this role, and was also a lady of karma ('Nin' means 'Lady'). They were known as the Lord and Lady of the Mountain – Iona when she was Mount Heredom.

Iona has a very special relationship with Venus, and Nin-khursag's title in its deeper meaning signified the gentle guidance and orchestration of the Divine forces from Venus of which she was mistress. Venus is the only planet of our solar system with a positive or sunwise spin, and she exerts a leading light within it. Jesus and Mary Magdalene both attained and perfected their supreme Nephilim status on Venus, which had an ethereal existence before it became physicalised as a part of our solar system.

Nin-khursag has remained pure and steadfast in her shepherding of the karmic forces, and is wise, compassionate and gentle, as is Father Saturn. He imprisons in order to liberate; he uses the death forces to release us into a higher form of life. He depresses in order to increase the strength of our spring. Enlil has reversed these God-orientated principles, because by doing so he can greatly increase and exacerbate the misery on Earth.

The plan for Earth was that Enlil and Enki should work together in brotherly harmony to shepherd the Saturnine and Mercurial forces into a ladder of ascension for the benefit of humankind, guided and overlit by Nin-khursag, who could command both forces. Enki is the keeper of the Mercurial potencies.

In the human body, which is a microcosm of the universe and of God's mysteries, Saturn sits at the bottom of the spine. His energies lock the Divine Light of higher consciousness into this centre, the root chakra, which securely earths and protects it.

Eventually, the light in the heart, our personal, individuated gift from the Godhead which is the essence of our humanity, will call that light upwards to meet Mercury, whose influences sit at the point of the throat: the top of the spine. Thereafter, the head is infused with the light rising from the bottom of the spine, which, melding with the light in the heart, envelops the head.

We then become a 'shem', our first soul structure, which is still there within us, although overlaid by the safety of the sturdy pyramid. Our head, lit by the heart, in spiritual terms shines like the 'highward firestone' at the top of the shems that the Sumerians built as physical structures on Earth.

We can at this point ascend into the heavenly realms whilst still on Earth, our higher consciousness released and radiant and carrying us upwards, yet safely rooted into the planet.

For this process to become possible, we need the forces of the Grail. But in addition the Saturnine and Mercurial powers within us must be in operative harmony to do their work in enabling the facilitation. This was Enki and Enlil's sacred task: to help us to bring the energies with which they had been entrusted into perfect accord and synchronisation within ourselves so that the spiritual organism God had perfected in the human being would take flame in all its glory. It would become 'fully human'.

Before the severing of the Grail, before the downfall of Enlil, we had achieved this wondrous process with Enki and Enlil's help; but, magical and marvellous as it was, we still had far to go for the process to be realised to the height of its perfection. That is why it is said that, when we achieve it for the second time, the Earth will be inundated with a greater radiance than ever before.

Jesus first came to Iona with his mother as a young boy of 12. Mary, his mother, had sailed to Britain with her great-uncle Joseph of Arimathea (Mari-thea, Mother God), her son Jesus, and her first child, Naomi, who was 14. They all alighted upon Iona.

Mary, the Virgin, was given this designation because of her purity. It referred to the light irradiating her chakras, the 'Seven Lamps of Heaven', which equate with the seven rays of creation and the seven rays of the rainbow, although the colours within the chakras differ from those of the spectrum.

Nevertheless, there is a link. The chakras shine with a pure white or golden light, and sometimes with a clear light in which there is a play of delicate colours, deeply lovely and mystical. Only the sanctified soul shines with the perfect light of its seven lamps of heaven. Whether a person has experienced sexual union or not is irrelevant to the status of the true meaning of virginity.

In one of the earliest copies of Mark's gospel, rescued in 1873 from a dark cupboard in St Catherine's Convent upon Mount Sinai by the 'Sinai Sisters', Agnes Lewis and Margaret Gibson, the text states clearly and unequivocally that Jesus was fathered by Joseph, Mary's husband. It then goes on to state just as clearly and unequivocally throughout the story of Jesus's birth and upbringing that Mary, his mother, was a virgin who gave birth to Jesus.

There is a passage in the same gospel, called 'the secret Gospel of Mark' when the text is left whole, which was removed from later versions. It describes a ceremony of love that John the Beloved underwent with Jesus after being raised from the grave as Lazarus, upon which he became 'John': a sacred titular designation.

After this ceremony, John became known as 'John the Virgin', as he is described in the Gnostic gospels. His 'seven lamps of heaven' had been lit by the holy rites he received, which comprised the final touch of hallowed flame to the tinder within the chakras prepared and refined by his soul.

Mark evidently understood the important definition of the word 'virgin', and his gospel, in the true translation of the meaning of 'virgin', makes perfect sense.

Mary undertook a different, connubial form of the ceremony of love with Joseph in order to conceive Jesus. It was a sexual rite in which there was no selfish desire, but only love. This was necessary for the male aspect of the mighty Nephilim soul that was Jesus to manifest in flesh – all had to be absolutely pure. In order to 'earth' Jesus properly, Naomi had to be born first to Mary, to open the door through which Jesus entered earthly conditions. The power of the Divine Woman, working through an earthly human soul, was a vital component of this great enterprise.

Mary Magdalene, the feminine aspect of this same great Nephilim soul, did not require such specialised conditions, because it is always easier for women to manifest than it is for men. Mary came through the union of Mary Jacob with Matthew Cyrus, a Hebrew priest.

Matthew Cyrus belonged to the secret order of priests known as Rex Deus. They were grouped under the names of archangels (Michael, Gabriel, etc.), and they ritually impregnated certain chosen young women, who were then married into influential families. The process ensured the bloodline could avail itself of the influence needed to counteract Enlil as far as possible in human society, and Rex Deus and its rites persist today.

Rumours of Rex Deus have led some to believe (not without manipulation from our favourite psychopath) that this organisation represents the fearsome and nightmarish 'Syndicate' that was an earthly representation of the circle of conspirators which Enlil set up countless years ago. In fact it comprises part of its antidote and exists purely to serve humanity, although some members do fall over their feet of clay, as in the case of Matthew Cyrus. However, the stumbling ones are quickly weeded out.

The Syndicate (sometimes erroneously referred to as 'the Zionist Plot') is a real and remorseless hidden organisation with worldwide underground links. These often manifest above ground in movements such as the Bilderberg group, who meet once a year under armed guard and dispense the white powder to invited guests who go on to seize worldly power soon afterwards, or the equally obscene Skull and Bones club, to which many American Presidents seem to have belonged.

The Syndicate is also involved in vast networked circles of ritual child abuse and other forms of extreme cruelty and degradation whose emanations are used as a direct power-source for Enlil's circle and the Naphidem. Some Jewish people are involved in maintaining the Syndicate and carrying forward its black torch; but then representatives of every nation and religious group are similarly involved; and Jewish people are certainly not over-represented.

It is well to take care not to scapegoat the Jewish people. We collude with Enlil when we do so. They offered themselves in self-sacrifice for the scapegoat role, because their group-soul saw that it was virtually inevitable that such a role would have to be fulfilled. But that arose from their nobility of soul, and does not serve as our excuse.

The priest who impregnated Mary Jacob fell from grace. He was from the Order of Melchisedek, one of the divisions of the Rex Deus brotherhood. He desired her, and deceived her into thinking that her impregnation took place under the usual circumstances. But it did not, and Mary Jacob was left pregnant without a prospective husband, because no marriage had been arranged. She joined Mary and Joseph's family (she was a cousin), and the two young women gave birth in Bethlehem within 11 days of one another (12 inclusive days).

Poor Mary Jacob was the reason why no proper lodgings were offered to Joseph and his wife; people were hostile towards this older man with two pregnant young women ready to give birth, only one of whom was his wife. They disapproved, and rejected the little party accordingly. Mary Magdalene's illegitimacy was also the reason why, later in life, she was condemned as 'harmatolos', 'one who misses the mark', and was spitefully spoken against.

Mary the Mother, Naomi, Jesus and Joseph of Arimathea came to Iona for the same reason that they travelled the rest of the British Isles together – to awaken the beautiful fountains of light that had been secured deep in the very soil of Britain, the Mystic Isle; so deep that it was as if they were imprisoned. They had to be released; and whilst Jesus and Joseph expressed the Sacred Masculine Principle in undertaking this holy work, Mary, with the help of Naomi, expressed the Sacred Feminine Principle and undertook the actual work of stimulating and liberating these fountainheads of God-light.

They were being made ready for the sweeping flame from the highest realms that would ignite them as an initiation into their brightest and most potent radiance once the Grail was reconnected. This could have happened in the first century, within a few decades of the holy family's visit and endeavour in Britain.

Sadly, because of its terrible shackles to Enlil's influence, the collective human spirit refused to embrace the liberty it was offered. Nevertheless, the great process of emancipation began when the Christ-Being touched down through Jesus and Mary Magdalene, who brought Sara-Tamar back to Earth.

The buried light had been infused into Britain, and especially into Iona, by the Master Craftworkers amongst the Nephilim, who had directed the Divine forces – the God-light – into the rocks that were escorted to Earth by the law of gravity. They are a spiritual guild from on high that extends to Enki and his co-workers.

The Divine light was protected and increased by the rites of the esoteric brotherhoods through the ages: the Druids, the Essenes, and others deeper back in time which are yet part of one whole. The secret sisters who know the sacredness of nature and the sanctity of the Earth were prominent in this process. This worldwide brotherhood became more exoteric as it fed into the Templars, and later into the Masons and the Rosicrucians.

It seems that the Holy family visited every natural shrine upon Iona that Fiona cherished throughout her lifetime. Upon Dûn-I, Mary the Mother let her soul wing into the heavens in devotion and prayer, accompanied by her children Naomi and Jesus, and her kinsman Joseph. From the haven in the rocks they watched the sun rise and were greeted by angels.

They drank from the Pool of Healing, and blessed it, and drew light like pearls from it; their serene faces were reflected in its tranquil depths. They took the fairy path up between Sgéur Iolaire and Cnoc Druidean where no ordinary mortal can go, and their feet shone with its radiance. They paid homage to the Port of the Coracle, where in future years a beacon of the temple of John would disembark with his cowled brethren and light a lamp that shines into our hearts today, reflecting the eternal radiance of Iona.

They knelt in spiritual rapture upon the green airidh that looked across the sea to Ireland, and murmured benisons over the Spouting

Cave, so that even the elemental creature within it was so struck with light that it began to understand the mystery of Love and felt the first tremor that will one day transform it into an angel.

Fingal's Cave received magical resonance in its depths from the music of their orisons, for many of these were given forth in song. The haunting melodies it sent across the waters were even sweeter from then on. The Giant's Causeway heard the enchantment of those songs and resisted the waves, its heart's desire to reconnect with the Isle of Staffa and so draw closer to Iona; for the rocks and stones of our Earth are resonant with feeling.

The Holy Family wandered in Port Ban, and blessed the hallowed light of the old gods that gave us our name: Hu, the God of Light and Manannan of the sea, for these ancient tales enshrine a secret. So close was Britain in its earliest days to India and the sub-continent in spirit, in ideas and philosophy and religion, that the Brahmins spoke of the sanctified land in the north as the seat of the fathers of the human race – the Hu-Mann being, the creature that came forth from the sea and became filled with the light of heaven.

To the Divine Forges their feet turned, and in that mystic place of pure spirit they communed with the Great Ones on Iona – Ain, Ar-Thor: the spirits of the Divine Woman and the True Father; Archangel Michael, Brigid, and the throng of bright angels led by the White Angel of Iona that danced upon its scarlet flame, who in time to come would teach Fiona how to pray to the Divine Woman.

And to a secret chamber they went which led beneath Iona's surface; a special cavern that they especially blessed, for one would come after them and be born in this place upon whom many hopes depended.

And then they repaired to the meeting-place of their hosts, where kind hospitality awaited the foot-weary travellers.

Their hosts were a community of Druid high priestesses; for Iona was their place of command, and their sanctuary.

CHAPTER 27

MARY MAGDALENE

The feminine community of Druids upon Iona worked with Mary, Jesus, Naomi and Joseph of Arimathea to undertake the partial reconnection of the Divine forces enshrined and buried there. This deeply sacred ceremony was a forerunner of what will one day comprise the Great Reconnection in its entirety.

A beacon was lit upon Dûn-I, to 'open the sacred eye' once more, a ritual was undertaken by the shore to greet the sacred sea, and a perambulation of the Machar (the sandy plain beyond the shore) was essayed. The procession carried tapers, and sang orisons. Angel voices sounded, as many as the stars, among their own. Mary and Naomi descended into Iona's chamber of secrets to complete the calling forth of the hallowed light of the Shekinah, of Mother God.

The next day, the party left amid loving farewells. The solemnity and the joy of far-reaching destiny touched them all. Mary and her daughter had lit a flame that would never go out on this consecrated island, and her son, working with Joseph of Arimathea, had courted that flame in the strength of his spirit.

When Jesus came again to Iona, it was with Mary Magdalene. Fiona tells a strange story that belongs to Ionian folklore about this compelling, enigmatic figure: that she roamed the world with a blind man who was her devotee, that her 'first husband' tracked her there, killed the blameless blind man and cut off her long red hair, and that she wept until she died.

The story ends (in Fiona's words):'One of Colum's monks found her, and took her to Iona, and she was buried in a cave. No-one but Colum knew who she was. Colum sent away the monk who had found her, because he was always mooning and lamenting. She had a great wonderful beauty to her.'

It is poignantly strange that the monk who carries her to the cave on sacred Iona begins to see visions of the Sacred Feminine (as if at last the scales are removed from his eyes), and his heart is struck with love and lament for what the world has lost. He is the blind man resurrected, in holy garb, with his eyes opened to the wonder of the Divine Woman, sorrowing because no-one can see his vision.

Iona knows all secrets, and they surface, in plain sight and yet unseen, in her storytellers' genius. There is no literal truth in the story, of course. It is entirely symbolic. Mary's remains lie nowhere on Earth, for her body was changed, and she ascended without the need to cast it off, in the same way that Jesus did. And yet the inner shrine of Iona, her sanctified 'cave', contains the sleeping potential of a treasure that will lead the world out of captivity.

When Mary Magdalene and Jesus came to Iona together, it was to clear and open the crown chakra of the world. The crown chakra is linked to the heart, and Britain is Earth's heart chakra. But Iona is the heart's link to the crown chakra.

They came before returning to their homeland for their three-year ministry, for Mary took an active, though hidden, part in this. It would culminate, of course, in the Crucifixion. But after Jesus's death on the cross, he was able, before ascending to the highest spheres, to open up the dimension that Noah and Enlil had so carefully sealed and to read, with Mary Magdalene, the contents of the emerald tablet.

Mary spoke them to John the Beloved, her brother, as if in a trance, and he made the transcripts into a book. It was called *The Book of Love*, also known as the *Lost Gospel of John*, and it was hidden away for safekeeping with nothing but a barely breakable code to point to its whereabouts.

The ceremonies in preparation for the coming of the Holy Grail which Jesus and Mary Magdalene enacted on Iona were deeply personal, and involved the rites of the sacred marriage; so we will not intrude with recounted vision. But a grace and a sweetness was renewed on Iona through them that will ever be a component of her peace, her magic and her abiding mystery. And it is because of those beautiful rites that the Divine Forges were activated again in the spiritual atmosphere of Iona, and Fiona was able to see them in a living dream.

They entailed ceremonies of calling upon, communion with and secreting within the sacred land of Iona the ancient living starlight, and blending within themselves the light of the sun and the moon.

Sara-Tamar, the daughter of Mary and Jesus, came to Iona as a young woman to facilitate the rescue and transcription of the emerald tablet, whose teachings must be embraced before humanity can fully reconnect with the Holy Grail. Only with Sara-Tamar enthroned at Iona's heart could the rescue of the emerald tablet be accomplished. She is the Divine Woman, and one day she will resume her Queenship within the Holy Mountain. She prepared the way for Naomi, the sister of Jesus, to return in our time and finally open the door she created in the higher ethers 2,000 years ago, so that this might come to be. Naomi has reincarnated and awaits the call to set out for Iona.

Sara-Tamar, in herself the Holy Grail, was the one prize the dark Syndicate craved. She had to be hidden away in Ireland, a country that holds a special spiritual force of protection. She went to Rome to correct the misconceptions of Paul, who fell desperately in love with her and finally espoused her teachings. Many documents attributed to Paul were forged, as biblical scholars with no axe to grind confirm. The idea was to attempt to hide the true scope of his teachings.

However, it has to be said that there were three great stages in the life of St Paul: his pre-Christian life, his early Christian life, and his post-Sara-Tamar life. Let us just say that there were distinct problems with the first two stages!

Sara-Tamar was thrown into a Roman prison for Christians, despite the remonstrances of Paul to Roman officials. He was himself promptly put under house arrest, as the authorities were afraid that he would attempt to rescue her with his own hands (they were right). There she starved to death, which broke Paul's heart, but also deepened and blessed it.

Her work at the eight stations of the Grail had been done, and Paul promised to bear onwards the torch that her father and mother had lit and that she had endeavoured to put into his hands, despite the incursions of hostile forces. Sara-Tamar's body did not remain in the Roman prison to be buried or discarded, because of course she ascended in the same way as her parents, her father before her and her mother afterwards.

John the Beloved Disciple went with his sister, Mary Magdalene, to Iona after they had lived for some years in France.

There he fell in love with Elaine, the High Priestess among the community of Druidesses on Iona.

CHAPTER 28

JOHN MARTINUS

There was a sorrow in this love that John the Beloved bore for Elaine, the High Priestess of the Druids on Iona. Each knew their destiny as the reading of an ever-present scroll within them. Yes, they were to be allowed to come together; but then they would part, for each had spiritual work to do in the world, and their bitterness – their gift of myrrh on the mortal plane – was that their paths led away from one another.

John spent much time in France, where he was preparing a small select group – a radiant seed – for the inundation of light that would shine, first through many secret brotherhoods in Europe, through the future Arthurian court, and then through the medium of the Cathars and the Templars a thousand years into the future. The edifice of their inspiration was bilateral with that of the Bogomils ('lovers of God') who came from the Baltic regions, where Miriam had dispensed her wisdom so many centuries ago to a magical brotherhood which had existed millennia before she vouchsafed her new revelations to them.

What linked the Cathars and the Bogomils was their Grail knowledge and the encompassment in their tradition of Miriam or Meretaten (Grace Cooke), leading back through the esoteric history of Enki and Ham (Zoroaster) and leading forward through Mary Magdalene and Sara-Tamar.

St Martin of Tours, celebrated on Iona, was a prominent Bogomil who initiated the French and Baltic connection during his lifetime in the 4th century and was a preserver of the Grail mysteries. Secrets associated with his guardianship wait to be revealed concerning America and Europe, and the rising to prominence of the Cathars. The red granite cross dedicated to him on Iona pays tribute to his early association with the Cathars, and his great contribution to the Grail quest.

It might be said that the Bogomils had their own particular take on these mysteries, and exoterically their beliefs are hard to fathom. Yet there was beauty and truth in them, and they responded to that radiant seed sown by John that took such flourishing root at about the time of the first millennium. Of course, there had been secret brotherhoods and communities in France and contiguous countries which had always embraced teachings from the emerald tablet, ever since it had been transcribed in AD 54. These communities became the Cathars.

And so a number of Bogomil Wise Ones, and with them their culture and ideas, made their pilgrimage to France, or, in John's time and in the Cathars' time, the Nation of Occitania as it was known then – the land of the sacred figure 8, the Sacred Marriage, relating to Jesus and Mary Magdalene, Enki and Nin-khursag, Mother-Father God. It was here that Mary Magdalene, her daughter Sara-Tamar, and John, lived together with Mary Jacob who was their mother and Sara-Tamar's grandmother, in a great network of limestone caves that stretched underground for 200 miles.

In these caves the Temple of John was born anew, earthed and consecrated. It was a Johannine Christian Temple, as it always had been, because the mighty Christ Being in the heavens, the Son-Daughter, had inspired and infused and directed the steps of Enki and Nin-khursag from the beginning.

Jesus and Mary Magdalene comprised the great vehicle through which this supernal consciousness would descend to Earth. John's emphasis was slightly different in that he represented the True Father, as Nin-khursag reflected the Divine Woman, the 'drop' of the Mother; but all served God, and the three ineffable aspects of God: Mother-Father-Child.

No truer servants of the Divine were ever born to Earth than Enki and Nin-khursag – except for two others; for Jesus and Mary Magdalene were greater souls, more exalted servants, even than these former shining ones, because they were of the purest Nephilim who, through the miracle of miracles, actually descended into fleshly form on Earth.

John's mission was to light a heavenly lamp that would shine through the years until, at last, the whole world would take flame. John's service was rendered to the Christ, although, as mentioned, he had his own emphasis that was part of the great mission. Until the world understood the True Father, and thereby the Mother, it would be impossible for it to understand the illumination of the Christ spirit, which is not a religion but will purify every religion, and will give clarity of vision, heart and understanding to those who prefer to follow no religion.

John had many books to write, for all the biblical documents attributed to John were written personally by him. Scholars say that his gospel was the latest to appear, but in fact there is just as much evidence to suggest that it was the earliest, as it draws on Gnostic sources that were already established well before the three-year ministry of Jesus.

John lived to be well over a hundred years old, and his death was no death, but the contractual passing on of an Avesa into another prepared and waiting body. Throughout his gospel he emphasises the role of women and demonstrates the significance of the number eight.

Agnes Lewis, one of the Sinai twin sisters who discovered the earliest extant copy of the gospels, noted with appreciation that, in the story of the woman at the well in John's gospel, Jesus is described as standing when he speaks to her, although he had formerly been seated. 'I like to think that our Lord would stand in the presence of a woman, as a mark of respect for her,' commented Agnes perceptively. She had certainly picked up on the Jesus and John link, leading back to Enki, the world's first Gentleman!

John, in his writings, also acted as Mary's faithful amanuensis, compiling the greatest book the world will ever know, for it will be the beginning of our journey to freedom. The book is a transcription of the emerald tablet, which Mary and Jesus read together whilst Jesus was in the higher worlds and Mary was still on Earth.

His ultimate sacrifice on the cross enabled him to unlock the hidden dimension in which Noah and Enlil had concealed the emerald tablet, and together, as if by satellite link, Mary Magdalene and Jesus drew out its wisdom in a flow of immortal words, which Mary spoke to John, their attendant scribe. The transcription was given to the world in Occitania.

However, as mentioned, the emerald tablet could not be transcribed until Sara-Tamar had reached the age of 21 (the 'trinity of seven'). At that time, she journeyed as a sacred ritual from Ireland, passing through Fingal's Cave to Iona, using the ancient causeway that once linked the two isles. Not until Sara-Tamar occupied the ancient throne upon Iona (an ethereal throne, located within the island in a secret chamber) could the process of transcription begin.

As she took her place upon the throne in holy Iona, the unholy dimension in which Enlil and Noah had locked away the emerald tablet finally crumbled away so that it lay revealed before Jesus. The light deep within its heart connected with the light of his consciousness, entering through the sacred 'ayin' or eye.

Yet it was not Jesus's consciousness alone that held the power to receive the light of the emerald tablet. Mary Magdalene, dwelling on Earth in her physical body, fused her consciousness with his in the perfect expression of their true identity – the Divine Androgyne. Only then could the emerald tablet be read, as if with the light of a spiritual laser. Mary spoke its language, translated into earthly words; and John transcribed them; but it was only through the link that Sara-Tamar provided with Divine Mother – the All – that the deed could be accomplished.

Not even Jesus's sacrifice on the cross could have sufficed to bring about this great miracle had not Sara-Tamar taken her place on Iona. As in olden days, when she had come to Earth as Derdekea or Ain – the Divine Drop of the Essence of Mother-God – it was her presence alone that could connect Earth with Heaven. Sara-Tamar: she who is the Divine Daughter; she who is, in her innermost essence and being, the blessed Holy Grail.

John wrote the book in Latin and it remained with Mary and her companions in the Languedoc. At a point in history when the Vatican seemed ready to free itself from its demonic allegiance (culminating in the time of Pope Urban VIII) it was given into the hands of the Roman Church. Sadly, the succeeding pope was very much in the clutches of Enlil and destroyed the book by fire, ritually cursing its ashes and consigning them, contained in a jar, into the river Tiber.

After John's original transcription, Sara-Tamar made two copies of it, also in Latin, the second of which was dispatched to Jerusalem for the use of the Church arising there under the leadership of James the Righteous. The book was eventually secreted in Chartres cathedral, where it will be discovered by one prophesied to find it within a year or so after the Grail has been reconnected (see the end of Chapter 32).

Certain valid documents will be unearthed in company with it, including the prophecies of Sara-Tamar; for Sara-Tamar was indeed a prophet and seer. It is her prophecy that predicts the discovery of the

Chartres copy of the transcribed emerald tablet (the *Book of Love*), and specifically who will retrieve it.

The initial copy of the *Book of Love*, first of all taken from Occitania to Ireland for safekeeping with Sara-Tamar in her dûn and thereafter borne back to the same region to be buried in a protected crypt within King Dagobert's family chapel (Rennes-le-Château), was finally laid to rest in St Margaret's Burial Ground within the precincts of Lincoln cathedral.

It is marked by the 28th tombstone there, dedicated with the name Raynor, ('regnal', 'ray of light', therefore 'Reign of Light' in its combined meaning), a little to the left beneath an open grassy space, in a crypt which once belonged to the church of St Margaret of Antioch, demolished long ago. It is sealed and protected, as it has been since the 12th century, when it was removed to England at the time of the Crusades.

The crypt is overlaid by the emerald covering of the grassy burial ground, and the subterranean tunnels which led to it have been purposely collapsed and filled with rubble. Its resting place is impregnable, and will remain so until the time is right for it to be retrieved, which will not be long in coming.

It will be recovered within a few years – five at most – of the discovery of its sister copy at Chartres. A great deal of documentation – including Sara-Tamar's prophecies – and a number of artefacts will be found with it that will greatly extend our understanding of its significance and mystery.

Due to the rules of her ministry, John the Beloved was able to remain with Elaine for only a short time, during which Elaine conceived a son. A ceremony of the Sacred Marriage took place between them to facilitate the conception. Afterwards, deeply sorrowful because he had to leave her behind but moved in his spirit with a new inspiration born from the depths of love, John parted from his Druidess.

He set out for Patmos, with all the wild Druidry of a magical prophet transferred to his grieving but stimulated heart. He was ready to write his second great book – *Revelation*. His third would be his gospel. The searing exquisite words and the transcendental cosmic visions of *Revelation* were given to him on Patmos, but his heart-pierced inspiration flowed from Iona and from his love who dwelt there with his son.

167

John Martinus was born to Elaine (pronounced 'Ellen') in the underground chamber secreted in Iona where he had been conceived. He spent two formative years within the Druidess community upon Iona, and then Elaine took him to Glastonbury, where he met his father for the first time.

Her little son remained there with him until his next mission called him away, but his mother stayed with him for some years and eventually initiated him into the mysteries of a secret temple within Chalice Hill, or Glastonbury Tor. Its location was within a great underground chamber with mystical connections to the hidden chamber within Iona.

John Martinus was a deeply spiritual man; a true mystic. St Columba mirrored many of his characteristics. He was known and loved by the people of the elements, the ethereal folk of Faery, who trusted him and worked with him. He took his mission of the true Christ Light – beautiful beyond imagining and recognised as a magical starlight of the spirit by the Faery peoples – deep inside the Earth, where there is a community of human beings who withdrew into the interior fastnesses of the planet during the time that Atlantis sank.

(Remains of Atlantis are still there, below the Atlantic seabed, but undiscoverable so far because the continual agonised quaking of the Earth for more than a century after the continent sank caused great mudslides and continent-wide sinkholes to occur below the waves. The constant quakes buried these rolling mudslides deeper and deeper, until the remnants of the Atlantis civilisation were interred so far below the seabed that it will require very advanced technology to locate them.)

These people who went within the Earth were taught the true teachings of Christ, and followed John Martinus so devotedly that they called their underworld country after him – St Martin's Land. They knew no war or strife or sickness.

John Martinus encouraged close and brotherly co-operation between this human community and the elemental people, who taught their human friends to eat so wisely, of such spirit-blessed crops, that they lived for centuries and their skin turned a beautiful, delicate shade of green, like a tree in leaf in the early spring. They were children of the emerald tablet, because John Martinus taught them his inherited knowledge of it.

They also shared a very special inheritance that encouraged their balanced spiritual expression of life to imbue them with this green colour. The deepest origin of this inheritance was from the green race of Perseus – the race of the Eagles who came to Earth as one of the six races who would join together to pass into and build her humanity (see p. 301). But the inheritance in its later stages also came from another planet in our own solar system, as we shall see.

John Martinus married an Occitanian princess related to his mother, the Ionian Elaine. He fathered the Merovingian dynasty, which was very much associated with the Elven race, as Lawrence Gardner attests in his remarkable works. This Elven connection was, of course, directly associated with John Martinus in that he fostered the links between the two races, whilst Elaine shared ancestral bonds with the Elven people, who were once a community on Earth.

St Martin of Tours, also celebrated on Iona as well as the enigmatic St Martin (John Martinus), was of his line. He was a key descendant of John Martinus, steeped in the mystery of France and Occitania, although he was a Hungarian army officer who, when in France, had sliced his military cloak in two so that he could give half to a naked beggar in the depths of winter. This slicing in two of a military status symbol for the sake of compassion and succour shows him to be a prominent John-man.

After this incident, St Martin, who longed for a contemplative, solitary life, was nonetheless persuaded to remain in Tours and become its Bishop, in which office he remained for the rest of his life. Tours is on the highly significant pilgrimage route to Santiago de Compostela, which leads from the cathedral there to Rosslyn (which we will examine later) and translates as 'Tower', the supreme virginal symbol of the Divine Feminine.

St Martin of Tours was Hungarian, as a number of John Martinus's descendants had established themselves in the region, drawn there by the settlement of Miriam's wandering followers. They belonged to the Dragon Court, with Egyptian links back to Miriam, her grandmother Tiye, and Tiye's grandmother Tuya who were of the secret sisterhood of this Dragon Queen Court which had been formally acknowledged, sponsored and protected by the Egyptian queen Sobeknefru. Its roots belonged to earliest Mesopotamia and even deeper into the past, and its members comprised the keepers of esoteric history and Grail knowledge. St Martin of Tours held high position in this court, although he travelled to France in honour of, and at the call of, his ancestors. He brought the first clearly defined Bogomil spirituality to France (although it was always bilateral) and established a precedent for others to make pilgrimage there.

St Ninian, who was a good friend of St Martin of Tours, dedicated his Scottish church, 'the White House', to his friend's memory. It was the beginning of an American association, because the Temple of John, which later included the Templars, cherished a hope that America could be built on the foundations of the teaching of the Temple.

The march of materialism has ensured that there cannot be any realistic chance of this until after the return of the Grail. Nevertheless, the ideals and hopes of the American nation were first birthed on Iona, for both St Ninian and St Martin of Tours, who were among the earliest brethren to cradle these ideals and hopes for America in their dreams, belonged to the Temple of John, whose mystic centre was Iona.

America was known to the esoteric brotherhood many centuries before Columbus. Jesus and Mary Magdalene had visited the country together; and we must not forget that in the far distant past, Scotland comprised a part of the land mass of that great continent. A link even exists between St Columba and Christopher Columbus, although only the saint was a holy man. One externalised the Temple of John successfully, the other did not, although the potential was there within him to have done so.

There is a mystery regarding St Ninian, St Martin of Tours, Iona and America, which is beyond the scope of this book but nevertheless waits to be revealed.

As mentioned, a very important branch of Tiâmat's special bloodline continued through John Martinus. The Merovingians comprised a descent of kings that were intimately associated with the Grail, and which constituted significant members of the Desposyni, the bloodline associated with Christ (Jesus and Mary Magdalene). There were no direct descendants of Jesus and Mary once Sara-Tamar had died childless, but of course the members of their extended families were numerous.

The Romans, both before and after the establishment of the Vatican, continually sent secret agents out into the world to assassinate any member of the Desposyni that they could hunt down. They were certainly successful in the case of the Merovingians. Members of this royal bloodline were obstructed with brutal relentlessness, until finally King Dagobert was killed by Church agents in a forest, impaled to a tree by a lance through the eye (symbolic of Roman attempts to put out the sacred 'ayin').

As a five-year-old child, Dagobert had been kidnapped and taken to Ireland after the death of his father, King Sigebert II. His kidnappers were apparently in league with their master, Mayor Grimoald, who was akin to a modern-day Prime Minister and who colluded with the Popish plot to stamp out the rule of the Merovingians in Gaul. He put his own son on the throne after the (contrived) mysterious disappearance of the little Prince Dagobert. But his kidnappers were in fact members of the secret Temple of John, who took Dagobert to Ireland, the only place on Earth where he would be safe. There, he was escorted to Sara-Tamar's dûn. She appeared to him in spirit, and gave the transcripts of the emerald tablet into his keeping.

Eventually, the young Prince Dagobert returned to France, where he reclaimed his father's throne and became king. His headquarters were at Rennes-le-Château, where he buried the transcripts of the emerald tablet in a vault in the crypt of the family chapel.

After his murder, his heart was removed at his former behest and buried with the Grail to protect it, for he was one of its chief guardians.

Sadly, after Dagobert's demise, the Merovingians fell into corruption through the pursuit of occult power. They became unworthy of the great destiny that would have been theirs if they had retained their gift of enlightenment from their illustrious ancestor.

Had they done so, they would have overseen the coming of the Grail in France and in Britain at the time of the rise of the Cathars and Templars, both Grail-endowed orders. Sorrowful to relate, their ethical ship went down and was lost. However, the St Clair family who settled in Rosslyn are also of the John Martinus bloodline (a branch that was fostered in Norway, so close to Iona), and they acquitted themselves very nobly indeed.

The Grail was taken to Lincoln, England, at the time of the Crusades, where in 2005, the writer and student of esoteric mysteries, Callum Jensen ('Dan Green') discovered its whereabouts. His belief is that it is not the emerald tablet that lies there, but the remains of Mary Magdalene, murdered when she was pregnant with the child of Jesus. His understanding of the story is therefore different from this one. Time will reveal all!

The death of John Martinus was never recorded. It is said that there are traces of his birth and existence within the secret chambers in Iona and in Chalice Hill in Glastonbury.

In fact John Martinus did not die, but lives on, a secret presence within our Earth. He is the Avesa Ham, who combined with Enki to enter a prepared body when Jesus and Mary Magdalene called their conjoined soul back into the body of the dead Lazarus. The soul who came forth was christened 'John the Beloved' by Jesus – John the Beloved who was Jesus's spiritual twin.

When John the Beloved's body had come to the end of its earthly life, John the Beloved (Ham/Enki) passed into John Martinus; and this soul transition was very significant indeed, as is discussed below.

Some of John Martinus's followers from our world (yet originally, long, long ago, from another) were led by him into the subterranean lands that he penetrated. His is the eternal spirit of John, he who walks in the ways of the True Father, and therefore understands the message of the supernal Christ in all its ever-unfolding dimensions.

There is one further mystery to be disclosed about John Martinus. His name, Martinus, means 'of Mars'.

The Temple of John within Egypt knew of this mystery. 'Cairo' means 'Mars'.

Vulcan, the great metalworker, forger and craftsman of the Gods, was the God of Fire, the element traditionally associated with Mars. Such is the classical legend. The esoteric legend tells us that Mars was once inhabited. We may be in the first stages of such a discovery through the space probe 'Curiosity', which has already confirmed that there was once 'sweet' water, water fit to drink and which is the basis of life, on Mars. However, the Martian civilisation was not physical, so no doubt positivist material science will not make much headway in its findings.

The Martians became entirely debased by the concept of the false Father (known on Iona as the Haughty Father). They were so relentlessly warlike that the planetary community had to be permanently removed (much as the Naphidem were removed from Earth) and all traces of their culture obliterated. The red surface of Mars is partly due to the wholesale subtle fires which engulfed their civilisation. There is nothing left of it now except a wandering spirit, which causes optical illusions, such as the stone face, the yeti, and the mermaid, all of which have appeared as illusory images upon the Martian surface.

This wandering spirit is the trace, the last breath, the drifting memory, of a great spirit belonging to Mars – its essence – which grieved for the deception that had been wrought upon its people. We might say that it was a planetary intelligence; but, as all intelligences are, it is a person.

The illusory images could be considered in the following terms.

The mermaid: the merry-maid, as Mary the Mother, Mary Magdalene, and Mary Jacob have often been portrayed; as Tiâmat has been portrayed: the Sacred Feminine presence whose dwelling is the sea; the essence of the bitter waters, whose spirit moved upon the deep, and who birthed us all.

The yeti: the missing link: the creature that arose after being selected from Homo erectus, and underwent the process of the application of a chakra system to its spine and etheric body, so that the human essence could eventually be transplanted into it: the rise of humankind.

The strangely androgynous face in stone that yet makes its point with its masculine aspect: feminine and masculine as one, with the face showing us the beautiful, poignant John-man: the ethically noble, gentle-man who knows that he is sourced in the Mother, and follows faithfully in the footsteps of the True Father.

Is the spirit of Mars trying to signal something to us – trying to tell us something: the way to evolve? What is this magical wizardry of optical illusion that plays upon its surface?

Determined that the people of Earth should not fall prey to the same terrible fate as that of the Martians, this good spirit of the True Father came to Earth to enter into and inspire Cain and the line of Ham (all of them Vulcanic Master Craftsmen). He came to forge the true man in the image of the True Father, imbued with the spirit of John: the

Demiurge or 'Higher Man' here on Earth, the 'Man of Light' who uses his craftsmanship and skills to aid, enlighten and liberate the Spiritual Man within.

Crucially, this Spiritual man, the John-man or the true man, constructs and crafts reverently from the divine material issued to him by Mother God (the Star Fire), building from that holy substance alone. All other material is steadfastly refused.

John Martinus was he who went within the interior of the Earth in his work to forge men's hearts anew. A great spirit inspired and filled him.

For he, John Martinus, who led a community of people that dwelt within the interior of the Earth, was indeed Enki; Enki, who was attuned to the grieving planetary spirit of Mars; who had fought long and hard to save its civilisation but who had been overcome in the end by Martian deafness and indifference to his efforts and his teaching, and who had come to Earth, overlit by the Christ being, to save us from descent into a similar fate.

Enki had a body on Mars as he had a body on Earth and a body belonging to the planet Nibiru, his home planet. His Martian self was grounded upon Earth in John Martinus; and he eventually took his present name, which is Fulcanelli: 'little Vulcan', in acknowledgement of his Martian connection.

John Martinus – John 'of Mars'.

CHAPTER 29

JOURNEY'S END

It is time to repair to Rosslyn Chapel, and discover its unknown link with the holy isle of Iona. There is also something hidden beneath the chapel, referred to as 'a great secret buried within Rosslyn'. We go in search of this treasure!

Rosslyn Chapel lies seven miles south of Edinburgh. It is an unfinished building; it was to have been on completion a much larger church with the present structure as its collegiate chapel. One point to be aware of from the beginning, however, is that nothing concerning Rosslyn is accidental. Everything about it makes co-ordinated statements in the service of an overarching enlightenment.

The building is unfinished; so are we, as an entity created by God; so is the dispensation to us of the emerald tablet; so is the mission of John, of Jesus and Mary Magdalene, of Sara-Tamar, the Divine Woman. They come to us to offer, not religion, but truth, truth for all humankind, truth that shall set us free. When all is finished, it will not signify an end, a sort of tomb-vault of perfection. Instead, the path will truly begin at last, revealed shining at our door.

The chapel was formally founded in 1446 by Sir William St Clair, of the family with famous Templar connections. The village surrounding it was built to furnish its craftsmen with convenient residences, because Prince William (Sir William St Clair, Prince of Orkney) assembled them from all over the world. The timber, interestingly, was shipped in from the Baltic regions.

The chapel took 40 years to build. We might note the time span in relation to the 40 years of Arthur's reign (called 'the Peace of Arthur'), the 40 regnant years of Solomon and also of his father, King David; the 40 days that Jesus spent wandering in the wilderness, and other significant designations of this esoteric number.

It is a time in which something eternal and of great import is rooted squarely and surely into the fabric of mortality and our mortal Earth. We can think of the spiritual Master Craftworkers hammering and chiselling, checking with spiritlevels to ensure all is straight and true, laying the cornerstone. Forty is the number of the builder, magical and esoteric and facilitative of bringing forth spiritual substance from the Eternal through into the mundane realm.

William St Clair died two years before his project was finished; and in the event the chapel remained a chapel in its own right and did not become the appurtenance of a much larger church. The correlation of the death of Moses before he reached the Holy Land is significant here.

William St Clair was interred within the chapel, baptising the new building with a royal burial and continuing a tradition of entombment within its vaults, prior to the raising of the chapel, whereby the corpse lay facedown (humbly venerating the Earth goddess) and coffinless in a suit of armour. It is said that Prince William's ancestors lay here, on this spot where Rosslyn Chapel was constructed. Like Iona, it was a royal burial ground.

This too bears meaning: the lordly line of the High St Clairs, associated with the Templars, were John-men of the first order and would wish to meet 'death', the Great Ascension, in their Enki-inspired garb of fish-scales, with their posture bowing to and honouring the Great Mother, in the place of their forefathers.

There is also a special reason for the assumption of this posture and why, on the last occasion that the bodies were examined, they were seen to have remained remarkably unaffected by decay, which will later be revealed. For now, we might think of the 20 interred bodies as a circle of pre-appointed guardians.

It is said that no-one can enter the chapel and fail to be touched by its beauty and mysticism. Tim Wallace-Murphy has described it as 'an enigmatic, arcane library of secrets, sculpted in stone and shrouded in mystery'. A native of Roslin village, returning from America after many years, relates how he stood 'in breathless rapture, gazing at the beauteous building, from the windows of which streamed a rich amber light, for the interior was filled by the glory of the setting sun...' Amber preserves everlastingly, in a clear golden medium, which also serves as an accurate way to describe Rosslyn Chapel.

The writer of an early guidebook said, '...the profusion of design, so abundantly shown everywhere, and the exuberant fancy of the architect strike the visitor who sees Rosslyn for the first time with an astonishment which no familiarity ever effaces'. Another admiring guidebook author quoted that the chapel is 'one of those Architectural wonders whose intricate beauties and peculiarities extort our imagination while they baffle description'.

Trevor Ravenscroft said of Rosslyn that 'The sculptures are magnificent manifestations of spiritual insight or vision, given substance in stone' and Douglas Sutherland described the chapel in an article he wrote in 1982 as 'A mediaeval masterpiece of masonry, containing some of the most exquisite carvings ever fashioned in stone...'

It is as if to experience the sight of Rosslyn Chapel's interior (and even its arresting and delightfully unusual exterior) is to be inspired to wax lyrical. And this is as it should be, for in penetrating the inner sanctum that Rosslyn represents we do indeed approach the 'Holy of Holies'. Perhaps this innate recognition is why many people have likened its architecture to Solomon's Temple, although mundane reflection equates it more with Glasgow cathedral than any other building. However, there are pointers within it that incontrovertibly relate to Solomon's temple.

Within the last decade or so, expectations have grown that Rosslyn Chapel would reveal its secrets. Ground-penetrating radar scanning shows that the vaults are intact and items are contained within them (as is to be expected even without the treasure), although to open them up would undermine the stability of the chapel.

First of all, it is important to realise that the chapel has already revealed one of its most significant treasures: a treasure which must be recognised and understood before we can proceed to what still remains a mystery. Rosslyn Chapel is ready to give us its first lesson!

Within the last few years, a remarkable discovery was made at Rosslyn Chapel. On the roof, twin beehives have been found behind two of its pinnacles, only one of which has an access hole. The entry point is an aperture in the centre of a carven flower embossed upon the stonework. Honeycombs have been found within, ungathered and ancient. It seems that the practical application of collecting honey was not the reason that the beehives were built.

The message of the twin beehives is that the chapel will offer us its golden treasure, the nourishment of its honey, of which we will be able freely to partake; but there is a golden treasure, twin spirit of the first one, which is similarly for our benefit, yet must never be accessed or disturbed but always remain sealed.

Dorothy Wordsworth, visiting the enigmatic chapel with her famous brother and describing the architecture and carvings of Rosslyn as 'exquisitely beautiful', was enchanted by these stone flowers that appear in multitudes in the chapel's interior as well as the one on the roof-pinnacle with its secret honey-gathering heart. 'They are so delicately wrought that I could have admired them for hours, and the whole of their groundwork is stained by time in the softest colours,' she recorded, in tones of a spiritual responsiveness that seemed almost to intuit their mystery.

Honey, flowers and the beehive are salient symbols of the Sacred Feminine, and were a code for the alchemists' art. Bees are also a symbol of resonance, which as we shall see is crucial in its significance.

Under the direction of Miriam, within the Ark of the Covenant as an active part of the beautiful golden Mercy Seat that Bezaleel wrought to protect humanity from the hideousness it encompassed, was placed a most mystical artefact: a pot of honey! It was placed within the shem or pinnacle that adorned the Mercy Seat as a sample of gold in a different form.

The symbolism of honey is both profoundly simple and simplistically profound.

When the 13th-century alchemist Michael Scot taught that honey falls from the air into flowers and is then collected by bees, he was not being whimsical and unscientific. He was in fact referring, via potent symbols, to closely guarded secrets regarding the distinction between the true and the false Ark of the Covenant (the one covers the other) and the vital connection between the human soul, the bee and our planetary life-support systems.

The 'honey in the air' is the divine gold of the spirit that enters us through our breath when we attune ourselves to the 'God-breath' or the 'Mother-breath', which is simply a method where each breath is imaginally drawn and released through the heart to a relaxed count of eight so that we enter the sanctified realm deep within.

Via this gentle 'God-breathing', the honey or divine gold falls into the 'flowers', which symbolise our chakra system, those points in the body (the ductless glands) where the physical is conjoined to the worlds of the spirit. In psychic vision they look like many-petalled flowers.

The most ancient alchemical secret of all is that the mystical honey flows from the Divine Feminine, and that it is necessary for human souls to absorb this substance to be united with God. Its potency was recognised as that of peace, harmony, love and burgeoning life; it was a form of the Star Fire – sweet, nourishing and golden.

What was secreted within the false Ark below the Mercy Seat and the honey was a counterfeit food made from the terrible white powder – a toxin or drug that inflamed the lower self and fomented rapacious aggression, war, misery and death.

Rosslyn's secrets teach us that we need to use the magic of the true Ark of the Covenant in overcoming the forces of our shadow self, manipulated by Enlil. The shadow enslaves us by filling our minds – our thoughts, emotions, percipience and attitudes – with fear, intolerance, distaste, harshness, dread, unhappiness, criticism and negativity, from which anger and even violence and desecration arise.

To counteract this dark invasion, we nourish ourselves with the food of the gods. This 'nectar of supreme excellence' is, in earthly terms, simply honey, for, as Michael Scot knew, honey has an unsurpassed ethereal counterpart that nourishes the soul, and the magic of the Sacred Feminine (known as the Star Fire essence in the Dew-Cup) dwells within it.

It is gathered from flowers, just as the Scarlet Priestesses of ancient temples were the flow-ers who fed the Star Fire to the earliest kings when the original human pattern of the androgyne was split; prior to the split this was done so naturally it was hardly discernible. It is indeed a form of natural gold. Most of all, it is a pure gift of nature.

However, although it is very good to take physical honey in balanced quantities, we can use its ethereal qualities with great effect to thwart the intentions of Enlil's dark interlopers. We do this by first softening, making gentle, the negative thoughts or feelings that come swirling into our soul-space – our mentality and emotional self. Soften and make gentle the way the inrush of negativity has made you feel.

Now turn the focus of the ayin – the inner eye – to the thought of honey. It is utterly sweet, like the balm of a new day or evening birdsong.

It is not cloying or saccharin-sweet, for its sweetness turns the soul to God. Its sweetness is the divine antidote to the burden of degradation and disgust, or the burning sting of distress, that the negative inundation has created within you.

Take the ethereal essence of honey, like an angelic thought, deep inside your mind and soul, into your emotional self, into your suffering nervous self. You can breathe it in using the Mother's Breath.

It will actually soothe away an acid stomach or a sense of bitterness in the mouth and throat. It gets rid of the deposits of misery and sullenness and general negativity that envelop us from within. It gets rid of the gloop and mire of mind-controlling influences. Take in ethereal honey, take in sweetness, and feed it to your heart and mind. Feed it to the ayin, and look out at the world through softened, gentled eyes, through sweetened vision.

Now let the honey flow from your heart and mind into your language. Dare to use this new language! It takes away the tongue's need to lash and flail. It transforms the wormwood in our everyday linguistic constructs. It cleanses and purifies. It is the secret of the true Ark of the Covenant. Let us feed from the Mother, and only from the Mother.

You can do the same with pain, sickness and irritation. Pour honey into the site of distress, ethereal honey from the gardens of paradise. It is the kiss of God, the touch of the angels. It will help you. Think of an inundation of honey, mellifluent, cradling you in gentle sweetness. Your very bones will respond.

Physical honey does not destabilise our blood sugar levels because it has been pre-digested in the stomach of the honey bee. It contains every vitamin, every mineral and every trace element in just the right quantities we need to sustain our life-force at its optimum level, ensure protection of the kidneys and avoid overtaxing the liver and bowel. It clarifies brain activity yet is a natural sedative.

Take physical honey in your diet, take ethereal honey in your daily meditations and whenever the need arises, and note how much better you feel! Honey, the essence of correct nourishment, is one of the secrets of the Grail, numbered amongst the Grail Hallows.

The alchemists say that honey is associated with Venus, and that the bees are its priests. Certainly they seem to hum with Tibetan monkish resonance! When the Grail teachings come to us in their fullness, they, like honey, will astonish us with their purity, their simplicity, and their power.

Meanwhile, Rosslyn bids us to feed only on what is pure, what comes to us from the bounty of nature. If we nourish ourselves on every level solely with the food that is in harmony with the Star Fire, with the Mother's heart, then the sacred golden honey will fall into our 'flowers', our chakras will be filled with light, and our 'Seven Lamps of the Virgin' will shine out with perfect radiance.

Having taken on board the message of Rosslyn's beehives, we can proceed to the heart of its mystery.

CHAPTER 30

THE SEVEN LAMPS OF HEAVEN

Tim Wallace-Murphy and Marilyn Hopkins, in their inspiring and knowledgeable book on Rosslyn, explain how the chapel is the culmination of seven ancient sites held sacred to the seven planets of astrology which equate with our chakra system. These locations were dedicated to the tutelary spirits or gods of the planets, which were seen as entities that help us in a very specific and direct way to achieve enlightenment.

Each one was the site of a Druidic planetary oracle, which eventually housed a Roman temple to its associated god, and ultimately a Christian church or cathedral. These Gothic buildings were constructed by the Knights Templar, an order of esoteric masters who possessed Gnosis – the inner knowledge of God.

The seven sites formed a route of pilgrimage for Gnostics and Christian mystics which began in Compostela in Spain and passed through France to culminate in Rosslyn, which was seen as the site of Saturn and as equating to the human crown chakra.

This is a vital discovery, and from the perspective of the story delineated in these pages it can perhaps be seen how a beautiful configuration of sacred sites came together to form a rainbow – the sign and symbol of the true covenant with Mother-Father God – feeding into Rosslyn so that the pure white light of the unified spectrum could flow forth, upwards and outwards, from the sacred site of Rosslyn, the symbolic crown chakra of this particular configuration.

However, it should be made clear that, according to what has been revealed to me, Rosslyn does not equate with the crown chakra. Nevertheless, although not a crown chakra or centre in itself, it does stand as crown chakra for the purposes of this all-important seven-site system, known as 'the apocalyptic configuration in stone'.

The system which has been applied to correlate the Compostela site in Spain with the first or base chakra, and Rosslyn with the last or crown chakra, belongs to Fulcanelli. From what is known of Fulcanelli, every system and idea that he delineates leads to the revelation of greater and higher truth. He is the latest incarnation of the Avesa Ham/Enki who became John the Beloved, then afterwards John Martinus, and many other figures throughout history both hidden and renowned.

Fulcanelli is a master of alchemy who spawned the idea early in the 20th century that profound secrets were to be discerned in the Gothic architecture of the great mediaeval cathedrals, and his gradation of the planets (with the moon as the lowest and Saturn as the highest) is certainly illuminating and thought-provoking – and an ingenious form of alchemy, as we shall see.

By applying his theories, Compostela ('field of the Star'), dedicated to the Moon, is seen as the starting point of the sacred journey to Rosslyn. (It is worth remembering at this point that Iona was once known as 'Ioua', 'the isle of the Moon'.) Along the path of this sacred journey, pilgrims devoted themselves to the purification and opening of each chakra. Moving on from the Cathedral of St James of Compostela, they visited the church at Toulouse and then the cathedrals of Orléans, Chartres, Notre-Dame de Paris and Amiens before finally arriving at Rosslyn.

The cathedral at Compostela is dedicated to St James the Greater, but underneath the floor of the cathedral lies a church dedicated to St James the Lesser, known as St James the Righteous. We might note that his memorial church lies underground in the manner of a footing and a base.

James the Righteous was, it seems, the man entrusted with the establishment of the true Christian Church by Jesus. Peter undertook this role; but in the Gnostic gospels Peter is more than once reported to have made an attempt on Mary Magdalene's life ('because he hateth all our sex', said Mary). He declared that women have no souls, and, in Mary Magdalene's gospel, it is Peter who tries to rouse the disciples against her. It is only the intervention of Levi that prevents what seems to be the threat of a violent physical attack against Mary.

The presence of a stone demon in many of the mediaeval cathedrals is believed by esotericists to represent Peter. When Jesus stated that one of his disciples was a demon, he referred to Peter, not Judas (see Chapter 4). Peter was Enlil's agent on earth, and opened the doorway for Enlil's countless touches on the tiller regarding Christian doctrine. St Peter with the keys of heaven is a fair representation – he won't let us in, and has no intention of ever doing so if he can help it! Moving Peter into place as head of the Church was a strategic manipulation by Enlil, ensuring that the over-masculinised Roman mentality would march domineeringly right into the heart of Christian doctrine.

When the pilgrims reached their journey's end at Rosslyn, they deposited on its altar the precious cockleshells, symbols of St James, that they had carried from Compostela. Although the cockleshell is particularly associated with St James the Greater, it is really an emblem of the site of the Moon oracle at Compostela and the moon's great link with the sea, sacred sign of Tiâmat.

Compostela was indeed the site of the Druidic oracle of the Moon, 'Ioua', feminine symbol and the start of the pilgrimage or the pilgrims' Alpha point. This signified the sacred marriage of the moon chakra or the Sacred Feminine principle with Father Saturn, the Sacred Masculine principle represented by the Saturnine chakra and the Druidic oracle of Saturn at the Omega point of Rosslyn. The whole point of the pilgrimage was to ritually and energetically conjoin the Alpha and Omega points representing the polarity of the seven-site configuration in stone leading from Compostela to Rosslyn. Again, it is worth noting that Rosslyn is the Omega point relative to this particular 'apocalyptic configuration in stone' pilgrimage only.

The cockleshell provides a link with Tiâmat, as it represents the merry-maids or the Sea Goddess. Botticelli painted Venus being born into manifestation from the sea on the beautiful dovetail scallop shell, very similar in form to the cockleshell. As well as the overarching significance of Venus, the painting is said to represent Mary Jacob, the mother of Mary Magdalene and direct descendant of Eve, Nin-khursag, Enki and, leading back through them, of Antu, consort of Annum and Enki and Nin-khursag's mother – and thus to Ain, Great Queen, Divine Daughter.

Some scholars think that the devotional depositing of cockleshells in Rosslyn Chapel indicates that its founder and its esoteric messages in stone issued from descendants of the Ebionite sect, a group of early Jewish-Christians who believed that Jesus was not born of a virgin, did not die on the cross, and was not a deity. The Ebionites were particularly associated with James the Righteous, their leader. The cockleshell is therefore associated with James the Lesser (the Righteous) as well as James the Greater.

The beliefs of the Ebionites also appear to have been held by the Knights Templar and by Arian Christians, associated particularly with the Merovingians, the Bogomils and the Cathars; yet these groups differed from the Ebionites in that they encompassed the deeply mystical aspects of Christianity markedly absent and lacking in the Ebionite sect. And in fact the unmistakable resonance of Rosslyn is that no rigid doctrines are portrayed within it, but only the articulate, uplifting and beautiful inspirations of many different paths to the Divine. Nevertheless, most people will probably agree that Rosslyn Chapel does not 'do' anti-mysticism!

Jesus did indeed give the establishment of the Christ teachings in Jerusalem into the hands of James the Righteous (or Just), his brother. Mary Magdalene, with Joseph of Arimathea, her little daughter Sara-Tamar and many of the disciples, meanwhile, sailed west to Britain and to France to establish the teachings there.

Jesus gave the Christ teachings into the care of James for a very specific reason. His purpose was to heal a dangerous schism that he perceived clearly even before it manifested.

Jesus himself gave the title 'James the Righteous' to his brother. He also said something that has proved a point of perplexity to scholars – 'James the Righteous, for whom heaven and Earth came into existence'.

He meant by this that James represented a certain kind of righteous person who, because of innate goodness, was the very reason why creation had come into existence – to facilitate the unbinding and unblinkering of the goodness that was the true and real humanity created by God so that human souls could be released into the freedom of their greater being. Heaven and Earth encompass and facilitate this process, and were created for it.

James was a pragmatist. He was a good and righteous man, but he understood spirituality as a set of mundane codes for living obediently and judiciously and didn't wish to move beyond the mentality of the Ten Commandments. When Moses dropped and broke the true sapphire tablet upon Mount Horeb (the Mount of Hathor) and accepted the false tablet into his hands, he sealed much of the human understanding of spirituality into this tomb of pragmatism. Had he been able to resist the taunts of Jethro, he would have carried down the mountain, not a 'set' of laws carved in stone, but a living spiral of laws leaping out from the radiance at the heart of the tablet, ever moving upwards into light rather than written in stone.

James definitely rejected the Sacred Feminine – the living wonder within the soul. He was a bluff man, and to him, things were cut and dried. He supported his brother Jesus, but he didn't 'get' the higher aspects of his teaching – their mystical, star-strewn initiatory path. All he understood of them was that they were a new take on Judaism, a way of making it better and more humane. He was unable to realise that they pointed out a new direction altogether – ultimately, decisively away from religion, at least in relation to its divisive, orthodox, controlling and indoctrinating aspects.

Therefore, James did see Jesus as just an ordinary mortal. Jesus was not a deity, of course; but James, brother-like, did not perceive the Nephilim light that lit his soul. As for being born of a virgin, that was ridiculous in his eyes. Mary his mother had given birth to many children, his eldest sister Naomi was her first-born, and after the death of his father Joseph, she had gone on to marry Zebedee and to bear more sons.

The true meaning of 'virgin', the purity of the seven lamps of heaven radiant within the soul, was not a concept James would have grasped. The conventional mistranslation of 'virgin' (caused by male repression towards women) suited him fine. And as for Jesus's death on the cross – James had seen and spoken to Jesus many times since the Crucifixion, so of course he thought no death had taken place. He missed the larger significance of everything – the shining marvel – almost entirely.

James was a devout and orthodox Jew, a truly good and righteous man; but he was not inspired and he was certainly not a Gnostic. It does seem very baffling that so many people seem to have become convinced that orthodoxy and Gnosticism were somehow one and the same thing within James the Righteous! They are not so much at opposite ends of the spectrum as entirely removed from one another.

Paul of Tarsus, the true Gnostic, after receiving his initiatory teachings from Sara-Tamar, entirely despaired of James the Righteous. He saw that James denied the mystical truth of Christianity and its veneration of the Divine Feminine. Paul, so misunderstood and deliberately falsified in his message and words as far as could be arranged, was, apart from John, Enlil's greatest threat among the disciples. Paul feared that James's stance was so dangerous, so steeped in mundane limitation, that, forgetting the very teachings he held so dear, he even made an attempt on his life.

It seems that Paul was indeed right to fear the danger inherent in James's obtuse attitude. But Jesus knew by the light of the love within him that to kill or even to attack personified misconception breaks spiritual law. Instead, we are counselled to embrace those who suffer from it. And so, James was embraced and given stewardship of the teachings so that he could create and embody a point that demanded resolution (i.e. a point which would intensify and rise up as if in suppuration so that it could be purified and healed).

Many people are represented by the symbol of James the Righteous today: good, just people who are unable to see beyond the end of their nose as far as spiritual truth and reality are concerned. Such limitation keeps us blind and imprisoned and vulnerable to Enlil; but, to heal the limitations of the righteous, heaven and Earth came into being. The plan of Creation was laid to lead us through the initiation of matter and its obtuseness and then to set us free.

Nevertheless, James's humane righteousness comprised the essential base upon which humanity's understanding of spirituality must properly rest. It was a very good and positive thing, just what was needed – except that a base is designed to be risen up from and not to take over the whole concept of the structure for which it provides a foundation, so that it remains forever a base!

We can also note, from his act in electing James the Righteous as the just and true base for humanity's rise into spiritual freedom, Jesus's deep knowledge that the base of Mount Heredom, God's Holy Mountain, had been separated from its peak; how that terrible rift was still a present, living energy within the soul of the world, and how it needed a special focus and outpouring of reconciliation and healing before the separated base and peak could find wholeness again.

Mary Magdalene, Joseph of Arimathea, Mother Mary, John and Sara-Tamar, who took the teachings to the West, comprised Mount

Heredom's peak, James the Righteous the bereaved base that, via the cruelty of separation, had forgotten all about that divine apex of enlightenment to which by rights he should rise.

The seven sacred sites of the planetary oracles configure to form a spiritual device whereby the point requiring resolution created by James the Righteous would achieve that active resolution by those who made the pilgrimage. Moved by Gnosis, these pilgrims started out at the moon-blessed Compostela site of St James, carrying the feminine symbol of the cockleshell. The power built into the cathedrals and churches on their way combined with the power of the planetary oracle sites and their own spirituality to create a reconciliation between the polarity of James at Compostela and the spirit of the Divine Feminine that fills Rosslyn.

In another sense, the feminine moon at Compostela was united with the masculine Saturn at Rosslyn. Literally either way, the drawing together of the polarities was achieved by the pilgrims and their heartfelt offerings. Until this healing reconciliation was accomplished, the chapel at Rosslyn could not be inundated with the rainbow potencies of the seven-site configuration at a higher level.

From my own findings, the following list describes some of the beliefs of the Templars, a secret remnant of whom are thought to have orchestrated the erection of Rosslyn Chapel:

They were devoted followers of the Temple of John, aiming to express its ideals through their Order; they believed that any religious devotion free from dogma, injustice and oppression was an expression of Divine truth; they were committed to the true teachings of Christ, whom they saw as a heavenly Being comprising both feminine and masculine aspects in perfect equilibrium; they believed that Jesus of Nazareth and Mary Magdalene reflected the example and teaching of this heavenly Christ Being to the highest degree, but Jesus and Mary themselves were understood to be human beings of the loftiest order and not deities.

They worshipped Mother-Father God, the Christ Being in the heavens, and the Divine Woman Sara-Tamar, who were all considered to be facets of the One God, they understood the true history of humanity and knew about Enki and Enlil; they did not believe that the Christ Being could be sacrificed or die, but they were aware of the sacrifice of Jesus and his suffering on the cross, which, through Sara-Tamar, restored the emerald tablet to the Earth. They were aware that he ascended and changed his bodily atoms into spiritual atoms, and that this marvel – the Holy Grail which was in essence the Divine Woman – was the basis for the restoration of an extraordinary spiritual science which could be expressed through enlightened physics and chemistry.

They revered Mary Magdalene as the living expression of the Mother who brought forth the Divine Woman as her daughter, but also regarded Mary as the designated channel for the feminine aspect of the Christ Being and thus claimed in secret that Christ still walked the Earth for many decades after the Crucifixion and that this Holy One made France and Britain her home. They knew of Sara-Tamar's existence on Earth and all it implied.

They possessed Enki's secret knowledge of divine smithship and Nin-khursag's Gnosis, which branched into many divisions of the 'underground stream', the hidden knowledge passed down through secret channels, and they were determined to build a global civilisation on heavenly principles rooted squarely into the Earth which knew no national or religious divisions.

They were committed to guarding Tiâmat's special bloodline, protecting the emerald tablet and the sacred Grail knowledge, and restoring the Grail to Earth. At the last, they had planned a coup to overthrow the seat of Peter within the Church and restore power to the true teachings of Christ, expressed so beautifully by Celtic Christianity. It was at this point that the Order was decimated by the earthly forces of Church and State. A small number of Templars escaped; they dispersed around the world, many taking refuge in Scotland. They ensured that the Templar treasures were preserved and did not fall into the hands of their enemies.

If you walk into the Baptistery in Rosslyn Chapel, you will come to two memorial windows, installed in relatively modern times. One portrays a winged airman of World War ll, standing on the white cliffs of Dover (symbol of white Albion, the mystic isle), flanked by St Andrew and St George, patron saints of Scotland and England. He stands looking to heaven touching his heart. His glove is rose-coloured, symbolising the rose within the heart – the sign of the Sacred Feminine. He is unmistakably a John-man. Opposite is a window portraying St Francis of Assisi.

These windows, created for reasons personal to the St Clair family, nevertheless comprise a prophecy. The spirit of the airmen will descend again to help Britain fight off the terrible incursions of Enlil (the motto of the St Clair family is 'Fight').

Every effort and sacrifice across the globe was equally valuable in overcoming the Nazis, of course (the Nazis were a direct manifestation of unmitigated Naphidem influence, led from behind the scenes by Marduk, who, as usual, was trying to get them back to Earth and needed specially bred 'Aryan' bodies for them to step down into). Yet a particular inspiration possessed the Allied airmen; it was as if they knew (as indeed they did at a subliminal level) that if Britain fell to the Nazi darkness, we would all be lost.

The airmen were reincarnated Templars; the public sensed as much when they were dubbed 'the knights of the skies'. The uniquely valiant spirit of the Templars will come again to help us to vanquish Enlil once and for all. The whole world will be freed; but Britain has a special mission in that she will lead the way. That is her responsibility and service.

With our own current leader and that of the most powerful nation on Earth having succumbed to the lure of the white powder, with our governments in collusion with Enlil's wiles, manipulations and diktat, we need the spiritual will with which the Templars are ready to infuse us. Ignorance and doubt regarding spiritual reality and our global destiny beset us now, but this will be swept away in the coming days.

England and Scotland will at last discover common ground, and will work together with all of Britain and eventually the world to turn back the encroaching tide. We will come to realise that St George is not just the patron saint of England, but of Britain (as he is of Portugal), and that he carries the energies of Mercury, the 'airman' or the winged god, our messenger and protector. It is the Mercurial influence, the messenger at the gates of the Sun, that will show us how to rescue ourselves from Enlil and facilitate our upward movement away from him and into the freedom of ascension. St Andrew, as the window portrays, is Mercury's helpmeet in this work.

The window depicting St Francis is an indication of the new spirit of compassion, simplicity, brotherliness, spiritual values, and the care of one another together with our planet and our animal brethren, which will ensue from our victory. The inspiration for his mission came to St Francis in a chapel dedicated to and depicting St George; and no saint was more devoted to the stories of King Arthur and the Holy Grail than this beloved holy man.

At his feet is a cockleshell (green to denote the emerald tablet), and above his head a star, showing that the coming spiritual revolution will be founded upon the true teachings of Christ, whose signs are the Star of Bethlehem (the peak of Mount Heredom) and the cockleshell (Mount Heredom's base): the conjoined and healed Holy Mountain which is the living, active Holy Grail and the symbol of ascended human consciousness.

St Francis embodies the spirit that conjoins the sacred peak and base in eternal unity. He holds the Dove of the Eternal to his heart – John, the Dove. More pragmatically, the window predicts that it will be in the time of Pope Francis that this great revolution of the spirit will take place.

The chakra teaching which best explains the influences of Enlil and Enki is an ancient one from the East (originally from Hyperborea). This places Saturn at the base of the spine, where he locks in the celestial light as guardian of its secrets and powers until Mercury has prepared the top of the spinal pathway and opened the gates of the chakra in the base of the brain. Mercury then conducts the light forces, through the heart, into the head. The Mercurial influences are seen as occupying the throat chakra, the centre dedicated to communication: the quality that this heavenly courier embodies.

When this process is complete, we have an image of the crozier transposed over the spine. Rather than merely the straight lance earthing our light downward into the planet (Saturn and Mercury working together), it comes up the spine and grows a curve to arch over our head at the crown chakra and complete itself at our brow chakra. We are led by Joseph of Arimathea, shepherd of the true Christian teachings, turning into Osiris, shepherd of brilliant stars.

And so we come to realise why the seven sacred planetary sites reach out arms of light to support this vital Saturnine site at Rosslyn, creating a configuration of the rainbow which designates the chapel as their Omega point. Pouring celestial light and strength into this focal point, they thus prepare and fortify it to embrace its destiny and become the Saturnine base or root chakra of the world: the point from which everything wondrous will arise.

We can read the reason why, within the culmination of Rosslyn Chapel, there exists a special power for cleansing, preparing and finally kindling the full radiance of the light within our 'Seven Lamps of Heaven'. But, in fact, the chakras that Rosslyn will especially empower and illuminate are the first five chakras, those leading from the bottom of the spine to the top – from Saturn to Mercury. At this point the impetus is transferred to Mercury, who takes over from here.

We see therefore that the heavenly energies must begin to ascend from the site of Rosslyn Chapel (the base or the root chakra) where they have been imprisoned for safekeeping by Saturn, to a spiritually designated height where the Mercurial forces await their coming. It is not a physical height that can be measured, but a vital ascension into an ineffable height. Is there a method of facilitating ascension of these light-bearing Saturnine forces within Rosslyn Chapel? Indeed there is; one which will be discussed in the next chapter.

The true Saturnine force will gladly release the divine light, which it has locked away in order to safeguard it until its time comes. The problem is that Enlil, a human being like us yet much more advanced than us, was once entrusted with the shepherding of the Saturnine forces, and he wants to make sure that the beautiful Saturn-preserved light stays exactly where it is – locked up! Then (so he plots) he can prevent earthly humanity from ever ascending and eventually exterminate it altogether.

Therefore, Rosslyn Chapel has a special task to fulfil. It must give a terrific spiritual boost to the imprisoned light to allow Father Saturn to take his power back from Enlil's encroachment and insist on its release at the proper time; for that is Saturn's role, which is why he is lord of karma, restriction, gravity and time, and his metal is the heaviest of all – lead. He imprisons and holds until the time is right for release, which is why he is guardian of the womb. This cosmic drama is all about birth – the birth of a new heaven and a new Earth.

Some distance away from Rosslyn Chapel lies Iona, the sacred mountain top, embodiment of the great beacon of the head-centres within the human chakra system and of the sacred eye (Dûn-I). This eye opens once the head-centres fill with light. It is not just the third eye, but the triangle which incorporates all three eyes – our two visible eyes and the invisible eye at the mid-point of the brow, which form a pyramid. When this eye opens, its fulfilled pyramidal structure carries it to the top of the head, where it sits like an apex.

Once, when Iona was Mount Heredom, when she had her base as well as her crown, she represented the ascensional power of the seven chakras within us: the heavenly ladder that we could ascend to enter into sublime worlds beyond our present-day understanding. But she was decapitated. She lost her base, and now she commands only the head-centres. The age-old powers are still there within Iona, waiting to be reconnected. But they can only be reconnected if what she lost so long ago can also play its part: if her base is reactivated so that every chakra is incorporated into her potencies.

Over 500 years ago, Earl William St Clair, last Prince of Orkney, set to and rebuilt that base. He rebuilt it where once before its destruction it had stood, not just as a base but as a holy mountain, when poignant Iona was the peak of beautiful Mount Heredom. Sacred power-points throughout Europe, and beyond Europe, Africa, connecting via Spain, came to his aid.

He called it Rosslyn Chapel.

CHAPTER 31

THE GREEN MAN

The little chapel of Rosslyn was dedicated to St Matthew. To reiterate, nothing about Rosslyn is accidental; and St Matthew is indeed highly significant.

To understand his significance, we need to turn to Zoroaster. Some scholars say that Zoroaster or Zarathustra, a Persian mystic, was born at the beginning of the 7th century BC, but many place him much earlier, perhaps even in the time of the Elamites, whose reign in Persia ended in 900 BC.

What is certain from the viewpoint of this story and from Laurence Gardner's researches in the secret archives of the Dragon Court is that Zoroaster was the biblical Ham, Enki's spiritual son and his direct descendant through Cain.

Ham (Zoroaster) and Ahura Mazda, the 'god' he served (Enki), worked together throughout the centuries in an astonishing partnership of devotion and self-sacrifice to humanity in order to guard and rescue it from the depredations of Enlil.

Ham was an 'Avesa', meaning that he used the Star Fire in such a way that, because of the purity of his light-body or soul, he was able to live indefinitely on the Earth.

Ham was in training for, or indeed engaging with, the release of Divine light through his Zoroastrian guise at the time when he had entrusted Shulgi (Shem) with acting kingship of Ur. We may be reasonably certain that Ham, in his absences from Ur, was frequently among the Elamites inhabiting west Persia and was honoured by them, for it was the Elamites that rose up in fury and conquered Ur (and the brand-new Babylon, unrecorded in this first instance of its history) when Shem ousted Ham and his son Canaan (King Ur-baba) from power.

Zoroaster (Ham) taught that to follow the guidance of Enki (Ahura Mazda), would lead us into Divine Light, and that to follow the guidance of Enlil (Ahriman) would lead us into suffering and darkness. From Zoroaster arose all the teachings on angels embodied today in religions across the world.

The priests of Ham's Zoroastrian teachings worshipped Annat or Ain, the Divine Woman, as an understanding of the mystical Being that was God. (Her worship was partly obscured so that it seemed as if Zoroastrianism had no feminine deity; but this was far from the truth.) Ahura Mazda and Ahriman were seen as supernatural guides: one heavenly, the other infernal.

The priests of Zoroastrianism were known as the Magi, and 'Zoroaster' became a titular designation for its high priest as the Order passed down the centuries. It was, of course, essentially the Temple of John. The descent of the priests was via a bloodline. The great King Cyrus of Persia – whose inspired reign endowed the country with the height of its famous magnificence and beauty of art, science, culture and scholarship – was associated with the Magi and was an ancestor of Matthew Cyrus, who (dishonourably) impregnated Mary Jacob with her daughter, Mary Magdalene. Matthew Cyrus was a member of Rex Deus, a hidden brotherhood of 24 orders of priests of Israel (with their origins in Persia, Canaan, Egypt and Mesopotamia), each headed by an angel.

Rex Deus in its later years (for its discipleship was of Enki and Christ) was known to follow and abide by the Gospel of Matthew alone, although it seems clear that the mysticism of the Gospel of John was also highly prominent in its thinking. There was a very particular reason for its dedication to Matthew's gospel. Whilst Rex Deus served the Temple of John, which had passed with the Order clandestinely into Judaism, its outer historical links were with Zoroastrianism. The Temple of John and Zoroastrianism were one and the same, but Zoroastrianism was Rex Deus's localised branch of it; and Matthew himself arose from the Zoroastrian Magi.

He was one of the three (Melchior) who came to visit Jesus and Mary Magdalene after their birth in the Bethlehem stable. The Wise Men remained clandestinely with the holy family (Mother Mary, Joseph, their son Jesus, and Mary Jacob, mother to Mary Magdalene, who had given birth first in the stable or cave in Bethlehem). They assumed the role of protectors of Jesus and Mary Magdalene, and indeed of their entire extended family, particularly at the psychic and other subtle levels of life.

Melchior's Zoroastrian link with Matthew Cyrus prompted him to assume this Greek name. He was the only one of the three Wise Men who became an outright disciple of Jesus, although Melchior's Magi brothers certainly paid heed to the teachings of Jesus and Mary Magdalene. The 'Jesus and John' teachings were entirely resonant.

'Matthew' means 'science', deriving from a Greek root meaning 'to learn'. As Fulcanelli tells us, Matthew espoused that pure science (not material positivism) which brings the whole being, the full arc of human intelligence, into beautiful orchestrated being so that the heart of mysteries may be unveiled to reveal their secrets. Rosslyn was built according to the illumination of that radiant arc of inspired intelligence, in the highest tradition of the Temple of John.

The Wise Men were delegates from the four branches of the Temple of John (Essenes, Druids, Therapeutate and Magi: one of their company, the Therapeutate brother, died from natural causes on the journey to Bethlehem). Their task was, in the tradition of John, the Wise Knight, to bow their knee in reverence, humility and obedience to the Divine Couple at their birth, and ritually to surrender what had been in the safekeeping of the Temple of John since the beginning of the revolt against Tiâmat in Eden, into the hands of Jesus and Mary Magdalene, who would now complete Enki and Nin-khursag's task.

This certainly did not mean that the Temple of John relinquished its task; far from it. But, if we can think of little bright Mercury hurtling around the sun at great speed in an orbit of devotional servitude, and the great sun shining just beyond him but within the orbital sphere of Mercury's encompassment (his soul), we receive an idea of Enki's (John's) relationship to Christ.

Enki has ever embodied Mercury down the ages – Mercury, the god who receives divine intelligence and direct spiritual succour from the sun, and is the messenger of the sun: its messenger within the stream of human consciousness, just as Archangel Michael and the Shekinah are its angelic messengers. Yet Enki is supported by and stands in the light of these mighty angelic beings. Enki, when we think of the great cosmic human entity made of stars which is God's creation – the 'Grand Man of the Stars' or the Vitruvian man – represents the human mind. The human heart is represented by Christ, the sun.

Enki served to prepare the way for the coming of Christ (Jesus and Mary Magdalene). Ham was Enki's faithful servant, as Enki was Christ's faithful servant, which meant that they both diligently served the Christ Couple. And Ham, now one with Enki in the higher realms, stood behind Melchior, who remained with the Christ couple to protect them and eventually to join their mission.

Melchior shielded them with the deepest and most ancient esoteric knowledge of the spirit, for his tradition was the oldest on Earth. We would classify it as magic today. He instructed the secret tradition of the Temple of John as it descended through John the Baptist and John the Beloved. Melchior was indeed a Merlinesque figure, for such a figure has stood behind every opportunity to reconnect the Grail, from Joseph the Dream Oracle to Merlin himself in the time of King Arthur.

Rosslyn Chapel is built in the magical tradition that Melchior upheld, which is Enki's and which embraces the golden thread ('the good and the true') in all religions, expressing the deep mysticism, the Gnosis, of the secret brotherhoods of the ages. Nevertheless, the golden thread is rooted in Zoroastrianism, although it flourishes in the noble aspects of Judaism, Christianity and Islam, especially the Sufi philosophy with its positive-spin stance (Enlil's regime is based entirely on negative-spin mode).

Melchior, as a triumphant John-man and perfect son of Mercury, holds forth the Caduceus. However, he encompasses Saturn in his esoteric embrace, for he is sage, prophet and holy magician. Merlin is Father Saturn's true son and is reflected in Melchior; and thus we can say, with perfect exactitude in the higher sense, that Rosslyn Chapel is the work of Merlin!

Melchior is our direct Merlinesque link with St Matthew's Chapel of Rosslyn. But Merlin is a figurehead, and it might come as a great surprise to discover just who the Merlin of Rosslyn Chapel actually is. As we shall see, Merlin will underpin and bless the coming of the Holy Grail, as he has always stood ready to do so ever since it was severed.

Enki worked tirelessly in the ethereal regions to prepare the way for the coming of Christ. He either dropped the dew of stories upon the world, entering human consciousness through dreams and visions, which described spiritual realities in sacred terms, or, with Ham's aid

(Enki's 'conductor' to Earth), he stood behind light-bearing souls who incarnated on Earth and incorporated a mythic journey into the path of their lives.

But even in the latter case, this mythic journey took place much more in the ethereal realms than it did in the region of the mundane. Enki was the devoted servant, the light-attuned Mind preparing the way for the coming of the Kingdom: his master, the transcendent Heart, the Christ.

Therefore, we have figures such as Horus, Osiris, Mithra, Krishna, Tammuz, Dionysus, Bacchus, Attis, Quetzalcoatl and Itu (the Hindu vegetation deity) and many, many more who appear throughout the course of mythology. All of them are masculine deities or heroes who mediate between heaven and Earth as a symbol of their acceptance, veneration and restoration of the Holy Grail within themselves. Their emblem and the emblem of the Grail is a holy plant or tree, and they are also connected with the moon, which ritualises vegetational growth: both powerful symbols of the Sacred Feminine.

All of them, too, are in particular associated with the planet Mercury and the Mercurial forces. Even Buddha, who before he came to Earth was known in Vedic mythology as Budha, god of Mercury, a 'green man' deity, has this Mercurial connection; and he certainly came to help us to prepare our minds for the great global event of heart-centred ascension. They were the Green Men, the Emerald Tablet Men, sourced in the holiness of the Mother, whose simple emblem on Earth was nature. El Khidir, an Arabic esoteric master who helped to build Solomon's Temple, was known as 'the Verdant (Green) One', because green is the colour of enlightenment in esoteric wisdom.

Osiris was said to be green-skinned; and the heroes and gods of the 'green man' mythology all bore Christic characteristics such as being born under an announcing star to a virgin in a cave in a manger on 25th December, attended by shepherds, being known as the 'King of Kings', 'the Saviour', 'the Redeemer', 'the Messiah', 'the Good Shepherd' and 'the Way, the Truth, and the Light', being sacrificed on a stake or a tree to bring peace to the world, and rising on the third day. Some of these heroes are even called Jesu or some other form of 'Jesus'.

The miracle of miracles was that after lowering its breast to whisper to Earth from heaven of the cosmic drama that would free us, an aspect of the Godhead actually descended into the literal pragmatism of our mundane world via an androgyne of the highest Nephilim to embody eternal truth on Earth. It shouldn't have been possible, not even in the knowledge stored in the annals of the halls of the highest supernal wisdom; but it was done. Some religious philosophers and mystics cannot believe it to this day; they think it must all be metaphorical; yet it happened.

The myths that Enki and Ham wove and embodied are evidence of the need for preparation, and Enki-John was ever he who prepared the way. For a reality to be birthed, as Enki knew, we must first hold it in our collective consciousness, in our God-given imagination.

A reverse operation is underway at the moment, whereby reports are put out on the Internet regarding projects of the adversarial forces claiming that mechanised human soldiers, horribly conditioned, are already in circulation, plus other disturbing 'truths' of the darkest magnitude. In fact these things are not true yet, but they are certainly waiting further down the road if we take the wrong turning. The mystic Lorna Byrne confirms that her angel guides are actually showing her a projection of these things, to help us to avoid them.

We must become aware of what the Green Man carvings within Rosslyn Chapel are telling us. There are 103 of them, and they smile out and look down in many places from the strange beauty of the chapel's interior – or do they actually leer? They might be smiling, or they might be leering, and that is the point we must tune into.

The Green Man carvings are not only representations of Enki with his star-trails of mythology, telling us of the Four Hallows of the Grail, which are Nourishment, Immortality, Healing and Fertility; they also symbolise the sacred Saturnine forces which Rosslyn enshrines. And they do more: they signify the Saturnine and Mercurial forces, the Alpha and Omega of the spine, alive and active and creating a force field of power that runs between them.

The trouble is that Enlil is there at the bottom of the spine, making his special contribution! Having unlawfully commandeered the Saturnine forces to a certain degree, he hopes (and the leer shows us how sanguine his hopes are!) to leap in and grab us at the last minute, just when we are ready for spiritual lift-off to the stars.

The Green Man mirrors the true Master Craftsman, another of Enki's aspects – the man who knows his Divine source is the Mother. Therefore, his crafting comes from the power of inspiration which comprises the harmonics within nature, an expression of the Mother. The Green Man or Emerald Tablet Man, being the true Master Craftsman, will not use any material for building other than pure and true elements of nature, carefully refusing the false and the unworthy.

The wisdom of the emerald tablet – what he takes from the Divine Feminine within the rites of the Sacred Marriage which provide him with the Star Fire – is the guidance he steers by and the essence he uses in his crafting. It gives him discernment. If a man refuses his emerald tablet inheritance, he becomes mechanistic, robot-like, with an arrogant desire to dominate nature and women. His joy becomes a leer. The death forces, instead of the light forces, are the material with which he builds himself and his world both inwardly and outwardly – as is largely the case today.

Enki and Nin-khursag, as the guardians of Gnosis, seem to hold up dualism as a condition of life on Earth. Yet it is not really dualism as polar extremes that characterises their teaching, but the discernment of the real from the false, wisdom from unwisdom. And there is a great catch in the possible interpretation of the Green Man.

Having lost the Star Fire, and with women, its dispensers, finding their direct access to Divine source confused and overshadowed by an illusion (their 'inequality'), men in some societies began to replace the essence in the Dew-Cup with hallucinogenic plants. These became a stand-in for the Star Fire. The malignant white powder was the real usurper, but Miriam's influence had imposed restrictions on its dispensation.

Sometimes the plant spirits, when utilised in this way, remain benign; very often they do not. And even when they are helpful, cosmic law requires that if we enter into a transaction where via biological necessity the plant is forced to serve us at the astral level, by the same token we bind ourselves to its service, which means that we become enslaved to elemental overlords.

This is because we are not using our spiritual faculties to properly interplay with the plant souls. If we approached them in this way, without coercion, as fellow souls, all would be well and we could learn from one another and ascend to realms of joy together. In the case of hallucinogenic plants, we use coercion if we breach their worlds by taking them as a drug.

Even though they are plants and we eat and drink plant substance to survive, such eating and drinking when practised only for bodily nourishment exists as a sound transaction and occupies an entirely different level of spiritual law to that which is transgressed when we take them as drugs.

To do so is really a form of materialism: a denial of the Sacred Feminine within – the Star Fire – which carries us into supernal worlds without any exterior or earthly aid. We do need bodily conditions to be addressed, just as we need quietude and our own space to meditate; but bodily conditions are all that should be addressed via physical application, otherwise the equation goes wrong.

It is as though using drugs is a statement that we believe our higher consciousness is a force that is separate from us and supplied to us by chemical exteriority, by the material world; as though it is a mundane, bodily, mechanical thing that would completely vanish if by some peculiar chance hallucinogenic plants were to disappear from the face of the Earth! Reliance on such exteriority is the same as thinking we can catch a plane to heaven; such mechanisation of approach to the soul and spirituality is right up Enlil's street, and one of the quickest ways he can reel us in.

Our higher consciousness is integral to us and within us, and its powers of ascension are thrown off course when we coerce plant souls and breach their inner worlds by force. Plant souls do not lift human consciousness to the highest heights by these means. Their worlds are astral worlds, worlds of great beauty that we can traverse when we are properly centred and functioning independently and interactively in our higher consciousness, rather than being bound hand and foot and hurled through a breach into them via a material stimulus.

That is Enlil's way, and he delights in the power he wields over us when we fall into such a trap. And of course, our destination is to penetrate far beyond the astral worlds to unimaginably sublime regions even whilst firmly anchored in our body. In that scenario, plant souls would need to hitch a ride with us, rather than the other way round!

Using hallucinogenics in a traditional and disciplined way, such as within the teaching of a tribe, might enable the human soul to become an adept magician; but it actually blocks the user from traversing the higher realms, beyond the distracting astral worlds, which are our human destiny, our priceless heritage. It gives us a Simon Magus status instead of a Star Fire status, and is ultimately a rejection of the Sacred Feminine.

You might know or have heard of particular souls who are very psychically skilled, but are perhaps veering towards darkness and are not very humanely enlightened. This is not the exalted magicianship that we find when we go for the true mark.

To test the validity of this view on drug-taking, you can simply make a request for your own higher mind to guide you. Ask for a sign, or for three signs (to follow the Druidic rule of three) to be given to you from your higher mind or from the highest spiritual realms to bring wisdom forth for you on this matter. Keep an open mind, remain observant without actually seeking the signs, and they will assuredly come in a way that is most relevant and meaningful to you.

Thinking of this second lesson of Rosslyn, Michael Scot and his honey comes to mind. The pure substance in the Ark of the Covenant was honey – the true 'entheogenic' or God-yield from the magic of plants which nourishes the body perfectly, eases the mind via harmonic laws of the universe, and purifies the system. Rosslyn's second lesson is really a further clarification and reiteration of the first.

There are 103 images of the Green Man in the chapel. If we remove the zero, we have the number 13. This is the Perilous Seat at the Round Table of King Arthur, the seat where none can sit if they harbour impurity because they will be struck with immediate death – or will put to death that which is good and pure and of the heavenly or higher aspects of the human soul.

The reason is that 13 represents half of a sacred symbol.

The symbol is the Caduceus, the Staff of Life, or the Holy Tree, around which coil, in perfect unison, harmony and equilibrium, the serpentine forces of the Divine Feminine and the Divine Masculine principles. Push the '3' onto the Staff ('1') and you will reveal the symbol. Thirteen is the moment of Gnosis, when (particularly) a man realises that he is only half a being.

If he is impure (resonant with Enlil), Enlil's death forces will immediately take him and claim him, either enslaving or killing him so that the moment of clarity will have its light put out and be destroyed. Enlil certainly can't cope with moments of spiritual realisation like this, and wants to ensure that their enlightenment won't advance any further into the soul of the 'sitter' – the 'seat' being a certain point of awareness in which the sitter has centred his soul – and thus release him from Enlil's dominion.

However, if the sitter is pure or strives to be pure, his whole being begins to cry out for his lost bride, like the Fisher King (Enki in another guise) praying for the healing of his agony, which is ever-present at the point where she has been torn away from him (his 'thigh' or his genitals). He realises that he is the 3 on the right-hand side of the Staff which needs to coil around it and call his other half (the Sacred Feminine) to him so that together they can create the beautiful figure 8, the flow of eternity.

The sitter's one great aim from then on is to attain the Grail, which is to restore the link between himself and the Divine Woman that is his higher consciousness and invests him with the power of ascension.

In a state of terror about this highly dangerous '13' state (only dangerous in his eyes if his captive manages to free himself via its enlightenment) Enlil has done what he does best. He has dropped a void between the Staff of Life or Holy Tree and the masculine soul who, called by the magic of 13, advances towards potential enlightenment. But with Enlil's void in place, 13 becomes 103, and the '3' can no longer see the Tree of Life, or understand properly what it is, or sound the call for his other half so that they can make the figure 8.

The void in Enlil's case is one that is fallen into by the questing but confused masculine soul. It is empty, dark and screaming, but the soul who is liable to fall into it will continue to see an illusion of the Tree and of wholeness. What was all that about imagining a moment ago that something desperately vital and precious was lost and needed to be recalled to him? That was just a dream. He can see what he needs now. Smiling and enraptured, he will take the alluring false food (the drug) rather than the Star Fire, symbolised by simple honey. It is only long afterwards, when it is too late, that he will realise where he is – trapped within a void.

There are currently three important and highly accomplished writers on the subject of Rosslyn, the inner mysteries and the Holy Grail, who are feverishly pressing us all to take drugs in relation to them! And the many faces of the Green Man leer, and their number is 103.

Bees and hives with their honeycombs are all around us in Rosslyn Chapel. The Verdant Man, Enki himself, counsels us to remember the bee that produces the pure food, symbol of and akin to the Star Fire, the true gold that should be fed to human consciousness. By calculation, the bee cannot fly. Its wings are too small and delicate for the gravitational pull of its heavy body of Earth. But the bee has a secret, which is a resonance chamber below its wings. With the help of its resonance chamber (the Word or the Holy Breath), it can fly. Ascension is achieved.

Let us heed the warning of the 103 leering Green Men. We have our own inbuilt resonance chamber that can be filled with the Holy Breath, and it does not constitute the use of hallucinogenic drugs. It is Enki who wields the Caduceus, and who offers us the Four Grail Hallows and the gift of flight through his teachings on the Star Fire and the true nature of God.

Enlil, leering below him, offers us their counterpart, the coercion and illusion of the Four Horsemen of Doom. He would love nothing better than to sit back and watch them trample us. Enlil has full mastery over the dominions reached by drugs – he is their Overlord.

I am fully confident that, being so near to the attainment of the wonder of the Holy Grail as we are, we will not go and pitchfork ourselves straight into the steel trap of the jaws of Enlil at the last moment!

CHAPTER 32

THE TREASURES OF ROSSLYN

From the point of view of the guidance I have received, the treasures of Rosslyn certainly exist. They are a vital part of the chapel's mysterious destiny. They must remain secreted at Rosslyn's base, for the whole of Rosslyn is the mystical base of Mount Heredom, the primordial holy mountain.

Rosslyn's treasures bless and sustain that base with a mighty spiritual power, and indeed the Grail could not come again to our world through the medium of Mount Heredom (Rosslyn and Iona combined: Rosslyn its base, Iona its peak) unless Rosslyn remains so sustained.

To ensure that the treasures would not be displaced, its builders were careful to construct Rosslyn Chapel as an edifice that would, in our time, disintegrate if its vaults were penetrated. The current owner of the property has confirmed that this is so, and that opening up the vaults would dangerously undermine the chapel. We need the chapel and we need its treasures to remain in place and undisturbed, so this deterrent is a measurelessly good thing. Earl William St Clair, indeed, when setting out to build the structure, received instructions regarding the inbuilt deterrent as a Divine ordinance through the vicarious channel of his architect, Sir Gilbert Hay.

When the upper vaults were examined recently, a single ancient cup or bowl came to light. Standing in the middle of the floor, it was a small nondescript vessel and was most probably a workman's cup. Nevertheless, it was placed there hundreds of years ago to send a message to those of today who contemplate the Rosslyn mystery that yes, indeed, they are on the right track. The Grail is to be found at Rosslyn. The beautiful edifice at Rosslyn is the most holy Grail Chapel or sacred body into which its returning spirit will one day be called so that it may take root once again on Earth.

What lies in the lower vaults is of great import to the people of Scotland as well as to the world. It seems a matter of regret that they cannot access it. However, all is not lost. Although a human-sized entryway cannot be made into the vaults without eventually destroying the chapel, it will be possible to insert a camera into the chamber where the treasure lies so that it may be remotely viewed in all its mystery and wonder.

This has already been attempted, but unfortunately the probing remote endoscopic camera encountered a fall of rubble and dust so that nothing but the debris was visible through its lens. However, this was because it was not the right time for the lower vaults to offer up a view of their wonders. We must not forget that the Rosslyn treasure has its guardians.

At the point on the chapel floor below a carved pendulum, hanging from the roof in the shape of an arrow and known as the Sinclair Engrailed Boss, there is a keystone whose position and significance were discovered by the writers Robert Lomas and Christopher Knight. It is this keystone which must be raised to admit the lowering of a remote camera into the deepest vault and thereby unveil the peerless mysteries of Rosslyn.

There is an enigma regarding the Crown Jewels of Scotland and the St Clairs. During an unsettled period in the country's history at some time shortly prior to 1544, the jewels were placed under the protection of the St Clair family and given into their keeping. The family was chosen as guardians because of the outstanding reputation of the 'Lordly line of the High St Clairs'.

The items that were placed in their care included the ancient Crown Jewels and a piece of the cross upon which Jesus had been sacrificed.

This relic, the 'Holy Rood', had been given to Scotland by Margaret, a Saxon princess who was brought up at the royal court in Hungary.

The Hungarian court was at that time the headquarters of the secret Dragon Court, the keeper of much lost and esoteric knowledge; and the name Margaret is allied to Morrigan or 'Great Queen', from which emerged the titular 'Magdalene'. Margaret was a keeper of the secrets of the Grail, allied to the tradition of St Martin of Tours, who was of a high-ranking Hungarian family.

Margaret was escorted from Hungary to Scotland in 1057 by William 'the Seemly' St Clair, a knight greatly respected for his chivalry and courtesy. She came to marry King Malcolm Canmore of Scotland, who was so delighted with the character of St Clair that he persuaded him to settle in Scotland. (Sir William hailed from Normandy, where his family was established, although they descended directly from Røgnvald the Mighty, a famous Norwegian warrior earl.)

William the Seemly, significantly, became Queen Margaret's Cup Bearer. It was, indeed, through Margaret's influence that Sir William was given the barony of Rosslyn. Having borne Margaret and the Holy Cross to Scotland and established a profound platonic friendship with her, having learned many wonderful things from her, it was at this point that deep within his soul, William the Seemly St Clair dedicated his future and that of his descendants to the service of the Holy Grail, so beautifully symbolised by the Dew-Cup containing the Star Fire, of which Queen Margaret's 'Cup' was an emblem.

The Holy Rood was part of Margaret's dowry. My guidance confirms that this stake, part of the Crucifixion Cross that symbolises the Tree of Life or the Staff of Life, is genuine, and that a guiding destiny led it to Rosslyn.

Queen Margaret also donated generous funds to ensure that St Columba of Iona was remembered and honoured, and that the lamp of enlightened faith he lit for the world did not flicker and die in humanity's collective memory.

A document exists entitled 'Acts of the Lords of Council in Public Affairs' dated 1545 which formally requires William St Clair of Rosslyn (a great-grandson of the founder of Rosslyn Chapel) to hand back the Crown Jewels and the Holy Rood, upon which he would be paid for his service of protecting them. In the same document, the Laird of Craigmillar, one of the Lords of Council, actually protests about 'the Laird of Roslin' and suggests that action should be taken against him for detaining the Crown Jewels.

One way or another, Sir William refused to give them back! He must have had royal approval for his decision, for nothing more is recorded about them, except that a year later, marking the centenary of the erection of the chapel, Mary of Guise, Queen Regent of Scotland and mother of Mary, Queen of Scots, wrote to him in markedly humble vein, thanking him for showing her 'a great secret within Rosslyn' and earnestly promising to protect him and his family for the rest of her life as their humble servant. Moreover, she swears faithfully always to keep the secret he has shared with her.

The Crown Jewels and the Holy Rood are not mentioned again, and the Queen Regent made Sir William Lord Chief Justice of Scotland some years later, so there was obviously very good feeling between the St Clairs and the royal household. Moreover, the 'replacement' Crown Jewels, called the 'Honours', were assembled at this time.

Intuitively, it seemed to me that Mary of Guise descended into the vaults with Sir William (the entrance into them would have been stable in those days, over 450 years ago) to be shown a room where the Holy Rood and the Crown Jewels were ceremonially laid out around an artefact of enormous significance. The sanctuary seems to lie in a cave, although it must comprise part of the area of the vaults.

Certainly the scrolls of King Solomon's Temple were there, though they were not the centrepiece of that carefully sealed shrine where the treasures now lie in silent majestic solitude, bound to an invisible spiritual duty that can nevertheless almost be felt palpably in the solemn atmosphere, as if a slow sonorous symphony rolled everlastingly through it.

The Queen Regent, Mary of Guise, was deeply moved by what she saw in that shrine, and never forgot it. The treasure was, indeed, consummately unforgettable.

The story of the scrolls is an interesting one. It seems that these were put in the possession of Earl William St Clair, last Prince of Orkney, some time before he began the project of the church (as it was to have been). They were passed down to him via succession, either from the St Clair family or from members of the knightly orders to which he belonged (the Order of the Golden Fleece and the Order of the Cockle) who had ancient Templar connections.

A year after work began on the chapel, there was a great fire in the castle keep, where Earl St Clair kept all his papers and spent hours of each day in rapt study of them in company with his erudite architect and friend, Sir Gilbert Hay, one of the finest minds of the 15th century and a man with a most intriguing history, as we shall discover. The earl was out riding with his ladies at the time. The chaplain, knowing his master's devotion to his papers, dragged four great trunks from the dungeon where they were stored and thrust them to safety, climbing down the bell rope to escape the flames once he had done so.

The earl, on Colledge Hill, was so distressed to see the fire devastating the square keep that he could not comfort his princess and his ladies; but after news reached him of his chaplain's heroism, he grew cheerful and went to soothe them.

In fact, the edifice at Rosslyn was being constructed with the utmost care and attention to detail by the earl and his friend Hay, who oversaw the project with marked meticulousness.

Their instructions were in part drawn directly and verbatim from the Temple scrolls and from a secret book, over 200 years old and rumoured in Scottish tradition to be lost, which guided them with regard to the scrupulous particulars of the building that must be erected to reconnect Mount Heredom's base with its peak.

The scrolls were dense with the esoteric knowledge of Ham, who had written them. They explained the situation regarding Enlil, and Mount Heredom, and what must be done to put things right. This knowledge was irreplaceable, although there was one concluding point that was missing within the scrolls, which will be explained. Nevertheless, we might thank the brave chaplain as we look down the centuries, because without his selfless deed, reconnection with Iona would have been rendered extremely difficult.

What, in practical terms, was the actual function of the chapel in providing the service of reconnection?

In his book, *The Venus Blueprint*, Richard Merrick reveals in a stunning exposition how Rosslyn Chapel was designed as a resonance chamber based on the ancient concept of the Holy Mountain which also incorporated harmonics expressed by the 'rose line' of the planet Venus. Observed from Earth, Venus tracks a pentacle pattern in the figure of a perfect rose in the sky every eight years.

This beautiful rose configuration is marked by Rosslyn's name. Known as Roslin in its earliest days, its barons (the St Clairs) often signed their name as 'Roselin', emphasising the idea of a Rose Line. This signifies a sacred bloodline, but also the geometry and physics of resonance as expressed in the harmonic science present within the design of the chapel, represented by the orbital pattern of Venus with its creation in the heavens every eight years of a perfect rose, the supreme symbol of the Sacred Feminine.

Richard Merrick shows that this rose hangs as a mystical star over the summit of the visionary Mountain that informs all ancient concepts of religion and esoteric understanding. Most wonderfully, this mountain was a mountain of cadence, a musical mountain. And accordingly, Mount Heredom herself was a hollow mountain, characterised by many voluminous chambers of resonance and living waterfalls within her.

It is awe-inspiring to think that, throughout the many-splendoured web of Earth's pantheons and mythology from the beginning of human life on Earth, all roads lead back to 'serene, sea-girt Iona', which once was Mount Heredom.

Richard Merrick's genius in discovering Rosslyn's 'rose-line' mystery and the secret of the chapel's in-built harmonic science and resonance chamber, miraculously embracing the principles of the resonance of bees, gives us a scientific outline of Rosslyn's potential. In its sacristy there is a large fireplace, which it seems was used in the distant past to heat the chapel for mystical rather than mundane reasons and will need to be similarly utilised in the future.

It is the alchemical process of heating and cooling which will provide the conditions required to produce the extraordinary acoustics that will lift the sacred site of Rosslyn into spiritual union with Iona, its peak. This cosmic principle of heating and cooling produced the magical stained glass of the Templars, into which the eye is drawn as if into mystical worlds. It is this same magic, applied to the acoustics and the harmonic science pervading the stone structures within Rosslyn, which will perform the wonder.

In 2007, Tommy and Stuart Mitchell, a father and son team (so beautifully relevant to the teachings of Enki or John, the true Son of the true Father) released news of a musical secret they had discovered in Rosslyn. They went on to compose strangely beautiful and haunting music which was drawn from codes hidden in 213 cubes in the ceiling of the Lady Chapel within Rosslyn.

The Mitchells discovered that the shapes carved on the faces of the cubes seemed to match a phenomenon called Cymatics or Chladni patterns, formed when a sustained note is used to vibrate a sheet of metal covered in powder. The vibrations from the musical note cause beautiful geometric designs to appear miraculously in the powder, like the resonance of the Word bringing forth Creation.

210

Stuart assigned a note for each of the 13 variations of the patterns on the cubes and orchestrated them to create a piece of music that he entitled *The Rosslyn Motet*.

This appearance of the number 13 is a sign of half the sacred Caduceus, symbol of healing, wholeness, and eternal creation, which can only take up its beautiful motion when its other half (the Lost Bride, or the Sacred Feminine) is called to it. Stuart called the Lost Bride to the '13', the number presenting itself via the pattern categories on the cubes in the Lady Chapel, by the creative effort of his composition and the faith he expressed in the hidden presence of the music. Its mystical essence, imbued with creative power, is the result.

Despite the arguments put forward that this music may not arise from the original design of Rosslyn Chapel because of missing cubes, and that restoration work wrought some changes to the interior in the 19th century, my own guidance certainly confirms that *The Rosslyn Motet* is an authentic garnering. It will need a little modification that makes reference to the esoteric mysteries of the Platonic solid upon which the frozen music was carved – the cube. Yet it faithfully embodies the magic of sound that, when all conditions are right, will within the spiritual spheres swell the flat pyramid in the design of the floor of the chapel into its proper dimensions and resurrect Mount Heredom.

We will hear the music of the spheres then, because the harmonies of the planets interweave through the energies that pass directly into Rosslyn Chapel from the seven sacred sites stretching from Compostela right to its heart. We need the concerted power of the solar system, representative of the seven rays of creation, to restore the lost Grail; and we will hear its orchestration in wonder.

It is worth noting that around 1850–60, when restoration of Rosslyn Chapel was finally completed, a plethora of clues suddenly arose out of the blue at Lincoln cathedral, where the tombstone marker at the site of the buried transcripts of the emerald tablet appeared, followed by Tennyson's memorial statue and a new stained glass window, all replete, if not positively crawling, with Grail pointers.

When the transcripts of the emerald tablet are recovered from Lincoln, when they are translated and disseminated and we have come to understand that which has been veiled from us, when Naomi, the sister of Christ, prepares and awakens the ancient powers of Iona and Rosslyn in readiness for their reconnection, when the old chapel at Rosslyn is lit again with underground fires and its hidden but revealed music soars aloft on honeyed wings, Mount Heredom will come alive again, and the Grail will descend to the Earth...such a holy thing, as Tennyson, the Grail poet, tenderly expresses it.

Trevor Ravenscroft predicted that a date of great moment was associated with the seven-site configuration that feeds into Rosslyn. After much exertion, Tim Wallace-Murphy and his team found a perfect astronomical alignment where the pattern in the heavens matched the configuration on Earth.

The date associated with the heavenly alignment is July 28th 2019 – no more than five years ahead.

That is the date when the great powers at Rosslyn will be activated, and the Holy Grail will return to Earth.

At last...at last!

CHAPTER 33

REVERSALS

There are three famous pillars within Rosslyn Chapel. They relate to the strange and disturbing murder that was committed within the building, which took place after their completion.

They stand at its east end, directly in front of an area known as 'the Holy of Holies'. Today they are called the Master Pillar, the Journeyman Pillar and the Apprentice Pillar, Masonic names given to them in later times because they certainly reflect a Masonic mystery. However, originally they were called, respectively, the Earl's Pillar, the Shekinah Pillar and the Prince's Pillar.

Earl William St Clair, who began the building project that started (and inadvertently ended) with the chapel, was the last Prince of Orkney. He died in 1484, two years before the chapel was finished. His son Oliver, the new earl, succeeded him, and although he completed the roof of the chapel after his father's death, he thereafter abandoned the project. It seems strange that he should lose focus in this way and fail to realise his father's plans, regarding which the prince was so passionate.

This history means that the Master Pillar, being the Earl's Pillar, must equate with the new Earl, Oliver St Clair; and the Apprentice Pillar, which is the Prince's Pillar, with Earl William St Clair, Prince of Orkney, as Sir William was the last man to hold this title. Between these pillars stands a much plainer pillar decorated with Cherubim: the Shekinah Pillar.

The Shekinah was a concept of Goddess described in Hebrew texts as 'hidden aspects of God' and as the wife of Jehovah ('I Am that I Am', meaning the continuous flow of life and consciousness that brings forth creation, as in the figure 8). The Shekinah was known as 'the feminine presence of God'. Standing between the Master Pillar and the Apprentice Pillar, she is the Tree of Life or the Staff of Life, ready to set the sacred figure 8 (the intertwining Feminine and Masculine Principles) in motion.

The Apprentice (and there was such an apprentice) understood this and hearkened to her call. With an outpouring of love and obedience in his heart, he carved his pillar with one half of the intertwining serpents in the form of vines (meaning the true essence or the true blood), and to make his point clear he set eight serpents around the base of his pillar with the coiling vines extending from their mouths.

Being a true John-man, striving for the highest, (we might remember Leonardo's painting of John the Baptist with his forefinger pointing upwards to signify ascension (the Grail), and remember too that Leonardo was a young man just setting out in his career at the time that the Apprentice produced his marvel) he wrought his work with filigree delicacy and exquisite craftsmanship. The Apprentice Pillar is an extraordinarily beautiful sight to behold.

There was now a '13' symbolism (half a Caduceus, or half of a figure 8 on a staff) present in the chapel, waiting for its completion as the entire Caduceus from the pillar at the other side of the Shekinah, and a 'perilous seat' was thereby formed. Through no fault of his own, the Apprentice, graced with the gifts of heaven and having faithfully answered the call of the Shekinah, lost his life.

In the south aisle there is the rendering of a most unlikely circumstance. On one side of an architrave are carved pictorial representations of the seven deadly sins, whilst on the other side the seven virtues are portrayed. Yet a 'mistake' by the mason has caused the virtue of Charity to be replaced by Avarice, portrayed fifth in line among the seven virtues! And when the other side of the architrave is examined which depicts the seven deadly sins, there, sure enough, sits an illustration of Charity!

So, the human tendency towards avarice is included as a virtue, whilst the opposite human tendency towards charity (and we may include tolerance, as well as compassionate giving, within the scope of charity) is shown as a sin!

How did the stonemason responsible for this blatant 'blunder' get away with it? It seems likely that the stonemasons' tradition of making a single deliberate mistake in the execution of a project to demonstrate that only God is perfect answers the question. Yet this ostensible reason for the mistake was in effect a secret nod and wink between the stonemason, Sir William St Clair, and Sir Gilbert Hay, the masterminding architect; for it seems that they used it as a front in order to reveal and illustrate a very important truth.

Our societies today, even supposedly the most democratic and humane, are taking a retrograde path into attitudes and policies that are more reminiscent of the Roman Empire and its love of earthly power (avarice) than communities built on the highest spiritual principles. The clash of East and West, of cultures within countries, show us where we are with regard to charity and tolerance. We can put a name to the source of the manipulations behind this retrogression.

Our human choices are our own, of course, and we cannot lay blame on other factors for what is ultimately our sole responsibility. If we started to blame Enlil for our own shortcomings in an attempt to refuse accountability, we would assuredly walk straight into his trap. Yet, when any human being sets herself or himself absolutely in league with the adversarial forces (Hitler, for example), then we are in trouble. And if that human being is vastly more advanced than ourselves, and has learned the art of indefinite life upon the earthly planes and the manipulation of powers beyond our ken, then we are in big, big trouble.

The mason's 'mistake' (there are no mistakes with regard to Rosslyn Chapel) confirms that the presence of Enlil is definitely here within the building! The reversed teaching on avarice and charity, cannily exposed by the apprised mason, is Enlil's favourite formula to lead us deeper and deeper into the entombment of materialism.

So, where is he? If we return to the three pillars, and look up at the top of the Master Pillar, we see a carved head, a little off-kilter (some have suggested that it appears as if hanged, which is a most interesting observation). There is a smirk upon the countenance of this head, but if it is examined close up it can be seen that the face is held in a grimace as if bursting with suppressed and immoderate laughter.

This, of course, is Enlil, who is convinced that he will have the last laugh. And we need to know the story of the pillars to understand why he is represented by the Master Pillar.

Here is Dr Forbes's rendition of it. He was a former Bishop of Caithness, and he gives the story in a document compiled in 1774, entitled *An Account of the Chapel of Rosslyn*:

'The Master Mason, having received from the Founder (Earl William St Clair) the model of a pillar of exquisite workmanship and design, hesitated to carry it out until he had been to Rome or some other foreign part and seen the original. He went abroad and in his absence an apprentice, having dreamt that he had finished the pillar, at once set to work and carried out the design as it now stands, a perfect marvel of workmanship.

The Master Mason on his return, seeing the pillar completed, instead of being delighted at the success of his pupil, was so stung with envy that he asked who had dared to do it in his absence. On being told that it was his apprentice, he was so inflamed with rage and passion that he struck him with his mallet, killed him on the spot and paid the penalty for his rash and cruel act.'

This report seems to be backed up by the fact that work on the chapel was delayed so that the interior could be blessed and cleansed after an act of evil-doing, and the carven head above the Master Pillar seems to be off-centre, as though hanged. Many people find the story difficult to believe, however (although my own inner guidance verifies that it is true), because it so closely reflects the great Masonic story of Hiram Abiff.

There is more to the story of Rosslyn's pillars than there appears.

Hiram Abiff was the great architect and builder of Solomon's Temple, the first Holy Temple to be built in Israel, which was left unfinished (as was the building at Rosslyn) after the death of Hiram under similar circumstances.

However, it is important to note that the Rosslyn story is a match in reversal, because Hiram was a Master Craftsman who was killed by his own apprentices within the Temple. That Temple was Solomon's Temple, built to shelter the world from the terrible Ark of the Covenant. Yet the same imbalance that declared itself in Solomon's time still persisted when Rosslyn was built, and so the drama happened again, only in reverse, because the Grail forces within Rosslyn are the veritable opposite of those contained in the Ark of the Covenant, the containment of which was one of the main reasons (some say the only reason) why Solomon's Temple was erected.

There is a story at Rosslyn that, in a magical way, the Apprentice Pillar is secretly Hiram Abiff's work. This fairy tale is actually an astounding insight, as we shall see. To understand fully how everything is as it is at Rosslyn, Hiram's story also needs to be told.

Firstly, we might contemplate the many pointers to reversals within Rosslyn Chapel. These indicate the distorted reverse-spin alchemy of Enlil (a very real and actual process), and how it continually sends humanity spinning into reversal as we strive so painfully and earnestly to make forward progress on our evolutionary path.

The carving at head height to the left of the altar to the Blessed Virgin in the Lady Chapel shows Lucifer the Fallen Angel as a reversed figure, his head pointing to the ground. He is bound by the two coiling serpents of the Caduceus, but in their reversed mode they are coiling away from one another in their opposite directions instead of uniting at their base and head in the figure 8 to create a living symbol of unity and love – the configuration of Creation.

Another hanged or inverted symbol occurs at a point where, in 2007, Jeff Nisbet revealed his discovery of an upside-down Lorraine Cross encoded into the ceiling of the chapel. Noticing a peculiar crowding of the architectural elements in the second and fourth courses of the five-course vaulted ceiling, he was able imaginally to push them into their proper harmonious spacing with his trained artist's eye, upon which the clear symbol of the Lorraine Cross was revealed.

The Cross of Lorraine was the first insignia bestowed upon the Knights Templar. Its two bars reflect the union of the feminine and masculine spiritual principles and are an emblem of the Hermetic maxim 'As above, so below', a teaching drawn directly from the emerald tablet. Although it was hidden away by malignant wiles, Enki and Ham (Thoth and Hermes) worked together upon the false emerald tablet that Enlil afterwards released into our world. They toiled to extract from it all the authentic knowledge and directives that Enlil had included from the genuine emerald tablet and had mixed in with his poisonous manipulations in order to carry off his deception. Ham then buried the false emerald tablet in a temple in Egypt, where its pulsing malevolence was subdued, imprisoned and guarded by a special priesthood.

The hermetic documents which Enki and Ham produced were also preserved in Egypt, and although their teachings underlie the founding of the esoteric and scientific knowledge of humanity today, a breath of Enlil's distortion has infused them and lingers still, despite Ham's most strenuous and very best efforts to eliminate these toxic traces.

This great work of editing by Enki and Ham has ensured our forward progress, albeit by a chequered route, for without some grasp of the teachings of the true emerald tablet, we would have wandered in utter darkness and fallen easy prey to the maleficent Anunnaki king long ages ago.

Enlil would much have preferred not to include anything of the real emerald tablet in his rendering of the false one, of course, but by cosmic law his task of subterfuge did not allow the complete suppression of the genuine article. It was only by extraordinary alchemical and scientific ingenuity that, with the aid of Noah, he was able to hide and distort what he could of its pure pulsations.

These depictions of inversions within the chapel, visible and invisible, are to show us that our present world is built upon Enlil's backward-spin alchemy. Its crowning glory is the ring that supplanted the canopy of ice, formed from water of exquisitely pure crystalline structure, which once surrounded the stratosphere of our planet to protect our consciousness from hostile invasion. Now, the sinister ring of Enlil thwarts and fools our higher consciousness into constant blindness and degradation.

Yet these depicted reversals inside the chapel are not there to spell out dreary predictions of humanity's inevitable doom. On the contrary, they herald the blessed day (so near!) when the cataclysmic reverse-event of severing the Grail from the Earth will itself be reversed.

Once, our planet spun sunwise, expressing the positive-force spin, like Venus; and one day it will again spin in perfect accord with this mystical planet, our great teacher and the source of human life in our solar system. (Nibiru, who seeded our Earth, was first seeded by Nephilim working with the Venusian forces.)

We have no need to fear this day, for it will bring, not destruction and calamity, but a wondrous new world.

CHAPTER 34

THE ENIGMA OF HIRAM ABIFF

In Masonic ceremonies relating to the Third Degree, the member seeking initiation undergoes a solemn procedure in which the crucial story of Hiram Abiff is ritualistically dramatised. Hiram Abiff is spoken of as 'the son of the Widow' among the Masons (pointing to the deeper symbolism of Mother God who has been brutally torn away from human consciousness by the severing of the Grail), and is seen as the founding member of the Masonic Craft. Hidden, esoteric Masonic wisdom, of course, knows that the honour properly belongs to Enki, although in the deepest sense Hiram and Enki were one, as we shall see.

Hiram Abiff was the Master Mason who was sent from Tyre by its king to oversee the project of the building of the Holy Temple of Israel. King David had been very eager to build the Temple himself, but the prophet Nathan had dissuaded him, pressing on him that the task properly belonged to his son Solomon.

King Hiram of Tyre (for we have a spiritual father-son situation pertaining to the pair, Hiram the Master Mason and Hiram the king, which appears again and again in the history of the Grail) was placatory in the affair. He supported Nathan's guidance (which had originated from Hiram the Master Mason) but sent rich materials so that David could build a great palace in Jerusalem (the House of David) as a consolation prize in foregoing his wish to build the Temple.

One of the main reasons for the founding of the Temple was to house the malignancy of the Ark of the Covenant. King David, in spite of Miriam's injunction (for the sake of damage limitation) long ago that only the priests should partake of Enlil's white powder, had himself partaken of it. This meant that if he founded the Temple, it would fail to contain the Ark's evil potencies, and the artefact would thus be enabled disastrously to influence history. In return for David's obedience, the prophet Samuel reveals a prophecy to him. "Your line shall live forever," he promises.

Hiram Abiff was ritually murdered within the unfinished Temple by three ruffianly apprentices who wanted to wrest the secrets of his Master Craftsmanship from him. When he would not surrender the secrets in his keeping, the apprentices took his life, enacting a strange ceremony in doing so, as though Hiram were being offered in sacrifice.

King Solomon ordained that Hiram should be buried beneath the Temple, and declared that the secrets he kept so close were lost to the world. However, in another Biblical translation of the story, King Solomon buries Hiram beneath the unfinished Temple but allows his secrets, to which he somehow has access, to be inscribed on his tomb and to be revealed only to those who attain the appropriate degree of initiation within the Craft.

There is undoubtedly a confusion regarding the referencing of Hiram which indicates that his provenance and identity were problematic and obscured. A full account of the skills of Hiram is given in 2 *Chronicles* 2:13–14. In response to an official request from King Solomon of Jerusalem to King Hiram of Tyre for men and materials to build a new temple, King Hiram (given as Huram in *Chronicles*) responds:

"And now I have sent a skillful man, endowed with understanding, Huram 'abi (the son of a woman of the daughters of Dan, and his father was a man of Tyre), skilled to work in gold and silver, bronze and iron, stone and wood, purple and blue, fine linen and crimson, and to make any engraving and to accomplish any plan which may be given to him, with your skillful men and with the skillful men of my lord David your father."

The name of the king and the name of the Master Mason are identical, and yet it was obviously not the King of Tyre who travelled to Jerusalem to build King Solomon's Temple.

In the New King James Version of the Bible, the phrase above identifying Hiram ('Huram 'abi') was translated as 'Huram my master craftsman'. Many Biblical renderings also interpret the 'ab' in 'abi' (the latter being the word that appears in the original scripture) as 'master', but older translations read it as 'father'. The –i suffix literally translates as 'my'; as in Hiram or Huram the king writing to King Solomon to say that he is sending his father, also called Hiram/Huram, to oversee and to participate in the building of the Temple. However, the meaning is rendered as 'of my father' in some of the older translations.

In 1723, James Anderson in his *Constitutions* apparently solved the problem by announcing that the textual dilemma would be resolved by reading 'abi' as the second part of a proper name, which he promptly rendered 'Abiff'. And so the naming of Hiram as Hiram 'Abiff' came into being, albeit unsatisfactorily as it comprises an entirely forced conclusion.

A figure stood behind King Hiram of Tyre, the king who took on a form of his name and who kept his secrets, serving him and calling him 'my master' and 'my father' and 'of my father', for this mysterious figure was indeed an ancestor, a master, and a king. His own mystical father and biological ancestor was the instigator of the line that produced King Hiram, as well as David and Solomon, although his identity could not be revealed in its entirety, for his story was too marvellous for ordinary mortals to understand.

This was the very same figure who forged an uneasy truce within the tribes of Israel and whose followers were faced with a great struggle ('naphtali', the name of his tribe) in order to preserve his teachings and his legacy, which were precious beyond all price.

In *The Hiram Key*, the authors Robert Lomas and Christopher Knight put forward the fascinating idea that Hiram was in fact an Egyptian pharaoh, King Seqenenre Tao II, who reigned just before the 17th Dynasty became the 18th. This date, of course, far precedes King Solomon and his Holy Temple, because his building of it took place after the death of King David, Solomon's father, much further forward in time than the turn of the 17th Dynasty in Egypt.

If we return to the same figure who influenced King Hiram of Tyre and travelled to Jerusalem to build the Holy Temple, we find in this intuitive story we are following that he is historically listed as the founding father of ancient Egypt, being the grandfather of its first pharaoh.

This same mysterious figure, after Egypt's sorry descent into warring and materialism and the loss of its glory to invading Asiatic tribes, helped it back onto the path of its spiritual destiny. He did this by enlightening the very pharaoh Lomas and Knight mention, King Seqenenre Tao II, and helping him to set all in place for the coming of the supremely important 18th Dynasty.

This was the dynasty which would give rise to Akhenaten, his son Moses, the sisterhood of astonishing women who were the real players in the drama, the inception of a unifying deity, and the establishment of the

Temple of John (Enki) in Egypt. Sadly, King Seqenenre Tao II lost his life in sacrifice in similar mode to Hiram Abiff and the Rosslyn Chapel apprentice. Yet he achieved his purpose, for he was a loyal servant of this all-important overarching figure.

Just as devoted to him was the later King Hiram of Tyre, who, as forecited, assumed a version of his name – the name with which the same enigmatic figure identified himself when he travelled from Tyre to Jerusalem to build the Temple which, had Moses been able to accomplish his true mission, would have changed the world forever. For, instead of a holy structure built to contain the vile energies of the Ark of the Covenant, it would have been erected as a Grail Temple, conducting the supernal forces from the resurrected Mount Heredom out into the world, just as temples located on all the stations of the Grail will disseminate this godly force in the future.

The name of this shining figure was, of course, Ham, son of Tubal-Cain, Hero of the Good Land, who was great-grandson of Cain, son of Enki the Wise, known in every historical artefact bearing his name as Enki the Great Artificer, Enki the Master Smith, Enki the Master Craftsman – Enki who was known later in Egypt as Thoth, 'Architect of Truth'.

Ham, Enki's direct descendant and his spiritual son, held a secret that allowed him to live for many centuries upon the Earth: his 'Avesa' secret that properly belongs to all of humanity but which, together with many others, has been denied and hidden. He lost his life when he was murdered in the unfinished Temple (which never was completed, just as Rosslyn Chapel lies unfinished) and the secrets that he has preserved for us are the secrets of Iona and the secrets of Rosslyn.

However, the story behind the story is that King Solomon himself arranged to have Hiram (Ham) killed, and the meaning of the strange ritualistic manner of Hiram's slaughter by the apprentices is a direct exposition of Solomon's knowledge of magic.

Solomon knew that in Hiram he was dealing with a man who was what Jesus and Mary Magdalene would have termed 'fully human', and it was no simple or straightforward matter to assassinate him. He was protected by the forces of light, and only a form of ritual drawn from the deepest (negative) darkness could succeed in dispatching him.

Even then, there had to be a point of weakness within Hiram through which the dark ritual could enter him – and indeed there was, which will be explained.

Solomon, initially devoted to Hiram, had grown jealous of him and saw him as a rival. The Queen of Sheba (Makeda) had come to Solomon to conceive a son by him, for this son would carry the special bloodline forward through the required channels. However, she needed to conceive and bear a daughter first, and Solomon's attitude to women was too predatory and materialistic for him to be able to call down the soul of this daughter into the womb of Makeda.

This hoped-for daughter was so exalted, of the essence of the Divine Presence to such a profound degree, that notwithstanding womanhood's mastery of physical manifestation, she could not descend through the blocking miasma of Solomon's voracious appetite – an appetite that began as a deep reverence and love for the Sacred Feminine Principle, but deteriorated into predation.

For this daughter to become incarnate, a mother and father of the highest spiritual stature were required, because her coming was to be the coming of Sara-Tamar, the Divine Woman, the blessed Holy Grail. It was planned that, like her prospective father Ham (for it was intended that Ham or Hiram should become her father), she was to assume Avesa-hood. She was to be given into the care of the secret sisterhood on Iona to take her place upon the throne of the mysteries there until Jesus and Mary Magdalene, rescuers of the emerald tablet, were born, which was planned to occur at an earlier date than the later one in Bethlehem.

Solomon was apprised of all this, and understood Hiram's role perfectly. Yet, with the sinister help of the emanations from the Ark, which carried Enlil's murderous wrath in the form of an advanced technology, he later fell prey to jealousy and rage, and could not bear the idea of Makeda's relationship with Hiram. Consequently, using more than earthly powers, he had Hiram (Ham) ritualistically killed in the Temple. This was the reason why it was never finished, and why (because its purity was breached) it could not contain all of the malevolent energies of the Ark, but had to share the burden with Ethiopia, the heartland of Makeda's royal realm.

The Sheban (or Saban) royal family were also descendants of Ham, as the Bible states; although the purposeful error claiming that Ham was the son of Noah remains (he was actually of the line of Cain, which was a different family to that of Noah). Makeda's realm was one of joy and abundance. It specialised in magnificent, spiritually uplifting architecture, for she and Ham, the Master Craftsman, had enjoyed a relationship of devoted love for many years and wrought the dominions of Sheba together.

Although theirs was a sexual love, it had to wait to be consummated until Makeda met with King Solomon. This was because there was a profound bond of brotherhood between Ham and Solomon, a bond which arose from Nin-khursag and Enki's bloodline and comprised a special soul pairing. Makeda's union with Ham had to encompass Solomon for it to be complete.

Makeda's son by Solomon would continue the Davidic line down to Jesus and Mary Magdalene. Her daughter by Ham would inherit his Avesa qualities and form a pure receptacle for the descent of the Divine Woman.

The spirit of Neelâta-mek, or Brigid, Ham's twin flame, entered Makeda at her birth. Makeda was known, as Brigid was known on Iona, as the Woman of Fire ('Makeda'), the Smith-Woman. Compassionate, wise, with gifts of healing, abundance, Divine knowledge and supreme feminine Smithship, she built her blessed realm with Ham's dedicated assistance.

The Bright Knowledge, Brigid's particular domain, flowed in radiant rivers of scholarship from Makeda's lands. The leading light of her peoples was the Sabian tribe, who, like the Druids, represented a spiritual college of learning based on Oannes's (Enki/John's) teachings. The Sabians of Harran, and the earlier Sabians long before them, formed one unbroken stream of distinguished excellence.

Their university in Baghdad was the centre of knowledge from which the Arab peoples derived their early global lead in science, technology, medicine, astronomy, alchemy, architecture and many other disciplines. The natural scholarship of the East was of course conducive to this development. Yet, nevertheless, it is possible to detect from existing history that Arabic learning originated with the Sabians, Makeda's people.

224

The Sabians, in AD 830, informed Caliph al-Mamum that their prophet was Hermes Trismegistus ('Thrice Blessed Hermes', so designated because he had three-quarters of all knowledge at his disposal). Hermes, of course, is Ham, thrice blessed because he possessed and disseminated three-quarters of the emerald tablet. The Sabians went on to name their holy book to the Caliph as the *Hermetica*, the secret writings of Thoth, who is Enki.

Perhaps one of the strangest aspects of this story is that Brigid of Iona is Neelâta-mek, she who breathed her spirit into Makeda. Brigid was the Fiery One, the Smith-Woman, Woman of Compassion, Woman of Knowledge, Divine Custodian of poetry and song. These were all Makeda's virtues; and some years ago it was discovered that Hebridean singing and orisons match the sacred tribal songs of a number of Central and Northern African tribes.

Mary Magdalene, who knelt in honour of Brigid on Iona, was Makeda's direct descendant. Brigid is seen as the feminine half of the Christ Being in the heavens, of Christ Consciousness, which filled Mary. She was both the Black Madonna and Brigid the White, the Shepherdess.

Makeda was not given time to conceive Sara-Tamar. Hiram died too soon. Sorrowfully, she concluded her mission with Solomon, and returned home pregnant with his son, too sad and disturbed by Solomon's cruel act ever to visit him again, or even to keep up any correspondence with him.

Solomon, bereaved and remorseful, wrote his *Song of Songs*, through which the spirits of Ham and Neelâta-mek (Makeda) sang in joy and in sorrow, for Solomon was both the agent of their union and their heart-rending separation. He had betrayed them; and yet within that peerless song are all the secrets of the mystical conjoinment of the Sacred Marriage, in itself a form of ecstatic ascension.

What was the weakness within Ham that allowed his life to be taken, even though he wielded the power of immortality? It was not a human weakness, but a chink in his armour of light that was caused by allying himself with an elemental being, a little man of the Earth element.

Such Earth spirits are associated with the powers of Saturn, the 'base' of Creation or the Earth herself. This particular little man of the Earth element (we know his kind in mythology as dwarves or gnomes, although some mistakenly call them demons) was, simplistically, half bad and half good. He was of the creative and goodly forces of Saturn, but, because Enlil had hijacked and distorted these energies for his own dark purposes, this little man was also bound by the Shadow.

We can recognise him in our own tradition as Rumpelstiltskin, the little man of wrath who spun gold (backwards) in order that a cotter's daughter might marry the king. His reward for his reverse-spin gold was the queen's future baby son – in other words, he wanted the kingly succession in his power. But the good forces in the little man actually desired to free the queen from her promise, so he gave her the option of revealing his name, a magical act which would liberate her from fulfilling her word. Consequently, he ensures that the Queen's handmaiden overhears him singing his name as he brews and bakes, making the white bread and the false wine with which to feed the baby prince the following day when Rumpelstiltskin is due to claim his prize; and so the royal succession is saved from the invidious white powder and wine.

The reason Hiram (Ham) had taken the little man into his service (thus weakening his own light-forces and forming binding ties with the elemental, which would weigh Ham down and remain attached to him until he was ceremonially released) was that he needed a certain secret that could only be revealed to him by the elemental.

Ham himself had been vouchsafed all of Enki's knowledge; he was assisted at all times by the angels and by the Christ spirit alive in his heart. Yet there was something missing: just one little nugget of information that he needed from the elemental worlds, from the region of Saturn's 'base' powers, to enable him to build the Holy Temple so that its Earth energies as well as its higher energies could successfully contain Enlil's terrible Ark – the Ark that contained the distorted powers of Saturn.

Knowing that it would endanger his life and enchain his soul, out of his astonishing love for humanity which has never faltered since he began his great mission countless years ago, Ham willingly sacrificed his safety and his freedom to learn the secret that only the Earth elemental could impart. The story that enshrined this noble truth was that the building of Solomon's Temple was assisted by 'demons'. And indeed it was by bending to his own deadly purposes the will of the elemental bonded to Ham or Hiram that Solomon was able to kill the Master Mason, via dark ritual.

Ham's (Hiram's) murdered body was indeed buried, with elaborate ceremony, under the Temple. Interred with him were his scrolls, which contained the secrets of his esoteric Master Craftsmanship. We can glean a dim idea of just how marvellous these were by remembering Uri Geller's ability to cause a seed to burst into life in the palm of his hand, and of Bezaleel's art (Ham again) in creating from a miracle of golden smithship a receptacle so magical and lovely that the Divine presence of the Mother, otherwise cut off from the Earth, could pour her spirit into, and dwell within, its pulchritude.

Ham's scrolls, as well as containing the magical secrets of the Divine within metal, stone, wood and the act of building and smithship (how Earth resonates with spirit), also told the story of Enki and Enlil, and how, throughout vast tracts of human history, Enki and Nin-khursag have always fought to the utmost peak of their valour and ingenuity for us just as Enlil has always tried venomously to destroy us.

The scrolls told of the Holy Grail, of the loss of Mother God, and the supplanting of Father God with a false understanding contrived to throw us off track. They told of the blessed androgyne who would come as a couple – as Jesus and Mary Magdalene – to conclusively rescue us from Enlil's darkness and restore to us the inconceivable Divinity of the emerald tablet.

They told of Sara-Tamar and how she was the Divine Woman, of how she would come again through the blessed androgyne Jesus and Mary Magdalene, and of how all other attempts to birth her but theirs had failed. They told of Mount Heredom, of her decapitation, of the sanctity of Rosslyn, of the imponderable promise of tranquil Iona.

And there was a secret that was put into a casket of engraved silver, and it was the secret that Hiram learned from the son of Earth.

The Ark of the Covenant was buried with Hiram, but not alongside him. A concealed entrance which led underground to Hiram's tomb was created, but none could venture near that sacred spot unless they had passed many secret initiations in the art of Master Craftworking. His tomb and the scrolls within it were sealed; but Ham (Hiram) was not in the tomb.

He had ascended, using the magic of the Grail; a magic which is for every one of us, Divine Mother's gift to all of her children, and which will soon be ours again.

CHAPTER 35

THE LAY OF THE LAST MINSTREL

What of the Queen of Sheba's son by Solomon? He was not Menelik I, the son who succeeded her, although she taught Menelik the secrets of the Temple of John and he was known as 'the Wise One'.

The legend that arose concerning Menelik's visit to Solomon and his subsequent purloining of the Ark of the Covenant is a tutelary myth. It concerns the later transportation of part of the Ark from Solomon's Temple to Ethiopia, where, as we have seen, the spirit of the Sacred Feminine was most beautifully and securely rooted into the Earth by a highly venerable custodian of it, linked to the great Makeda, Queen of Sheba.

Only this special feminine strength in Ethiopia could successfully contain part of the Ark in tandem with the remainder of it contained by Bezaleel's Mercy Seat and the Holy Temple in Jerusalem.

Solomon's son, born to the Queen of Sheba, was the prophet Elijah. Ham came to earth again through Elijah, after his murder in Solomon's Temple. His great-grandson was Jonah, into whom, via his Avesaship, he entered at the appropriate time, which was marked by Jonah's miraculous swallowing and expulsion by a whale. Jonah was returned to Divine source and then reborn as Ham via the great cetacean.

Elijah's ascent to heaven in his 'fiery chariot' was a manifestation of the Grail; and the story of his legacy of his mantle to Elisha, next in the line of descending John-men, was an indication that, on ascension, he gifted his etheric body with all its esoteric knowledge and secrets to one who would continue to carry the torch.

It was of Elijah's line that both Jesus and Mary Magdalene (who were cousins) were born. It was at this point that the gateway to the sun (embodied in Mercury, or Enki and Ham, the John-men) was flung wide open due to Enki and Ham's long toil, and the spirit of the sun itself descended to Earth through Jesus and Mary Magdalene.

A line of magicianship may be perceived here, from Enki and Ham, Great Artificer and Master Mason respectively, down to Jacob (who was a mage), through Joseph the prophet and dream reader, through Moses who changed rods to serpents, through Solomon, demon-controller of esoteric power and wisdom, to Elijah, Elisha, Jonah and others including the Magi, to, ultimately, Jesus the miracle worker.

It is important to note that there exists both an exalted magicianship, where the invocant works inwardly with – and only with – the Star Fire; and a lower magicianship, where the invocant imposes the wishes of his or her ego upon a given situation and works with dubious forces to realise them.

To demonstrate the difference between the two, Simon Magus is illustrated in the story of Jesus as a man who mirrored his path but turned his craft to materialism and created the crime of simony by attempting to buy and sell enlightenment for material profit.

Perhaps, then, it is not so much of a mystery that one of Enki/Ham's later manifestations was as Michael Scot, the famous Scottish wizard who was known in his time as the most renowned and feared alchemist and sorcerer of the 13th century.

Michael Scot was indeed Ham, back again to help us, and naturally he was an entirely good man. He was a mathematician, astronomer and scientist of genius as well as a mage. The reason he was so greatly feared and that a cloak of darkness seemed to hang around him was due not so much to his considerable and recognised occult powers as to the persistent presence of the same little earth elemental, half bathed in light and half steeped in shadow, who had revealed to him the final secret that Ham needed to build Solomon's Temple.

The little entity could not be thrown off until Ham was ceremonially released from bondage to him; but in fact this was a good thing (though not very pleasant for poor Ham), because the grim, diminutive Saturnine being had one more secret to divulge – how to reconnect Rosslyn with Iona!

Again, Ham (Michael Scot) had almost all the necessary knowledge and skill at his disposal; but he needed his strange little servant to place in his hands a certain key. He needed to know how he could perform the alchemy required to create the necessary etheric bridge between land and sea to reunite Rosslyn and Iona.

No-one ever knew where Michael Scot died, the year or manner of his death, or where he lies buried, although his grave is rumoured to be at Melrose Abbey – and equally rumoured not to be there or anywhere. He retired from public view and allowed a considerable number of years to elapse (in which he remained characteristically busy throughout the course of several identities) before he reappeared in recorded history as the architect Sir Gilbert Hay, good friend of Earl William St Clair. Together, they built the chapel as a great work of alchemy, the most important ever to be undertaken on our Earth.

As the engrailed cross of the St Clairs silently pronounces, their line is the line of the Grail kings. The Grail kings were leaders who worshipped within the Temple of John and understood that their power was sourced in the Mother, the All. They were men of great honour and vigour and might, who yet would bend their knee in humility to the Divine Feminine, to the heart. Their bloodline protected the Grail secrets.

The heart of the Norwegian earl who founded the family first opened to the Culdee monks, the monks of Columba (the name 'Columba' translates as John, meaning 'dove'). These monks arose from the great Druidical community on Iona, who gradually became Christianised after the visit of Jesus, his mother, Joseph of Arimathea, Mary Magdalene, Sara-Tamar and John the Beloved to the isle. John Martinus, the latter's son, who made frequent return visits to Iona, the place of his birth, and who espoused the true Christian faith, was seen as one of their own.

A number of Culdees after Columba's death were seized on Iona by Vikings and became the captors of the earl, who had his domain upon the coast from where the Iona-bound Norsemen set sail and returned.

His family was open and enlightened enough to learn from them, because all its members were descendants of Elaine the Druidess and John Martinus. Its bloodline conferred on them certain advantages that they mustered the spiritual strength to utilise. Later marriages and a French connection initiated them fully into the secrets of John (the true Church of Christ).

Their Grail kingship was fully conferred on them when William the Seemly St Clair escorted Princess Margaret and the Holy Rood from Hungary to Scotland to marry King Malcolm Canmore. The design of the engrailed cross that they adopted as their sign and symbol is to be found within the heraldic escutcheon of Ham, curved a little to produce the C of the St Clairs. It is the mark of selfless protection to the death.

231

Michael Scot, having changed his identity to Gilbert Hay, built all of his esoteric wisdom into Rosslyn. His masons carved representations of maize around a window arch within the chapel as a symbol of America, for America (North and South) has a special destiny. It is the great continent which will be the first land on a grand scale (Britain will lead the way on a smaller scale) to unite the six very different races who came to Earth from the stars to learn to live in love and brotherhood – the whole purpose of our Earthly civilisation.

These six races are represented in St Matthew's sigil: the ox, the eagle and the lion, all culminating in the hu-man of Earth. In the sigil's correct representation, the eagle carries the serpent in its claws.

The eagle, in symbology, grants the gift of ascension by embracing the principle of Wisdom, signified by the serpent. The sigil promises that we as earthlings – born of the Nibiruan blood of the serpent people and combining in ourselves the serpent, ox, lion and eagle – are evolving by bodily facilitation of the ape to create a new cosmic humanity that will ascend via the wise eagle, whose sign is the winged disk. We are the serpent in the eagle's claws.

The reason that there are only four beasts within the sigil to represent the planetary races which assembled on Earth is that four of these races belonged to two planets which each supported two of the totality of six.

Within the window arch carved with maize, the stonework and the top windows create the beaked face of Quetzalcoatl, the Maya maize god who shares many characteristics with Christ. Quetzalcoatl shows us the Christ spirit in tutelary symbolic guise, for he is a plumed serpent (the winged dragon), the serpent and the eagle merged into one: the great emblem of ascension, of the Grail. And it is an incontrovertible sign that both North and South America must return to their Native American roots to be enabled to achieve their golden destiny.

The fabled lost Aztec treasure, said to be worth 600 billion dollars, is real and waits in protected concealment to be discovered and to fund the great coming together and rebirth of the Native Americans of the North and South continents. Such a beam of spiritual power, healing and wisdom will be released by the mighty resurgence of these peoples that the world will be struck with wonder. That resurgence will be a resurrection that dispenses glory and blessing to us all.

The stars which adorn the American flag are a direct transposition from the roof of Rosslyn Chapel, where five-pointed stars cluster in just such a configuration. The flag was designed with Rosslyn Chapel in mind.

Michael Scot wished it to be known one day that he built the spiritual device which will reconnect Mount Heredom. His name was a tribute to Scotland and to the potent presence of Archangel Michael upon Iona and in Scotland, and indeed throughout the entire land-mass of Britain. (Ham always uses symbolic names in his reappearances, such as Sir 'Francis Bacon' [a play on 'Ham'] and 'Fulcanelli', meaning 'little Vulcan'.)

He has left his documents regarding the esoteric and practical construction of the chapel and his true identity in two secret places, one behind the fireplace in the Sacristy of the chapel and another within the chapel itself, which I will not reveal publicly because it would just feasibly be possible to surreptitiously retrieve and make off with them!

Michael Scot, who is our stalwart friend Enki/Ham, shining champion to all humanity throughout the ages, has left his papers in two hidden but accessible places so they will provide evidence which will strongly indicate that it is worthwhile to lower an endoscopic camera into the vaults of Rosslyn. What the world sees there with wondering eyes will persuade it that we really do need to investigate what lies below the marker gravestone within the grounds of Lincoln cathedral!

Michael Scot's secret book, his *Book of Knowledge*, lies upon the shrine hidden within the vaults which is laid out ceremoniously with the Holy Rood, the Scottish Crown Jewels and the lost scrolls of the Temple. What they all surround as their centrepiece will be revealed shortly.

Sir Walter Scott, a descendant of Michael Scot, wrote his ballad *The Lay of the Last Minstrel* to tremendous acclaim at the end of the 18th century. Its mystery, poignancy and lyricism enthralled the public; but when read with full understanding, as is now possible, the entire resonance of its symphonic music will roll out its emancipated magic for all those with ears to hear.

Strangely enough, the admiring public agreed unanimously upon one flaw in Scott's composition – the presence of the little earth elemental in the story! Of course his inclusion is crucial; and Scott explained in his defence that the 'goblin' associated with the famous Scottish wizard, both of whom feature in his ballad, was the very reason it was written. A friend of Sir Walter Scott, a Scottish noblewoman, had asked him to retell the story of Michael Scot and his goblin as a favour to her.

The ballad is rich with tutelary symbolism. Michael Scot is 'buried' in a hidden tomb in which there burns a great light associated with his lost *Book of Secrets*, which is actually in his tomb with him, although its destiny is to be recovered. The goblin is in his service, and is a conscientious and dedicated servant who remains in the human world after Michael Scot's death. However, there is also something sinister and unpleasant about the goblin. Whenever he expresses this side to his character, he cries "Lost! Lost! Lost!" in a malevolent tone and promptly vanishes. He is, of course, referring to the Grail.

The ballad progresses, telling the stories of Scotland's troubled and warring past, where blood and gore are conspicuous because of the grievous loss of the Grail (never cited directly). At last, Harold, a young man stirred by such tales since infancy, takes centrestage. He is the minstrel or bard of the St Clairs, and within Rosslyn's environs he 'had learned a milder minstrelsy' than that of war and conflict as his heart opened to the spirit of place pervading its land and family. He tells a tale of love and loss, not of violence and bloodshed.

Harold's lay is that of Rosabelle: 'beautiful rose'. Yeats wrote about this 'rose upon the rood of time', this 'most far-off, secret and inviolate rose' who is the Divine Woman, the Holy Grail...and also Iona, Mount Heredom's peak, waiting to be made whole again. Rosabelle's identity remains secret so that our hearts may know her.

The lay tells of her desire to cross the sea to Rosslyn's halls, because of her 'mother who sits alone' (the dispossessed Goddess), her father who will 'chide if Rosabelle herself does not pour the wine' (the Masculine Principle waiting to be offered the Star Fire) and because her lover will lead the ball and ride in the ring that night (the dance and the procession of the Sacred Marriage, to which the idea of the ball or 'ring' – the eternal circle – is essential and which cannot take place without Rosabelle).

The unknown remonstrator begs her not to attempt to get to Rosslyn under the prevailing conditions, warning her of omens that predict she will not succeed. That night, a strange rose-light, like a spirit fire, falls over the castle, the chapel and the lands of Rosslyn, a rose-coloured light brighter than the full moon. The music of the sea swells, but plays a dirge for Rosabelle, for she did not reach Rosslyn. She is in the sea. "The sea holds lovely Rosabelle," laments the minstrel.

A grief like no other falls upon the listening company when his lay is finished, and the goblin, who sits among them, vanishes with his keening cry, this time articulating, not his usual refrain of "Lost! Lost! Lost!" but instead, "Found! Found! Found!" The secret is out. The wizard has been given the hidden formula as to how to connect Iona with Rosslyn. The Grail that was lost will be found.

The shade of Michael Scot then appears and illuminates the goblin in a flash of lightning to hold him in his power, for now that the goblin has delivered his precious secret, the goodness within him has been imparted and only evil remains. He must not be allowed to escape and wreak mischief.

Somehow the company understands the situation, and that Michael Scot, having won his secret, is now in need of ritual release from the goblin. They proceed to Ambrose Abbey, the site of Michael Scot's 'grave' (the place where he is attached to the elemental), and with orisons, hymns and liturgy, perform the holy ceremony that will release him and give him peace and freedom.

The fruits of his life are the promise that Rosabelle in the sea (Iona) will be reunited with Rosslyn. He has set everything in place so that it may happen.

What lies at the centre of the holy shrine within the vaults below Rosslyn Chapel?

The answer is astounding, because it is the emerald tablet itself. The transcripts of the emerald tablet lie in wait for our discovery in the form of a book in a stone chest buried in the grounds of Lincoln cathedral. Their channelling into book form was the joint effort of Mary Magdalene, Jesus, Sara-Tamar and John the Beloved. Yet they knew that the artefact itself, blessed and sacred beyond the measure of our earthly comprehension, must remain where it had always been – within Mount Heredom.

In the days of Eden, the emerald tablet had crowned the holy mountain by dwelling at its peak, in fact a little beyond its peak at the point equivalent to where the 'soul star' chakra is positioned above the head in our human chakra system. It was present within Eden (which was linked directly with the apex of Mount Heredom), at the centre of Eden's royal court, where it was placed after it had been usurped by Enlil from Enki.

Enlil could not harm it or remove it, of course; it was utterly beyond his power to do so. But, with the help of Noah the ingenious scientist and alchemist, by his darkest ingenuity they were able to hide it in a hidden, impregnable dimension. Enlil's bright idea had been to conceal it in the base of Mount Heredom.

When Jesus revealed and unlocked the obscured dimension in which the emerald tablet was hidden via the power of his willing sacrifice, he knew that it must not be disturbed, but remain where it was so that Mount Heredom could one day be reconnected.

After he and Mary Magdalene, via the necessary stabilising force that was Sara-Tamar, had read it, and John had transcribed their words, Jesus once again 'covered it over', so to speak, that it might await the day when it could be placed upon its shrine and safely locked into the vault that was to guard it. Sara-Tamar travelled to Iona and dwelt in her seat of power there, surrounded by Druid priestesses as though she were a flame, to enable her mother and father to read and speak its words. Without her presence and power, it could not have been done.

The emerald tablet was the 'great secret within Rosslyn' that Mary of Guise, Scotland's Queen Regent, saw when Earl William St Clair escorted her down to the chapel's vaults. The marvel of the Temple Scrolls and Michael Scot's lost *Book of Secrets* were there as well, of course, as they are today (to say nothing of the Holy Rood and her own Crown Jewels!). Yet it was the wonder, the beauty, the magic and the all-pervasive holiness of the emerald tablet, accompanied by the Holy Rood that brought it back to us, which struck a chord deep in her heart that never stopped vibrating.

The emerald tablet is the supreme Crown Jewel of our Earth, of humanity itself. The original Crown Jewels of Scotland are very ancient and are associated with the guardianship of Ain and Ar-Thor.

That is why the Crown Jewels of the country to which it was vouchsafed so long ago must lie around it in protection and veneration, in company with the Holy Rood, part of the actual cross which was the sacrificial implement by means of which Jesus won back the emerald tablet for us.

There it dwells within that ring of power; the priceless and matchless gift that Mother God brought forth from her heart to preserve and ultimately save her children when they decided, thousands of years in the past, to cut her off from human consciousness, to try to banish and kill her, and to call her weak and inferior, a night-hag, and a whore.

It was her gift of all-embracing, everlasting love, deepest mercy, and profound and perfect forgiveness; of hope for our hearts and surety for our future.

That was her reply to us.

CHAPTER 36

'WHERE MY LOVE IS, THERE WILL MY RETURNING BE'

And so we return to Iona's dreaming shores, where the little island waits in the vastness of the ocean, under the vastness of the skies. There is a clear sense of the turning of the stars above her, as though Iona were some central timepiece.

There is a legend, sourced in Iona, that Saturn, Lord of Time, lies bound beneath the sea between two rocks nearby. And it is the release of this beautiful Saturnine energy into its true pristine channels that Rosslyn will achieve and Iona will receive. It is currently chained and repressed into twisted distortion, and has been so for millennia. But the shadow will be overcome, and Iona will be free again. And she in turn will set us free.

Fiona, speaking from Iona's timelessness, asks a question:

'Do you, too, not hold Iona, motherland of all my dreams, as something rare and apart, one who has her own lovely solitude and her own solitary loveliness that is like no other loveliness? In your heart, as in mine, it lies as an island of revelation and of peace.'

Dreaming that someone someday will write a history of Iona that reveals the island's secret, Fiona speculates on how that may be achieved:

'And, at the last – with what lift, with what joy – it will tell how once more the doves of hope and peace have passed over its white sands, this little holy land! This little holy land! Ah, white doves, come again! A thousand thousand wait.'

A thousand thousand? Like a mirror-reflection expressing eternal regression, that number might mean any number.

Perhaps it might mean somewhere in the region of almost seven billion.

Iona – under the sign of the dove.

***

'Nothing is covered up that will not be uncovered, and nothing secret that will not become known.' *Matthew* 10:26

APPENDIX

FIONA MACLEOD

The spirit of Fiona has certainly been with me as I wrote this book. Although having worked for many years on the uncovering of the story that the book discloses, it was within her beautiful writings on Iona that I first began to discern Iona's secret. It revealed itself not in a pragmatic sense but as a hovering spirit.

There is also a secret to be revealed about Fiona, a secret already known, but of which some readers may not be aware. I hesitated to include this information when introducing Fiona at the beginning of the book, because to have done so would have made it extremely difficult for readers to perceive and encounter her reality.

Fiona expressed herself through William Sharp, the Victorian writer who was part of W.B. Yeats's literary circle. But she was not a literary ruse or a pseudonym. I am convinced, I even dare to say I know, that Fiona was and is absolutely real. Her testimony is the voice that speaks through her works.

William Sharp's boyhood was evocative. He ran away with the gypsies, he saw fairies, and he encountered Brigid. But with him always was Fiona. He learned to see through her eyes and judge with her discernment.

When Fiona manifested directly through him in later life, both William and she were forced to endure the punishing resistance and agony which has been carefully and maliciously put in place to ensure that the androgynous human spirit does not re-conjoin. It cost William his sanity sometimes; and always the suffering was almost unendurable for both. Yet Fiona came to him and through him, and for the sake of the highest in himself, William Sharp persevered.

Sometimes, when Fiona descended, he would develop what seemed like nursing breasts. Sometimes, Fiona would make love to him 'as a man lies with a woman' as if she were fertilising his whole being, filling him with her fecundity.

No-one knew of Fiona's 'real' identity. She became internationally famous as a writer of spiritual beauty and literary distinction, her work lit with exalted soul-allurements that led readers to a breakthrough into poignant worlds of the spirit. She was presented to the public as William Sharp's cousin (obviously no-one ever met her in person), and he continued to produce his own separate works.

When it became known that Fiona Macleod 'was' William Sharp, his public were unforgiving. Fiona's work was condemned as nothing more than a deception and she was termed 'the Celtic siren'. Both she and William Sharp were forgotten very quickly, as if in embarrassment.

What the world could not know was that William Sharp would not have told the truth if he had claimed that Fiona Macleod was nothing more than a pen name. He asked a friend to say to the world on his death that Fiona too had died, as he was her vessel. If he himself had masqueraded as her true identity, he would have broken their androgynous link and killed Fiona's presence and voice within him.

To me, Fiona is a writer unequalled in beauty and evocation, and it was the obtuseness in our global mentality (which is lessening nowadays) that led the world to judge her as it did.

There could be nothing more exquisitely appropriate than that a human spirit which so bravely embraced its androgynous nature, no matter what the cost in suffering and the flails and scourges of the world, should accompany me in my quest to reveal this story. I consider myself honoured to have enjoyed her company and support.

ACKNOWLEDGEMENTS

My sincere thanks to Michael Revill, who helped me to confirm many important points in this story; to the Grail Circle and their 'John-man'; to Stephanie Sorréll, for her delightful piece on Iona; to Lionel and Patricia Fanthorpe, who with their Foreword came riding as rescuers of the book when its fate hung in the balance; to Dianne Pegler for her intuitive insight that the visiting Wise Men remained behind to protect the Christ mission; to Sharula Dux, for her information regarding the apparent absence of the remains of Atlantis; and especially to Fiona Macleod, who was with me every step of the way.

FURTHER READING

Nahmad, C, and Revill, M, *The Coming of the Holy Grail: The Exact Location of Heaven's Treasure and the Promise of its Retrieval*, (under new contract – please contact Claire Nahmad via Facebook for details)

Dunford, B, *Vision of Albion: The Key to the Holy Grail*, Sacred Connections, 2008

Wallace-Murphy, T, and Hopkins, M, *Rosslyn: Guardian of the Secrets of the Holy Grail*, Element Books, 2000; Thorsons, 2009

Harris, C, *The Lady Mary's Pilgrimage to South West Britain*, FastPrint Publishing, 2011

Merrick, R, *The Venus Blueprint: Uncovering the Ancient Science of Sacred Spaces*, Evolver Editions, California, 2012

Green, D, *The Murder of Mary Magdalene*, 11th Dimension Publishing, 2013

Macleod, F, *Iona*, Floris Classics, Dufour Editions, Republished 1996

Scott, Sir W, *The Lay of the Last Minstrel*, Birlinn; Bowhill Edition, Republished 2013

INDEX